Freedom of
Expression
AND
HUMAN
RIGHTS

Freedom of Expression

AND
HUMAN RIGHTS

Historical, Literary and Political Contexts

LIAM GEARON

sussex
ACADEMIC
PRESS

BRIGHTON • PORTLAND

The right of Liam Gearon to be identified as Author of this work has been asserted
in accordance with the Copyright, Designs and Patents Act 1988.

2 4 6 8 10 9 7 5 3 1

First published in 2006 in Great Britain by
SUSSEX ACADEMIC PRESS
PO Box 2950
Brighton BN2 5SP

and in the United States of America by
SUSSEX ACADEMIC PRESS
5824 N.E. Hassalo St.
Portland, Oregon 97213-3644

This work contains a substantial number of website addresses. Every effort has been made at the time
of publication to make sure that these addresses are accurate, but the author and publisher
wish to point out that website addresses and links sometimes change over time.

British Library Cataloguing in Publication Data

A CIP catalogue record for this book is available from the British Library.

Library of Congress Cataloging-in-Publication Data

Gearon, Liam.
Freedom of expression & human rights : historical, literary and political
  contexts / by Liam Gearon.
    p. cm.
  Includes bibliographical references and index.
    ISBN 1-84519-158-7 (hb : alk. paper); ISBN 1-84519-089-0 (pb : alk. paper)
  1. Human rights. 2. Freedom of expression. 3. Human rights—Religious
aspects. 4. Freedom of expression—History. I. Title: Freedom of expression
and human rights. II. Title.

JC585.G43 2006
323.44—dc22

2006002447

Typeset and designed by G&G Editorial, Brighton & Eastbourne
Printed by TJ International, Padstow, Cornwall
This book is printed on acid-free paper.

Contents

Part II
Freedom of Expression and Human Rights
Contemporary Historical, Literary and Political Contexts

Part III
Appendices

I
Charter of the United Nations (1945)

II
Freedom of Expression in International Law
The United Nations and Related Regional Inter-Governmental Instruments

III
UNESCO
Convention Concerning the Protection of the World Cultural
and Natural Heritage (1972)

IV
UNESCO
World Heritage Sites List (Results by Country)

V
United Nations
*Special Rapporteur on the Promotion and Protection of the Right to Freedom
of Opinion and Expression*
THE MANDATE

VI
United Nations
*Special Rapporteur of the Commission on Human Rights on Freedom
of Religion or Belief*
THE MANDATE

VII
United Nations
Declaration on the Elimination of All Forms of Intolerance and of Discrimination
Based on Religion or Belief (1981)

VIII

Freedom of Expression
*Inter-Government and Non-Governmental Organisations:
Internet Sources*

IX

The Nobel Prize in Literature
Awards 1901–2004

X

A Typology of Dissent *and* A Typology for Interrogation of Dissent

Foreword by Alastair Niven

Issues of free expression define the character of our times. If the 1930s were about tensions between the large doxologies of left and right, or the 1950s about cold war neurosis, or the 1980s about the rise and rise of market forces, in the first part of the Twenty-first Century international debates have sought to ask how much constraint can be willed upon a free society in order that it is adequately protected. As Oscar Wilde might have put it, the loss of freedom is the price of liberty.

Liam Gearon's remarkably clear and balanced book may surprise some readers. In a discussion of human rights over the centuries we expect to find Thomas Paine and John Stuart Mill. If we are not Pope Benedict XVI, we can see a case for Martin Luther. Plato and justice, St Augustine and conscience, Marx and economic liberty: each is a natural subject for the book. But Adolf Hitler and Chairman Mao? Their writings are analysed with scrupulous fairness, though the author's conclusions will shock no one. Tyrants they were, but with a mass appeal which challenges us to ask what exactly we mean by free expression. The cruelty of their authoritarian regimes, forcing popular consent, cannot completely explain away the mass appeal of what Hitler and Mao asserted. When members of the intelligentsia disagreed, they did not survive for long, but were they the only advocates of free speech or were not the crowds chorusing their approval also believing in the same principle? Some would argue that they were coerced into the rallies that bolstered Nazism and the Cultural Revolution, but is this enough of an explanation? Is free speech not very often the articulation on a comprehensive scale of ideas a liberal westerner would rather were never uttered?

This is a book of paradoxes. Political theory has been full of them through the centuries. As Thomas Hobbes observed, we agree to work together as social beings for reasons of self interest. Hobbes was explicit about the problem, partly semantic but also moral, which confronts anyone who writes about free expression. Does it not mean one thing to one person and the opposite to another? 'They that approve a private opinion, call it opinion; but they that mislike it, heresy: and yet heresy signifies no more than private opinion'. When private becomes public, the fat is in the fire. Liam Gearon indicates how the United Nations faces such equivocations on a daily basis. Aspiring to a global sharing of discourse, it must accommodate cultures and political traditions of very differing hues, without appearing to give preference to any one. In the act of open and free debate, regimes unpalatable to the democratic instinct have an equal right to be heard. Rights and democracy are not necessarily bedfellows.

Indeed, there is a danger that states will deny the potential of individuals by insisting on a rulebook of acceptable and unacceptable language and attitudes. Ali Mazrui, in his disputatious novel *The Trial of Christopher Okigbo*, says of the eponymous poet, 'He was the kind of man whose personality depended not on what he looked like but on what he was, complete with his beliefs and the idiosyncracies of his powers of articulation'. Suppress these, either tyrannically or in the name of the public good, and the character of the person is destroyed.

I write this Foreword as the current President of English PEN. As Dr. Gearon notes, this organisation has played a significant role in campaigning in the United Kingdom against the Government's proposals to make the incitement of religious hatred an offence [February 2006]. Again we recognised the paradox in every well-intentioned person's position on this. No reasonable person supports incitement. English PEN feels that existing legislation recognises this. Our problem was twofold. We felt that the legislation was being proposed with one religious group in mind and that it was being introduced in order to placate a possibly unrepresentative section of it. Secondly, we feared the consequences in terms of the right to criticise, to use irony, to say controversial things and to tell stories, whether as jokes or films or plays or novels. Common sense prevailed and the Government's measures were defeated, but in the process many nuances of the free expression debate were aired. Would that we had had this book to help us, with its calm and assured discussion of the history that lies behind our prevailing anxiety today.

When I was a student at Cambridge forty years ago I took a course called 'English Moralists'. It included Plato and St. Augustine as well as Aristotle. The classical tradition in this country made honorary Britons of the most improbable people. Dr. Gearon does not appropriate his subjects in this way. The spirit of his book is generously internationalist. I commend it thoroughly.

ALASTAIR NIVEN

Preface

There where one burns books, in the end one burns men.

HEINRICH HEINE

Each age defines, extends and retracts the limits of freedom of expression; but it is only in the modern period that liberty to express ideas, beliefs, and so forth, has become defined as a right. It is the twentieth century — a century that saw the rise of a regime that began with the burning of books as a precursor to the burning of people — which remains pivotal to the development of freedom of expression as a universal human right defended in international law. No longer simply a matter of legal or political or philosophical rhetoric, the balance between security of the state and the freedom of the individual has rarely been so urgently debated as in recent times.

Today, more extreme conflicts over freedom of expression have become integral to wider debates about life in open democratic societies committed to international human rights. In the United Kingdom in 2005, there were generalized political claims for new laws against words or speech likely to provoke religious hatred and/or glorify terrorism. Such proposed laws have been challenged by those claiming legal powers that would curtail freedom of expression. Post-7/7 2005 there are intense media discussions centring around the UK government proposals to accuse of treason those who speak out against Crown or country, patterns of restriction for free speech, which are arguably mirrored in the post-September 11 Patriot Act in the United States. Post-9/11 2001 and post-7/7, democratic governments and the international community have thus struggled with the problem of how to maintain national and global security while retaining individual liberties. Freedom of expression, therefore, remains central to the debate about the nature of freedom in an open society.

Yet from Plato to Mao and to the present era of the twenty-first century, the contingent limits of freedom of expression, as philosophical idea and historical reality, represent a tremendous diversity of notions and circumstances. One might perhaps expect this across a period of twenty-five centuries. There are, however, perennial patterns, more often of violent than of benign conflict. Often these patterns are repetitions of similar conflicts, many such conflicts seeming to last in various guises perpetually. The history of ideas, like the history of cultures, appears to be a history of human conflict as much as of human creativity. The tension between creativity and conflict arises most notably — both most profoundly creative and profoundly conflict-ridden — when what is at stake is a fundamental view of the world.

Worldviews — cultural, ideological, theological — are what give a culture coherence; worldviews also give rise, as history shows, to most bloody consequences — conflicts between religion and secularism (however these are defined), conflicts of inter-religious worldview, intra-religious schism, within and between religions, and those varieties of philosophical and political ideology (call it rationalism, humanism, the Enlightenment) which focus more on a belief in human nature than on ideas of God.

For example, the secular inclinations of the European Enlightenment set its humanist faith (what Mill called the religion of humanity) in those features of the modern world — science, technology, reason — which it helped create. It was a faith in its own abilities, the abilities of humankind, to make humankind's condition better; the set of circumstances created by modernity could not but help to ensure conflict with the religious systems that although it did not intend to replace, it did seek to surpass. The resultant tendency was for one worldview to struggle for dominance over another, often resulting in the attempted suppressions of the views of the other. For example, from the Counter-Reformation in the sixteenth century until the opening of the Second Vatican Council in the latter part of the twentieth century the Roman Catholic Church had set itself resolutely against the worldview of modernity, and its Index of books forbidden to the faithful included works of literature and philosophy as well as science. This is but one example of how a radical difference in worldview can have an effect upon the limits of freedom of expression. In the early twenty-first century other religious traditions, versions of a militant Islam, have taken on the mantle of the fight against modernity. *Freedom of Expression and Human Rights: Historical, Literary and Political Contexts* presents a series of such historical cases through examination of a particular text from each historical period and draws out what the implications were and often still are for freedom of expression.

Each historical period has its own dominant worldviews — religious or irreligious, theistic or atheistic — and these often define, with varying degrees of openness or accommodation, the limits to freedom of expression. Study of freedom of expression in historical, literary and political contexts reveals much about the nature of the limits placed upon freedom within a particular period. The General Introduction presents a tentative 'typology of dissent'. It attempts to establish a pattern of and for the analysis of such worldviews, and the conflicts over freedom of expression when one or other particular view of the world is subject to suppression.

Throughout all historical periods, from ancient Greece to today's virtual realities, text remains central to the definition of freedom of expression — its limits, the boundaries of what can and cannot be said, written or even thought. This book is an examination of some of these issues surrounding freedom of expression in historical context. Analysis centres on the issues of freedom of expression for specific historical eras and examination of a key text — philosophical, religious, and/or political — from that time. The premise of the book is based upon the idea that one such text from one such historical era can reveal the particular tensions of the age in which it was written. The text thus defined often determines the worldview of those willing to accept its limits. There are always limits to freedom of expression; indeed freedom of expression presumes its limit.

Freedom of Expression and Human Rights: Historical, Literary and Political Contexts is divided as follows: A General Introduction considers the events from

1901–2001 most cataclysmic in terms of the extreme repression of freedom of expression — notably through genocide — and at the same time the emergence of freedom of expression as a universal and legal human right.

In Part I a series of literary and historical case studies provide some insight into the great diversity of contexts — again, philosophical, religious, political, legal — through texts that help to define the age or the historical circumstances in which the text was written: from Plato's *Republic* through Saint Augustine's *Confessions* and Luther's *Ninety-Five Theses* to Thomas Paine's *Rights of Man* through to Mao's *Little Red Book* and the emergence of the era of the United Nations.

Part II analyzes the 'state control of freedom': how, in the UN era, governmental agencies and inter-governmental organizations (IGOs) maintain, monitor and often limit freedom of expression. The final chapter in this section provides a critical overview of non-governmental organizations (NGOs) and their role in challenging governmental, inter-governmental and other authorities seeking to repress freedom of expression. Part II reveals how fully freedom of expression has become integral to modern political and indeed everyday life but also how diversified are the means and media (electronic, hyper-reality, virtual) in which freedom of expression is evident and contested, repressed and defended.

Each chapter in Parts I and II contains, in addition to extensive sources for further reading, a range of authoritative electronic sources for advanced research, including access to primary historical texts and contemporary legal documents.

Part III provides a comprehensive range of appendices on freedom of expression — including international legal standards, inter-governmental organizations, non-governmental organizations, and so forth. The main body of the book cross-references to these appendices and provides systematic rationales for their inclusion. The appendices — cross-referenced throughout the book — will serve as a useful resource for activists as well as academics, journalists as well as researchers, and as a general resource on freedom of expression.

Freedom of expression is always most difficult to constrain in open democratic societies in which it is both widely accepted and taken for granted. New challenges to national and global security have, though, in turn challenged easy assumptions about freedom of expression, and the balance between rights such as freedom of expression and freedom of religion or belief. The danger is in becoming reactive and responding to the pressures of current day political crisis, without recognizing historical or political precedent, nor recognizing the key textual (broadly literary) sources where issues over freedom of expression have been most evident in the past, and which in turn can provide insight into and the means of resolving such problems in the present. *Freedom of Expression and Human Rights: Historical, Literary and Political Contexts* presents, therefore, a wide-ranging, critical analysis of freedom of expression, its definition, its repression and its defence; and no less a celebration of that which is worth protecting. On 7 July 2005 I was walking out of Tavistock Square when the bomb exploded. *Freedom of Expression & Human Rights* is dedicated to all those who died and were injured on that day in London.

Reference

Apignaresi, Lisa (ed.) (2005) *Freedom of Expression is No Offence*. London: PEN/Penguin.

Acknowledgments

I would like to thank Anthony Grahame and Cora Bailey at Sussex Academic Press for support on all aspects of the editorial work on *Freedom of Expression and Human Rights*; and to express much gratitude also to academic colleagues who commented on earlier drafts of the manuscript, including Dr Tina Beattie, Dr Kevin McCarron, and Dr Darren O'Byrne.

WAR IS PEACE
FREEDOM IS SLAVERY
IGNORANCE IS STRENGTH

George Orwell, *Nineteen Eighty-Four*

General Introduction
One Hundred Years of Censorship
1901–2001: From the Nobel Prize to the Twin Towers

It was a pleasure to burn.

RAY BRADBURY *Fahrenheit 451*

In *Fahrenheit 451*, Ray Bradbury's ([1953] 1996) novel of the future, a majority of the populace spend significant amounts of time watching mind-numbing soap operas on large television screens in every room of their house. The few individuals who read are persecuted. 'Firemen' are employed by the state to hunt down and burn all books. The book's title is taken from the temperature at which paper burns. Those found reading are arrested, imprisoned, persecuted.

The protagonist Montag is a fireman whose life changes when he begins to read the books he is employed to burn. The book ends with Montag on the run from the authorities and taking shelter with an underground group who live outside the urban conurbations in rural hideouts, each taking a role in retaining the literary heritage by memorizing parts or the whole of the classics of world literature. Implausible as it might seem to remain sanguine that the classics of world literature could be retained in the collective memory of a group of literary outlaws, Bradbury's narrative combines many of the historical features of censorship and the restriction of freedom of expression. There is something elemental in the fire that seems so completely to destroy a book and something so consistent in the alliance of fire as an instrument of the censor, and the destroyer of cultural artefacts: from the Inquisition (when it was not only the books but heretics that were burnt) to the burning of books in Berlin and other German cities in 1933 (in the period when Nazis burnt the creators of culture as well as their artefacts, burnt people as well as books), to the indirect and often unintended consequence of burning libraries in times of war (Karolides, Bald and Sova, 1999; Raven, 2004).

The dramatic situation of *Fahrenheit 451* might not have seemed that distant from the America of the 1950s at the time when Bradbury wrote the short novel: the world had witnessed the burning of the books in 1933 ending with the revelations of Auschwitz and Belsen in 1945; obsessive watching of the relatively new invention of television was prevalent; the un-American Activities Committee was in full swing in 1953, and as yet was unrestrained by any backlash (Webb and Bell, 1997; Anghelescu and Poulain, 2001). For Bradbury was writing at a time when Senator McCarthy was busy if not burning books then ruining the careers of those creative American talents who might have written them, thus obviating the need for the incendiary. The origin of the term McCarthyism was in a 29 March 1950 cartoon by the *Washington Post* to parody the excesses of the anti-American activities committee. Indeed, ironically it was the televizing of the trials that put an end to the previously unsullied reputation of McCarthy. It was in 1954 that the trials were televized for the first time, when mass television was becoming the norm, and networks needed to fill afternoon television slots. On television, the injustice of the manner of the investigation became fully apparent for the first time to many Americans and a backlash began against McCarthy (de Koster, 2000, cf. Foerstel, 2002).

This was also the time when Arthur Miller's *The Crucible* was written and performed. Ostensibly about the witch trials of Salem in late seventeenth century Massachusetts, there were few who could not recognize the parallels between the false persecutions of those alleged to be witches in Miller's play and those accused of Communist calumny against the United States in early 1950s America. In his notes, written half a century later for *The Crucible*, Miller suggests that 'The Devil or diabolical associations are used by all political sides to justify their cause', and that:

> The Catholic Church through its Inquisition, is famous for cultivating Lucifer as the arch-fiend, but the Church's enemies relied no less upon the Old Boy to keep the human mind enthralled. Luther was himself accused of alliance with Hell, and he in turn accused his enemies. To complicate matters further, he believed that he had contact with the Devil and had argued theology with him. I am not surprised at this, for at my own university a professor of history — a Lutheran by the way — used to assemble his graduate students, draw the shades, and commune in the classroom with Erasmus. At this writing, only England has held back before the temptations of contemporary diabolism. In the countries of the Communist ideology, all resistance of any import is linked to the totally malign capitalist succubi, and in America any man who is not reactionary in his views is open to the charge of alliance with the Red hell. Political opposition, thereby, is given, an inhumane overlay which then justifies the abrogation of all normally applied customs of civilized intercourse. (Miller, 2000: 249–250)

Miller usefully summarizes here his intentions in writing the play and ably contextualizes for us the recurring trends in the history of freedom of expression. *Fahrenheit 451*, like *The Crucible*, was written mid-way through the century as free expressions of ideas and ideologies left ravages of devastation, and to unparalleled proportions.

The twentieth century began somewhat more optimistically than the start of the twenty-first. If you had been living in an English village in the first year of the twentieth century as a doctor or a lawyer or a university professor, with a comfortable bourgeois lifestyle — perhaps still maintaining lip service to a Christian creed in which, post-Enlightenment, you could scarcely believe in, at least not fully, any longer — you could be forgiven for thinking you lived in a great age of human progress. At the beginning of the twenty-first century such illusions are harder to maintain.

Admittedly, across Europe the past few centuries had witnessed revolutions and wars, and many states had witnessed the violent overthrow of monarchies and aristocracies. Communism was an ideology and, a force to be reckoned with, if only to placate the workers upon whom your wealth depended. Intense nationalism and patriotic fervour were still prevalent but all nations in the modern era depended upon a strong sense of such nationalism and patriotism to engender identity within their citizens or subject. Newer, fairer, progressive forms of democratic principles had become the norm; and even if women did not have the vote, even if the British Empire was a force whose conclusion could not be envisaged, it was a benign civilizing force throughout large parts of the Earth. Yet somewhere there were the fears of how the application of new technologies might be applied for ill rather than human progress, especially the application of science to technological efficiency and potency in warfare. It was warfare, 1914–1918 and 1939–1945, that was to shatter the illusions of millions — first the trenches, then the death camps, and the bombing of civilian populations in cities across Europe. Nothing in the 'dark continent' of Africa, so named by the European colonizer, had any parallel. The cradle of ancient and modern civilization, of reason, of democracy, became the heart of barbarity.

Alfred Bernhard Nobel (1833–96) was a Swedish chemist and engineer, who pioneered the use of high explosives such as nitro-glycerine and accidentally discovered dynamite (1866). Before the beginning of the twentieth century he seemed to recognize that scientific discovery had the potential for both positive and negative effects. The inventor of dynamite was fully cognizant that the seemingly optimistic twentieth-century dawn might presage both the light of progress and the shadow of its antithesis. He could not de-invent dynamite, for which he foresaw terrible military uses, but he could attach his name to arguably more enlightened advances, especially in science but also in culture, particularly literature. Fraught with the excessive fortune made from the sale of the elements of mass destruction, he put to good use his legacy by establishing the Nobel Prize; the award still dominates as a mark of international achievement in the arts and sciences as well as in peace. The first Nobel Prizes were awarded, perhaps appropriately, in 1901, at the beginning of a century that was to see science and technology put to such ruinous good use.

The Nobel Prize in Literature is in many ways central to our considerations of freedom of expression because it makes a constructive positive link between the ideal of literary output and the making of a better world. In prior centuries religions and states had been responsible for the repression of writing. This was a relatively easy process in the days before the printing press when the authorities would not have found it difficult to ban a book (say a heretic such as Arius, condemned in 325 by the Christian Church at the Council of Nicea), and then to destroy extant copies that happened to have been handwritten. Still in the same period, books that had been around for longer and thus had more opportunity of having been copied, the classics of Greek philosophy perhaps, might have been destroyed less systematically as they had hundreds of years in which to be copied and distributed. One could name and excommunicate a heretic, for example, and have his books burned quite easily without trace. After the printing press however, when books became exponentially more numerous, the process of destruction required the most certain and systematic mode of destruction, and the enemy of all libraries, fire. (Although fires of course had famously laid to waste the ancient library of Alexandria.) Indeed the post-printing press period coincided too with the period in which books not favoured were burnt along with their authors. The post-printing press period also coincided with the increasingly systematic repression of books. Perhaps the most famously systematic list was that of the Vatican's Index of Prohibited Books which lasted from the Counter-Reformation — when the books of Protestants and non-Christians needed to be systematically detailed — until the late twentieth century, by which time (the last

Index was 1946, and it became an historical document from around 1966) the Catholic Church had essentially given up not on the process of restricting reading by the faithful but on the impossible task of listing all the books the faithful should not read.

Yet until the Nobel Prize in Literature there had been nothing before on the international scale that had marked down the *positive* contribution of writing to ideals of a *better* society, rather than seeing writers as a source of its potential corruption. The prize was and continues to be given for works of an ideal, moral nature, works that contribute to humankind's understanding of its own condition and its place in the universe. (The Nobel implicitly recognizes that literature as much as science contributes to our knowledge of our place in the world.) This has meant, naturally, only a particular sort of literature becomes eligible for selection, only works with high moral and philosophical ideals can be nominated, and this is itself a contentious aspect of the prize. Much great, classical modern literature has remained unrewarded. The list of excluded potential Nobel Laureates sometimes reads as a much more distinguished list than those who were so recognized, and the name of Nobel laureates, especially early Laureates, are today obscure figures in the backwaters of national cultural history rather than global figures in the world of culture and the arts.

◆   See Appendix IX   ◆

The Nobel Prize in Literature

PAGE 217

◆   A list of Nobel laureates in literature from 1901 to 2004, and links to the kinds of literature that the laureates represent   ◆

The writer must be living to receive the Nobel Prize, so Shakespeare cannot appear; yet writers also considered controversial (ideal in the wrong way perhaps) or risqué in their day are also absent from the list — James Joyce, F. Scott Fitzgerald, D. H. Lawrence, even Graham Greene. Each reader will find surprising omissions; and while some award recipients bring pride to their nations, today they might be obscure or unknown internationally. Time of course has the effect of eroding reputation and only the next one hundred years will tell whether those presently in the limelight will remain acclaimed or eclipsed by decades to come and the talents that these bring. Still the Nobel Prize for Literature remains an important benchmark for the contribution the arts might make to *bettering* the human condition (Feldman, 2000). If the First World War shattered any cosy hopes for optimism about human progress, the Second World War confirmed fears perhaps previously unimagined such as the use of scientific and technological advances to make death more efficient.

Nevertheless the text remains very often the focus for repression and the means of facilitating repression, as well as the means of establishing basic human rights, or indeed, any political or theological position (cf. Tighe, 2005, on the broader position between writing and responsibility). For example, twentieth-century political history would have been utterly different but for the existence of three classic texts: Karl Marx and Friedrich Engels' *Manifesto of the Communist Party*, Adolf Hitler's *Mein Kampf* and Chairman Mao's *Little Red Book*. These texts — epitomes of intolerance as much as of materialism and militant atheism — are foundational to the violence of the twentieth century, and most influential in their attempts to limit freedom of expression.

A surprisingly limited number of texts have indeed had a profound effect upon the entire conceptual history and political development of freedom of expression. Yet the twentieth century has an especially important place in the development of the idea of such freedom, instituted by mid-century as part of international statute as a basic human right. Thus the utopian ideals of the UN's founding 1945 Charter and the 1948 Universal Declaration of Human Rights enshrined freedom of expression in Article 19, but also in Article 18, concerning freedom of religion or belief. We might therefore remind ourselves of simple, key historical landmarks in the twentieth century that provide for the preoccupations of the twenty-first: here we find the struggle for the dominance of ideology (meant here as a political belief) and theology (meant here as a belief in a world dominated by God, by religion, and possessed at least of the possibility of the supernatural); for instance, from the 1917 Revolution in Russia to the rise in 1933 of the Third Reich in Germany (both anti-religious ideologies) to their consequences in genocide. And genocide arguably remains the ultimate in cultural silence (Ball, 1999; Charny, 1999; Chorbajian and George, 1999; Bartov and Mack, 2001; Lorey and Beezley, 2002; Power, 2003). The case can be stated extremely by reference to history of the Third Reich: the burning of books in Berlin in 1933, those texts injurious to Nazi sensitivities to the views of 'Jews' and 'Communists', was a precursor to the imprisonment and systematic torture in subsequent months of Nazi power and to a violence which led directly to the racial laws and the concentration and death camps. A single book, *Mein Kampf*, can be said to be a prime impetus for the mass extinction of millions (Rose, 2000; Raven, 2004).

Genocide thus remains the quintessential extreme of cultural silence. Freedom of expression — or rather its denial — does not witness any greater extreme than genocide. (The Universal Declaration of Human Rights, amongst the most influential of modern writings by a committee, was largely written in response to totalitarian excesses.) Genocide can be defined as the systematic elimination of a population undertaken for reasons of ethnic or racial identity. One of the most utterly disturbing reflections of the World Conference on Human Rights must have been 'its dismay at massive violations of human rights especially in the form of genocide' and the clinical-sounding 'ethnic cleansing' (Para 28). These statements came two years before the worst single genocidal incident since the Holocaust with the slaughter in Central Africa, and especially in Rwanda. Indeed a review of the approximate statistics for mass slaughter of targeted populations *since* the 1948 Convention on the Prevention of Genocide makes particularly depressing reading.

The figures detailed overleaf represent both immense human suffering — even the rounding up or down of figures is itself disturbing — and a considerable failure of political systems in the UN era; on Sudan, and other contemporary ethnic and nationalistic as well as global conflicts, see www.un.org.

The Universal Declaration of Human Rights contains 30 short articles that express basic rights such as that to life and freedom from torture, but also articles which permit freedom of expression, in aesthetics, in conscience, in ideology, in religion. The universal Declaration of Human Rights was approved by the UN General Assembly on 10 December 1948. The Convention on the Prevention and Punishment of the Crime of Genocide was approved on 9 December 1948. In many regards, the latter is foundational to the former, historically and in contemporary context. Few regimes intent on silencing a cultural minority will remain content with the censorship of writing (Saunders, 2001; de Baets, 2001; Jones, 2001; Rose, 2000; Raven 2004).

The Mass Slaughter of Targeted Populations *since* the 1948 Convention on the Prevention of Genocide

Date	State	Victims	Deaths
1943–1957	USSR	Chechens, Ingushi, Karachai	230,000
1944–68	USSR	Crimean Tartars, Meskhetians	57,000–175,000
1955–77	China	Tibetans	Not available
1959–75	Iraq	Kurds	Not available
1962–72	Paraguay	Ache Indians	90,000
1963–64	Rwanda	Tutsis	5,000–14,000
1963	Laos	Meo Tribesmen	18,000–20,000
1965–66	Indonesia	Chinese	500,000–1 million
1965–73	Burundi	Hutus	103,000–205,000
1966	Nigeria	Ibos in North	9,000–30,000
1966–84	Guatemala	Indians	30,000–63,000
1968–85	Philippines	Moros	10,000–100,000
	Equatorial Guinea	Bubi Tribe	1,000–50,000
1971	Pakistan	Bengalis of Eastern Pakistan	1.25–3 million
1971–9	Uganda	Karamajong Acholi, Lango	100,000–500,000
1975–79	Cambodia	Muslim Cham	
1975–98	Indonesia	East Timorese	60,000–200,000
1978–	Burma	Muslims in border regions	Not available
1979–86	Uganda	Karamanjong, Nilotic Tribes Bagandans	50,000–100,000
1981	Iran	Kurds, Bahais	10,000–20,000
1983–7	Sri Lanka	Tamils	2,000–10,000
1993–4	Bosnia	Mainly Bosnian Muslims	200,000
1994–5	Rwanda	Tutsis	500,000–1 million
2003–5–?	Sudan	Tribal groups in Darfor	Not available

Source: adapted from Ryan, in Gearon, 2002.

In the first days of September 2001 the United Nations held in South Africa a World Conference on Racism and Xenophobia. Tensions had been evident between various factions for the brief duration of the conference. There was not full agreement on the proposal from Arab representatives that Zionism should be regarded as a form of racism. There was no consensus on the vexed question of reparation especially by those presently rich, industrialized nations that had profited economically from the historical injustices of slavery. Yet there was seemingly broad agreement on the idea that discrimination on the basis of race, gender, culture and religion was an infringement of a moral universal. If all could not agree fully on how to compensate for the evils of the past, or agree on how to resolve present difficulties, this United Nations conference ended by at least giving an impression that disparate countries and cultures were in agreement about broad principles, ethical universals now commonly categorized as human rights. The heading of the Human Rights Watch press release on 10 September read: 'Anti-Racism Summit Ends on Hopeful Note' (HRW, 2001); how different the world was to seem twenty-four hours later (Sarat, 2003; Williams, 2003). Few can deny that the events and aftermath of 11 September are symptomatic of a wider, historical struggle over values, what is sometimes called the clash of civilizations (Huntingdon, 1992), a clash made more apparent in the post cold-World War period (Ryan, 2000; Haynes, 2001). But struggle over value — and the imposition of one set of values — has been evident since the beginning of empires.

From the idealistic foundation of the 1901 Nobel Prize for Literature to the world crisis engendered by the destruction of the Twin Towers in New York on 11 September 2001, free expression of ideas, beliefs and ideologies has been central to the development of the last hundred years or so of world history. We might also note the wider context of this history of an emergent culture of human rights: the Charter of the United Nations gave rise to a range of declarations of human rights, often centrally involving basic freedoms of expression.

◆   See Appendix I   ◆

Charter of the United Nations (1945)

PAGE 157

What also emerged within the international community was a consciousness that civil and political rights must also coincide with social and cultural rights. It was for this reason that the founding of the United Nations in 1945 coincided with the founding of UNESCO, the United Nations Educational, Scientific and Cultural Organization.

◆   See Appendix III   ◆

UNESCO

Convention Concerning the Protection of the World Cultural and

Natural Heritage (1972)   PAGE 169

◆   Appendix IV   ◆

World Heritage Sites, listed by country   PAGE 179

Developments in the last three decades of the twentieth century and the opening of the twenty-first have shown UNESCO giving high priority to the protection not only of cultural rights but the protection of cultural *sites*. Arising from the 1972 Convention on the Protection of the World Cultural and Natural Heritage, UNESCO has developed a massive international system of protection and preservation of world heritage sites (see overleaf for appendix cross-reference).

Even if the utopian — civil and political — ideals of the international community in the twentieth century are as yet unfulfilled in the twenty-first, the protection of wider social and cultural rights and freedoms has remained a collective responsibility.

The twenty-first century is encountering forms of tension and repression which relate to theological and religious perspectives in conflict with such universal civil and political, social and cultural rights. More often than not the tensions revolve around conflicting worldviews, often of an ideological or religious nature. Religious and ideological systems tend then to be just as often the victims of repression in freedom of expression as the instigators. There remain many states that deny freedom of expression of any dissenting cultural or religious nature: the twentieth century witnessed, as the twenty-first century continues to witness, intolerance of political and religious difference on a grand scale, often in the name of God (Bartov and Mack, 2001; Gearon, 2002), but as often by atheistic regimes, by Hitler, by Stalin, by Mao. It is modes of worldview which have remained the major source of tension over freedom of expression. It was for such a reason that the UN appointed in the 1990s two special rapporteurs, the Special Rapporteur on the Promotion of the Right to Freedom of Opinion and Expression and the Special Rapporteur on Freedom of Religion or Belief.

◆ See Appendix V ◆

United Nations

Mandate of the Special Rapporteur on the Promotion of the Right to

Freedom of Opinion and Expression   PAGE 201

◆ Appendix VI ◆

United Nations

Mandate of the Special Rapporteur of the Commission on Human Rights on

Freedom of Religion or Belief   PAGE 202

◆ Appendix VII ◆

United Nations

Declaration on the Elimination of All Forms of Intolerance and of Discrimination

Based on Religion or Belief (1981)   PAGE 203

Tensions around freedom of expression follow seemingly perennial patterns throughout millennia, to which the case studies in this book — from Plato to the United Nations — provide ample testimony. In this regard, a typology for such complexities is useful not simply to reduce literally to type situations of greater complexity but to enable us to see generic patterns through the history of cultural ideas, which is also the history of freedom of expression. We might term this a 'typology of dissent'.

A Typology of Dissent

The following are the conceptual contexts in which dissent of a prevailing worldview is likely to occur, and in which issues of freedom of expression, particularly its repression, are also to be expected.

1. The **religious** (philosophical, political, metaphysical, sacred worldview, often but not necessarily theological, often but not exclusively idealistic) in dialogue or conflict with the **ideological** (necessarily philosophical, political, often but not necessarily secular, rationalistic, non-metaphysical and materialistic)
2. Inter-religious (religion in dialogue or conflict with religion)
3. Intra-religious (religion in dialogue or conflict with its own tradition)
4. Inter-ideological (philosophical–political dialogue or conflict with other such)
5. Intra-ideological (philosophical–political dialogue or conflict with its own tradition)

* Appendix VIII contains a full list of Inter-Governmental and Non-Governmental Organizations that deal with freedom of expression.
* Appendix IX provides a list of Nobel laureates in literature from 1901 to 2004, and links to the kinds of literature that these represent.
* See Appendix X for a development of this typology.

The risk of such typology is superficiality, to take two and a half thousand years of cultural history and examine it by one theme — freedom of expression — and mark this down for significance too large for its apparently minor status. It is arguable, however, that freedom of expression has always risked being perceived as of apparently minor status, something in the way of a cultural luxury (Magee, 2002; Scanlon, 2005). For instance, in a time of war or famine, the notion that 'I have the freedom to read what novels I choose to read' or follow a particular religious creed would hardly seem a priority when my life is threatened (Magee, 2002). Yet this is not always true; indeed, throughout history people have been willing to sacrifice their life for a cause which they think will achieve a greater end (Post, 2003; Sarat, 2003); civil wars and world wars have been fought on such principles, for right or wrong, and, as is often said, the right to oppose prevailing opinion is often the first casualty (de Baets, 2001; Jones, 2001). Religious traditions have within them martyrs who have been willing to die for a cause, and even the idea of killing others while serving that cause is not rare; the Crusades in the Middle Ages were fought on these principles, and early Christianity was founded on martyrdom and persecution, in the days before it possessed the powers of states and empires.

The existence of freedom of expression remains a critical and critically significant barometer for other forms of freedom and basic human rights (Forsythe, 2000; Lerner, 2000; Jones, 2001; de Baets, 2001; Arnheim, 2004; Smith, 2005); and the denial of freedom of expression broadly understood (censorship, the denial of the right to religious belief and practice) is often a precursor to abuse of a more outwardly violent kind (Rose, 2000; Raven, 2004).

References

Arnheim, M.T.W. (2004) *The Handbook of Human Rights Law: An Accessible Guide to the Issues and Principles.* London; Sterling, VA: Kogan Page.

Ball, H. (1999) *Prosecuting War Crimes and Genocide: The Twentieth-Century Experience.* Lawrence: University Press of Kansas.

Bartov, O. and Mack, P. (eds) (2001) *In God's Name: Genocide and Religion in the Twentieth Century.* Oxford: Berghahn Books.

Bradbury, Ray [1953] (1993) *Fahrenheit 451.* London: Flamingo.

Charny, I.W. (ed.) (1999) *Encyclopedia of Genocide*, forewords by Desmond M. Tutu and Simon Weisenthal. Santa Barbara, California: ABC-CLIO.

Chorbajian, L. and George, S. (eds.) (1999) *Studies in Comparative Genocide.* Basingstoke: Macmillan.

Commonwealth Secretariat (2003) *Freedom of Expression, Association and Assembly: Best Practice.* London: Commonwealth Secretariat.

Cox, Michael, Booth, Ken, and Dunne, Tim (1999) *The Interregnum: Controversies in World Politics 1989–1999.* Cambridge; New York: Cambridge University Press.

de Baets, Antoon (2001) *Censorship of Historical Thought: A World Guide, 1945–2000.* Westport, Conn: Greenwood Press.

de Koster, Katie (2000) *Readings on Fahrenheit 451.* San Diego: Greenhaven Press.

Forsythe, David P. (2000) *Human Rights in International Relations* third edition. Cambridge. Cambridge University Press.

Gearon, Liam (2002) *Religion and Human Rights: A Reader.* Brighton & Portland: Sussex Academic Press.

Feldman, Burton (2000) *The Nobel Prize.* New York: Arcade.

Foerstel, Herbert N. (2002) *Banned in the USA: A Reference Guide to Book Censorship in Schools and Public Libraries.* Westport, Conn.; London: Greenwood Press.

Forsythe, David P. (2000) *Human Rights in International Relations.* Cambridge: Cambridge University Press.

Haynes, Jeffrey (1998) *Religion in Global Politics.* Harlow: Longman.

Hermina, G.B., Anghelescu and Poulain, Martine (2001) *Books, Libraries, Reading and Publishing in the Cold War.* Washington, D.C.: Library of Congress, Center for the Book.

HRW (2001) 'Anti-Racism Summit Ends on Hopeful Note'. New York: Human Rights Watch.

Jones, Derek (ed.) (2001) *Censorship: A World Encyclopedia*, four volumes. London: Fitzroy Dearborn.

Karolides, Nicholas J., Margaret Bald and Dawn B. Sova (eds) (1999) *100 Banned Books: Censorship Histories of World Literature.* New York: Checkmark Books.

Lerner, Nathan (2000) *Religion, Beliefs, and Human Rights.* Maryknoll, New York: Orbis.

Lorey, D.E. and Beezley, W.H. (eds) (2002) *Genocide, Collective Violence and Popular Memory: The Politics of Remembrance in the Twentieth Century.* Wilmington, Del.: SR Books.

Magee, James J. (2002) *Freedom of Expression.* Westport, Connecticut: Greenwood Press.

Marshall, Paul (ed.) (2000) *Religious Freedom in the World: A Global Report on Freedom and Persecution.* London: Broadman and Holman.

Miller, Arthur (2000) *Plays: One*, introduced by Arthur Miller. London: Methuen World Classics.

Orwell, George [1945] (1949) *Animal Farm: A Fairy Tale.* Harmondsworth: Penguin.

Orwell, George [1949] (1954) *Nineteen Eighty-Four.* Harmondsworth: Penguin.

Post, Stephen Garrard (2003) *Human Nature and the Freedom of Public Religious Expression.* Notre Dame, Indiana: University of Notre Dame Press.

Power, Samantha (2003) *A Problem from Hell: America and the Age of Genocide.* London: Flamingo.

Raven, James (2004) *Lost Libraries: The Destruction of Great Book Collections Since Antiquity.* Basingstoke: Palgrave Macmillan.

Rose, Jonathan (ed.) (2000) *The Holocaust and the Book: Destruction and Preservation.* Amherst: University of Massachusetts Press.

Ryan, S. (2000) *The United Nations and International Politics.* London: Macmillan, 2000.

Sarat, Austin (ed.) (2003) *Dissent in Dangerous Times.* Ann Arbor, MI: University of Michigan Press.

Scanlon, Thomas (2005) *The Difficulty of Tolerance: Essay in Political Philosophy.* Cambridge: Cambridge University Press.

Sellars, Kirsten (2003) *The Rise and Rise of Human Rights*. London: Sutton Books.
Sarat, Austin (ed.) (2005) *Dissent in Dangerous Times*. Ann Arbor, MI: University of Michigan Press.
Saunders, Frances Stonor (2001) *The Cultural Cold War: The CIA and the World of Arts and Letters*. New York: New Press.
Smith, Rhona K.M. (2005) *Textbook on International Human Rights*. Oxford: Oxford University Press.
Tighe, Carl (2005) *Writing and Responsibility*. London: Routledge.
Warburton, Nigel (ed.) (2001) *Freedom: An Introduction with Readings*. London: Routledge.
Webb, W.L. and Rose Bell (1997) *An Embarrassment of Tyrannies: Twenty-Five Years of Index on Censorship*. London: Victor Gollancz.
Williams, Mary E. (ed.) (2003) *The Terrorist Attack on America*. San Diego: Greenhaven.

Selected Electronic Sources

BEACON FOR FREEDOM
www.beaconforfreedom.org offers an outstanding historical resource covering key critical periods, country-by-country, but also dealing with the most infamous and long-lasting ideological and theological forms of repressions — some may find offensive the conflation of the Roman Catholic Church, the former Soviet Union and Nazi Germany. For instance, it contains selected international libraries, reports, articles and other relevenat links.

AUSTRALIA
Office of film and literature classification: http://www.oflc.gov.au
Search the OFLC database: http://www.oflc.gov.au (and follow links)
Guide to Law Online (Library of Congress): http://www.loc.gov/ law/guide/australia (and follow links)
National Library of Australia: http://www.nla.gov.au (and follow links)
Electronic Frontiers Australia Inc. On Censorship and free Speech: http://www. efa.org.au/Issues/Censor (and follow links)

CANADA
IFLA/FAIFE World Report: Libraries and Intellectual Freedom: http://www.ifla.org (and follow links)
National Library of Canada: http://www.nlc-bnc.ca (and follow links)
A Chronicle of Freedom of Expression in Canada: http://www.efc.ca (and follow links)
Guide to Law Online (Library of Congress): http://www.loc. gov/law/guide/canada (and follow links)

DENMARK
FAIFE: http://www.ifla.org/faife (and follow links)
IFLA/FAIFE World Report: Libraries and Intellectual Freedom: http://www.ifla.org/faife (and follow links)
The Royal Library: http://www.kb.dk (and follow links)
Guide to Law Online (Library of Congress): http://www.loc.gov/law /guide/ denmark (and follow links)

FRANCE
National Library of France: http://www.bnf.fr (and follow links)
Guide to Law Online (Library of Congress): http://www.loc.gov/ law/guide/france (and follow links)

GERMANY

IFLA/FAIFE World Report: Libraries and Intellectual Freedom:
   http://www.ifla. org/faife/report/germany (and follow links)
National Library of Germany: http://www.ddb.de (and follow links)
Guide to Law Online (Library of Congress):
   http://www.loc.gov/law/guide/germany.html

IRAN

National Library of the Islamic Republic of Iran: http://www.nli.ir (and follow links)
Guide to Law Online (Library of Congress): http://www.loc. gov/law/guide /iran.html

ITALY

IFLA/FAIFE World Report: Libraries and Intellectual Freedom:
   http://www.ifla. org/faife/report/italy (and follow links)
National Library of Italy: http://opac.sbn.it (and follow links)
Guide to Law Online (Library of Congress): http://www.loc.gov/law/ guide/italy (and follow
   links)

JAPAN

IFLA/FAIFE World Report: Libraries and Intellectual Freedom:
   http://www.ifla.org/faife/report/japan (and follow links)
National Diet Library: http://www.ndl.go.jp (and follow links)
Guide to Law Online (Library of Congress): http://www.loc.gov/law/guide/japan (and
   follow links)

NORWAY

Freedom of expression in Norway — article National Library of Norway: http://www.kb.nl
   (and follow links)
Guide to Law Online (Library of Congress): http://www.loc.gov/law/ guide/norway.html

PERU

National Library of Peru: http://www.binape.gob.pe (and follow links)
Guide to Law Online (Library of Congress): http://www.loc.gov/law (and follow links)

POLAND

National Library of Poland: http://www.bn.org.pl (and follow links)
Guide to Law Online (Library of Congress):
   http://www.loc.gov/law/ guide/poland.html

RUSSIAN FEDERATION AND THE SOVIET UNION

National Library of Russia: http://www.nlr.ru (and follow links)
Russian State Library: http://www.rsl.ru/defengl.asp (and follow links)
Guide to Law Online (Library of Congress): http://www.loc.gov/law/ guide/russia (and follow
   links)

SOUTH AFRICA

IFLA/FAIFE World Report: Libraries and Intellectual Freedom:
   http://www.ifla. org/faife/report/south_africa (and follow links)
National Library of South Africa: http://www.nlsa.ac.za (and follow links)
Guide to Law Online (Library of Congress): http://www.loc.gov/law/ guide/southafrica (and
   follow links)

SPAIN

IFLA/FAIFE World Report: Libraries and Intellectual Freedom:
   http://www.ifla. org/faife/report/spain (and follow links)
National Library of Spain: http://www.bne.es (and follow links)
Guide to Law Online (Library of Congress): http://www.loc.gov/law/guide/spain (and follow
   links)

TURKEY

IFLA/FAIFE World Report: Libraries and Intellectual Freedom:
   http://www.ifla. org/faife/report/turkey (and follow links)
National Library of Turkey: http://www.mkutup.gov.tr/index-eng (and follow links)
Guide to Law Online (Library of Congress): http://www.loc.gov/law/ guide/turkey.html

UNITED KINGDOM

IFLA/FAIFE World Report: Libraries and Intellectual Freedom: http://www.
   ifla.org/faife/report/uk (and follow links)
British Library: http://www.bl.uk (and follow links)
Guide to Law Online (Library of Congress): http://www.loc.gov/law/guide/uk (and follow
   links)

UNITED STATES

IFLA/FAIFE World Report: Libraries and Intellectual Freedom: http://www.ifla.
   org/faife/report/united_states (and follow links)
American Library Association: http://www.ala.org/cipa (and follow links)
Challenged and banned books: http://www.ala.org (and follow links)
Guide to Law Online (Library of Congress): http://www.loc.gov/law/guide/us (and follow
   links)
Library of Congress: http://www.loc.gov (and follow links)
Banned Books Online: http://digital.library.upenn.edu/books/banned-books (and follow
   links)

VATICAN CITY STATE

Guide to Law Online (Library of Congress): http://www.loc.gov/law/ guide/vatican (and
   follow links)
Vatican Library: http://www.vatican.va/library_archives (and follow links)
Index Librorum Prohibitorum, of 1949: http://www.univ.com.br (and follow links)

GENERIC ELECTRONIC SOURCES OF REFERENCE

Biography.com offers an immense range of historical and biographical detail of 'the greatest
   lives, past and present'.
Columbia Encyclopedia: http://education.yahoo.com (and follow links) source of a range of
   research and reference topics, including politics, philosophy and the arts.
Encyclopedia of Literature and Politics: Censorship, Revolution and Politics, Westport,
   Connecticut: Greenwood. M. Keith Booker's three-volume resource is available as an Ebook:
   www.greenwood.com (and follow links).
Oxford Dictionary of Nationa Biography: www.oxforddnb.com is an authoritative source of
   historical and biographical detail that requires a subscription account.
Oxford Reference Online: www.oxfordreference.com offers an outstanding and authoritative,
   online subscription source of reference, incorporating prime material on art, politics, religion
   and writing.

Stanford Encyclopedia of Philosophy: http://plato.stanford.edu is an encyclopedia is author-itative and is a marvelously useful work for general reference in philosophy.

The Internet Encyclopedia of Philosophy: www.iep.utm (and follow links) is an authoritative source on philosophy and politics.

United Nations: www.un.org is the immensely rich hub of the United Nations organization, important for its links to international politics and law, especially human rights

Wikipedia: http://en.wikipedia.org is a 'multilingual Web-based free-content encyclopedia' and is 'written collaboratively by volunteers'. It contains a wealth of useable information on a range of topics, biography, history and politics. It is not peer-reviewed, and within certain goodwill parameters, can be freely edited online, and thus any sources should be checked against other reliable, peer-reviewed written or online sources of information.

If you only visit one website on writers in the twentieth century, go to

The Nobel Prize in Literature   www.nobelprize.org/literature

The Nobel website presents an immense range of historical material relating to Nobel Prizes, and of particular interest here are those offered for Peace and those offered for Literature. The Literature Prize contains the acceptance speeches of numerous acclaimed writers who often present their own insights into not only their own work but also that of the political circumstances in which they were writing.
www.nobel.org and www.nobelprize.org/literature

◆   See also Appendix I   ◆
Charter of the United Nations (1945)

PAGE 157

Classic Texts on Writing and Dissent

Political, Literary and Historical Contexts
in Freedom of Expression

PART

I

Plato (c. 427/8 BC – c. 347 BC)
The Republic

> So much then for stories of the gods. We have settled, it seems, which of them our young children may hear and which they may not, if they are to grow up to honour the gods and their parents, and to hold friendship dear.
>
> PLATO's *The Republic*

Consciously or otherwise, freedom of expression is defined by the limits any age places on its liberty. For its treatment of freedom within a fiercely stratified society, *The Republic* has attracted immense attention over many centuries from political philosophers for the model of the utopian state Plato presents within it (Gracia, 2003). As the ten books of *The Republic* are also concerned with the training of those who should rule, educationalists have also found much of interest there (Haworth, 2003). For the modern reader, the most consistently outrageous aspects of *The Republic* are its comfortably elitist attitudes and totalitarian tendencies (Coleman, 2000; Jackson, 2001; Eyres, 2001; Appignnanesi, Heidegger, 2002, 2003). These attitudes and tendencies manifest themselves nowhere more dramatically than in the many passages devoted to the expulsion of poets and their writings from the ideal state. In classical Greece, the poet was much more than simply a 'creative writer' and was often regarded as a seer with epiphanic or prophetic or even religious insights (Lebetter, 2001; Murray and Dorsch, 2000; Asmis, 2004). Plato is incensed at the damage that he believes such figures can represent for the state.

Karl Popper's *The Open Society and Its Enemies* remains without doubt the most notable and systematic attack on the outrage of Plato's totalitarianism (Popper, 1946). Our task is to look specifically at those passages in which Plato's totalitarian impulses manifest themselves through the repression of the poets and thereby freedom of expression — artistic, literary, religious — and how Plato thus places the stability of the state over the freedom of the individual and individual freedom of expression. These questions remain integral to modern statecraft, as noted in the Preface. For such reasons, Plato is an early manifestation of an enduring historical controversy, of a political problem that will not, perhaps cannot, go away (Monoson, 2000; Lane, 2001; Mitchell and Lucas, 2003; Pappas, 2003). *The Republic* thus remains foundational to any historical and contemporary consideration of censorship and freedom of expression (Barasch, 2000; Levin, 2001; Babonich, 2002; Nadaff, 2003).

Plato the Author

Plato was born in Athens around 427/8 BC. His mother was Perictione and his father Ariston. It is likely that after his father's death in childhood, Plato grew up in his mother's second husband's house, Pyrilampes. Perictione's brother was Charmides, her cousin Critias, both political extremists favouring the wealthy oligarchic structures of which they were an influential and integral part. Both Charmides and Critias were friends of Socrates. Politics and philosophy were major factors in Plato's development, and were to dominate his later life and career. The boy of an oligarchic family who lost his father in childhood, it was the influence of Socrates through which Plato filtered all his philosophical and political views. At around forty years of age, Plato founded the Academy, a critically open and prototypical model of the university for around twenty-five centuries (Ebenstein and Ebenstein, 2000; Brickhouse, 2004).

Unlike Socrates, Plato left a vast corpus of writings. The works are for the most part in the form of dialogues, and hence of consciously dramatic effect. The dialogues invariably involve Socrates as protagonist. Plato is himself entirely absent from them. In addition to the inconsistencies of view between the early and later writings, this absence of the persona or authorial Plato presents considerable difficulties for interpretation. It is possible that Plato was relaying the views of historical figures of his time and as an author might be attempting to remain neutral in regard to the action that unfolds. For the most part, however, the views of Plato are presumed to originate from Socrates, his old mentor and teacher. If there are inconsistencies of philosophical or political standpoints — through early (*Euthyphro, Phaedo*), middle (*Republic*) and later (*Sophist, Statesman, Theaetetus, Laws*) dialogues — the authorial voice of Plato consistently leads us to sympathize with Socrates and his view rather than that of his interlocutors (except those sympathetic to Socrates himself).

In terms of stylistic and literary differences between the different periods of Plato's writing, the early dialogues are said to have stronger dramatic qualities: what more so than those on the last days of Socrates? The later dialogues are possessed of more carefully deliberated philosophical reflection, born of long reflection and experience, and of an ageing philosopher's weakening extremism (the *Laws* is less rigidly authoritarian) and softening towards sentimentalism (the *Symposium* reflects on the famous 'Platonic' forms of love, and indeed the praiseworthy role of poetry here).

In terms of Plato's politics, the early dialogues represent a diatribe against the Athenians for condemning Socrates. In the middle dialogue of the *Republic* Plato's own statecraft is harsher and even intolerant, more forbidding of democracy and the rule of the people in general. By the later *Laws* the Athenian visitor (and we can presume the voice of Plato) is sympathetic in regard to the democracy he observes there.

Although there remains considerable scholarly debate over dates and the wisdom of a strictly defined progression in the philosopher's works, for these reasons (literary style, philosophical content, political attitudes), Plato's dialogues can, then, be divided into a three-fold schema — early, middle and later works. The early (sometimes referred to as 'Socratic') dialogues are often ascribed as: *Apology, Charmides, Crito,*

Euthydemus, Euthyphro, Gorgias, Hippias Major, Hippias Minor, Ion, Laches, Lysis and *Protagoras*. The middle dialogues as: *Phaedo, Cratylus, Symposium, Republic* and *Phaedrus*. The later dialogues as: *Laws, Sophist, Statesman, Timaeus, Critias* and *Philebus*. The philosophy expressed by Socrates we might deduce is the philosophy of Plato; whether the philosophy of Plato is that of the historical Socrates is, as we have intimated, certainly more questionable:

> Many contemporary scholars find it plausible that when Plato embarked on his career as a philosopher writer, he composed, in addition to his *Apology* of Socrates, a number of short ethical dialogues that contain little or nothing in the way of positive philosophical doctrine, but are mainly devoted to portraying the way in which Socrates punctured the pretensions of his interlocutors and forced them to realize that they were unable to offer satisfactory definitions of the ethical terms they used, or satisfactory arguments for their moral beliefs. (Kraut, 2003: 7)

The *Dialogues* relating to the last days of Socrates are those which are likely to represent most closely an 'historical' picture of Plato's great mentor. Socrates' death by hemlock, a common method of execution in Athens, was at the charge of corrupting the young for permitting them philosophical freedom, leading them to impiety. This charge and the manner of his death demonstrate, as much as any dialogue of Plato, the extent and limits of Athenian freedom of expression. Indeed, the governance of a city upon 'democratic ideals' is shown to result in such injustice and is one of the reasons we see Plato in the Republic favouring the philosophical elite as the ideal form of government, even if later he modifies his views:

> Just as any attempt to understand Plato's views about forms must confront the question whether his thoughts about them developed or altered over time, so too our reading of him as political philosopher must be shaped by a willingness to consider a deep antipathy to rule by the many. Socrates tells his interlocutors that the only politics that should engage them are those of the anti-democratic regime he depicts as the paradigm of a good constitution. And yet in *Laws*, the Athenian visitor proposes a detailed legislative framework for a city in which non-philosophers (people who have never heard of the forms, and have not been trained to understand them) are given considerable powers as rulers. Plato would not have invested so much time in the creation of this comprehensive and lengthy work, had he not believed that the creation of a political community ruled by those who are philosophically unenlightened is a project that deserves the support of his readers. (Kraut, 2003: 7)

The shift in Plato's polity is matched by a shift in his interpretation of the role of the poets, which is gentler, more mellow in the later Plato than the earlier. This can be seen clearly between the *Apology* — where Socrates points out the poets are wise about things which they are not — to the Republic — where they would be banned from ideal state — to the *Symposium* — where poetry is praised for its contribution to 'Platonic' forms of love.

Yet the key premise, the great Socratic–Platonic philosophical ideal, unshakable more or less throughout the dialogues, is that this world represents only inadequately a more perfect other-worldly ideal. The earthly form represents only in imperfect mirror 'form' the ideal pattern from which it is derived, for every imperfect representation on this earth there is a heavenly form from which is derived its idea. Plato's famous metaphor of the prisoners in a cave — drawn from his Republic — illustrates this. Imagine prisoners restrained in a cave with only shadows from a fire to give them a sense of the world and its forms; people, Plato says, see the world just like this, seeing simply the shadow form of the world of experience rather than experiencing the world in itself, the heavenly perfection of its ideal form. (This idea had without doubt its most powerful expression in the post-Platonic Christian world when the idea of a Platonic ideal was taken and used by Christian theologians to suggest that the world in which we live and suffer is simply an imperfect form of the world of heaven. We should see therefore not the pleasures of this earthly body but those of the soul, of the spiritual.)

It was on the ground of such philosophical ideals that Plato based his polity. Utopias are often forged from the idea of an imagined past that never existed. This does not mean that such pasts are bad models for the future, only that they are necessarily unrealizable, just that they are unlikely to be realized as material reality in any foreseeable present.

Plato, the *Republic* and Freedom of Expression

The terms freedom of expression and human rights are almost entirely the products of the modern age and they do not sit naturally in the *Republic*. That Plato spent so much time on repressing poets in *The Republic* (Books II, III and X) might allow us to deduce that there was a proliferation rather than a shortage of them. For him poets are a corrupting and corrosive influence upon society and centrally because they are a weakening influence upon the character of individual men. The disruptive function of poets is not likely to have been an ironic device, though Plato's totalitarian intolerance often appears imbued with humour.

Like the vast majority of Plato's writings the *Republic* exists in the form of a dialogue, in what has been usefully described as 'the dramatization of reason' (McCabe, 2003). In the *Republic* it centres on the question of the nature of justice. Here Thrasymachus argues that justice is only what serves the powerful; Glaucon argues that it is a matter of self preservation. The state is to be divided into guardians, rulers (and their auxiliaries), and workers: the guardians of the state need to be philosophically inclined and a large part of the *Republic* concerned with their training; the rulers, those with political power, are decision makers, supported by auxiliaries who help against defence from outside forces; the workers provide for the necessities of life.

It is Socrates — always the presumed mouthpiece of Plato — who attempts to show that justice is good and good in itself. Plato moves from what is good for the individual to what is good for the state and vice versa with ease. What is good for one is presumed good for the other, and what is bad for one is likely to be bad for the other. Poets are not the only casualties amongst those influences seen to be pernicious. In the *Republic* there is no personal property, no attachment to family — essentially abolished — and 'defective' children are to be disposed of. In Plato's *Republic*, only philosophers and kings or rulers trained in philosophy have the necessary skills to be able to guide or rule the state. Unlike the famous metaphor of the prisoners in the cave who see the world as if it were play shadows rather than seeing the world as it really is, in reality it is not simply a poor reflection; philosophers love the truth and have at least the capacity to see the world as it is. There are four models of government which Plato outlines and dismisses: the timocracy (a martial state, which parallels the hated Sparta dominated by military honour); the oligarchy (government by a rich and powerful elite); democracy (government by the rule of the people by the people, and which Plato considers leads to the ultimate in chaos); and tyranny (government in which the ruler has absolute power).

The argument against the poets presented in the *Republic* is a simple one and it is based much less upon aesthetic judgment — though Plato's distaste for Homer is apparent — than political expediency, for which Plato has gathered a deserved repu-tation for ruthlessness over twenty-five centuries. It is nevertheless Plato's judgments upon poetry that govern his polity and the clash of aesthetics and politics becomes unavoidable:

> Then we must speak to our poets and compel them to impress upon their poems only the image of the good, or not make poetry in our city. And we must speak to the other craftsmen and forbid them to leave the impress of that which is evil in character, unrestrained, mean, and ugly, on their likenesses of living creatures, or their houses, or anything else they make. He that cannot obey must not be allowed to ply his trade in our city. For we would not have our guardians reared among images of evil as in a foul pasture, and there day by day and little by little gather many impressions from all that surrounds them, taking them all in until at last a great mass of evil gathers in their inmost souls, and they know it not. No, we must seek out those craftsmen who have the happy gift of tracing out the nature of the fair and graceful, that our young men may dwell as in a health-giving region where all that surrounds them is beneficent, whencesoever from fair works of art their smite upon their eyes and ears an afflu-ence like a wind bringing health from happy regions, which, though, they know it not, leads them from their earliest years into likeness and friendship and harmony with the principle of beauty. (Plato, 1935: 84)

Two major arguments espoused by Plato against poetry and the poets — and by this definition against free expression — are, first, that the poets misrepresent God and the activity of the gods (they give a false and irrational theology) and, second, that the poets make 'men' emotionally and intellectually unfit for the operations of the state.

In this first case, Plato presents the voice of theological reason, 'that God is simple and true in word and deed, he does not change himself; nor does he delude others, either in phantasies or words, or by sending signs, whether in waking moments or in dreams' Once this is accepted, there arise the canon 'determining all speaking and writing about the gods is that they are not magicians, and do not change themselves, or deceive us by lies, either in word or deed'. From this then comes the challenge against certain passages in Homer which infringe this theological logic:

> Though we find much to praise in Homer we should not praise him for his story of the sending of the dream of Agamemnon to Zeus . . . When any one says things about the gods we shall be angry, and shall not give him a chorus; nor shall we allow our teachers to use his poems to instruct the young, if our guardians are to be god-fearing and godlike so far as man may be. (Plato, 1935: 65)

These notions become canons, and there is the declaration that these principles should be used, as Plato would use them as laws. Homer is used as an example of poetic excellence, and if the argument works against Homer it can and should be used against the lesser poets. On the second notion, that poets make 'men' psychologically and mentally unfit for the State, we might cite the following passage also from Book III:

> Then we must also get rid of all the fearful and terrifying titles belonging to those subject, 'wailing Cocytus,' and 'loathed Styx,' and 'infernals,' and 'sapless, dead,' and all the words of that type, the very sound of which is enough to make men shiver. These will probably be useful enough for other purposes, but for our guardians we are afraid that this shivering fear will make them more emotional and softer than they ought to be. (Plato, 1935: 67)

Art and all forms of artistic imitation encourage that which under normal circumstances we would not find admirable; for example, we might weep at a tragic event in a play, but, at least in an ancient Greek context, 'the law says that it is best to take misfortunes as quietly as possible and not to grieve, because the good and evil in such matters are not certain, and to take them hardly makes things no better for the future; because no human affairs are worth taking seriously; and finally, because grief is a hindrance to that state of mind to which we should come in our troubles as quickly as possible' (Plato, 1935: 307).

The passages that must also be excised are those which represent such weakness in political leaders, so that — as we learn in Book II — we must from the poets 'strike out the weepings and wailings of famous men':

> if our young were to take such passages seriously, instead of laughing at them as bad poetry, unworthy of their subjects, it would be difficult to make them feel that they themselves, who are but men, are above those actions, or to make them rebuke themselves if it should occur to them also to say or do such things. They would lose their sense of shame and their hardihood, and weep and lament loudly over the most trifling misfortunes . . . and that we must prevent, as our argument has taught us, and we shall follow it till someone shows us better . . . (Plato, 1935: 69)

Undoubtedly unequalled for extremes are the means by which the physicians of the body and the soul are to judge as fit for only death those physically unfit or spiritually unsound:

> So the virtuous man, it appears to me, and not the wicked makes the best judge . . . Along with [such] judges you will give the city doctors . . . and the two professions will tend the souls and bodies of such of your citizens as are of sound nature; but for the rest, they will permit the unsound in body to die, and actually put to death those who are incurably corrupt in soul. (Plato, 1935: 111)

This is ironic, and fearfully so, for a man who left Athens after the execution of his mentor, in dismay and disgust at the State imposed death of Socrates.

Art conforms to Plato's theory of forms since that which is imitation cannot by its nature be truth, but only its shadow, and attacks build momentum until the final chapter: 'By Zeus, is not this imitation concerned with something that is third from the truth?' (Plato, 1935: 305). Worse, though, the poet is seen to be a danger to society in imitating 'what appears to be beautiful and ordinary and ignorant people' yet 'without knowing wherein each thing is bad or good' (Plato, 1935: 304). And in regard to such dangers, Plato recognizes that it is not the mediocre but the most magnificent of artistic and literary talents about whom the state should be concerned. As the acknowledged narrator of Greek history and letters, it is Homer who becomes the continued target of Plato in Book X.

> We must examine tragedy, and Homer its leader, since people tell us that tragedians know all arts and all things human that relate to virtue and vice and things divine. For a good poet, they say, if he is to make a beautiful poem on his subject, must do so with knowledge of that subject, or fail altogether . . . their productions are appearances and not realities. (Plato, 1935: 300)

The fear is that imitation of that which is not ordinarily desirable — in the *Republic* those weaknesses which the theatre is keen to re-present — may appear on the streets:

> And with regard to sexual desires, and anger, and all feelings of desire and pain and pleasure in the soul, which we say follow all our actions, you observe that poetic imitation produces all these effects in us. They should be withered, and it waters them and makes them grow. It makes them rule over us, when they ought to be subjects if we are to become better and happier, instead of worse and more miserable . . . when you find Homer's admirers saying that this poet has educated Hellas, and that in questions of human conduct and culture a man ought to read and study Homer, and organize his whole life in accordance with the teaching of this poet, you must be friendly and kind to such people — they are as good as they know how to be — and agree that Homer is the most poetical and the first of the tragic poets, but be quite sure in your mind that only such specimens of poetry are hymns to the gods or praises of good men are to be received into the city. If you receive the pleasure-seasoned Muse of song and epic, pleasure and pain will be kings in your city instead of law and the principle which at all times has been decided by the community to be best. (Plato, 1935: 310)

In an argument adapted to theological purposes that Augustine will use against the creative arts in his *Confessions*, Plato thus concludes that imitative arts and their representatives have as little place in the republic as villains:

> Then we may justly lay hold of the poet and set him over against the painter; for he resembles him in producing what has little value for truth, and also in associating with a similar part of the soul, which is not the best. And so we may now with justice refuse to allow him entrance to a city which is to be well governed, because he arouses and fosters and strengthens this part of the soul and destroys the reasoning part. Like one who gives a city over into the hands of villains, and destroys the better citizens, so we shall say that the imitative poet likewise implants an evil constitution in the soul of each individual; he gratifies the foolish element in it, that which cannot distinguish between great and small but thinks that the same things are sometimes great and sometimes small, and he manufactures images very far removed from the truth. (Plato, 1935: 308–309)

In the *Laws* Plato takes a more conciliatory approach to the poets, allowing those who would contribute to the harmony and well-being of the city to enter. Yet there is more to Plato's rejection of poets than an extreme polity. It is central to the consideration of freedom of expression here, for we find that Plato's objection to the poets is not simply for the corruption of their literary skills upon the individuals within the state. As Elizabeth Asmis comments, this 'subordination of poetry to politics has offended many readers of Plato from antiquity to the present':

> Plato's quarrel with poetry takes its start in the fact that Greek poets had a crucial role in the creation and transmission of social values. It was traditionally believed that poets, like prophets, were inspired directly by the gods with wisdom about the human and divine condi-

tion. It was the prerogative of poets to make known the past, present and future to their contemporaries and future generations by oral performances of their poetry. Prose writings and books did not become common until the fifth century BC, and even then the primary method of publishing a work was oral performance. The poems were chanted or sung, usually to instrumental accompaniment, at gatherings that ranged from private affairs to celebrations held by an entire community or region, such as the dramatic festivals of Dionysius. Most occasions had a religious setting, and many poetic performances were a form of religious worship. (Asmis, 1999: 338–339)

Plato's battle against the poets is as much that between philosophy and theology as between philosophy and art.

Asmis also points out that today Plato's parallel attacks would be upon the over-prevalent influence of rock concerts, television soap stars and the cult of celebrity, that:

Plato's view of the quarrel between poetry and philosophy involves a third group, the sophists. Their name 'wise men' which soon became a source of derision, showed that they considered themselves heirs and rivals to the poets. In Plato's *Protagorus*, Protagorus (fl c. 450 BC) leader of the first generation of sophists, proclaims that he was the first person to claim a place openly within the Greek tradition of educators (316–317c). As heir to the poets, he considers the most important part of education to be the criticism of poetry (338–339a), and he illustrates his contention by attacking a well-known poem by Simonides. In their challenge to the poetic tradition, the sophists used a new weapon, prose. Partly, they discovered new possibilities of language in prose; partly they attempted to capture the power of poetry by modeling their prose on poetic usage. One new use of prose was to engage the listener in an exchange of questions and answers, with the main aim of scoring a victory by forcing the respondent to agree with whatever is proposed. Socrates' dialectical method is a development of this invention. The sophists were also the first to teach methods of argument. Unlike the poets, they claimed no authority for their teachings except their own 'wisdom.' They emphasized the practical utility of their teaching which they regarded as the culmination of a series of inventions devised by humans for their own advancement. (Asmis, 1999: 42)

In broad terms, Plato's attack on the poets in the *Republic* is symptomatic of a wider rivalry between the supposed superstition of religion and the rationalism of philosophy.

Summary

Though Plato's influence on his pupil, Aristotle, is all pervasive, Aristotle's philosophy of literature and the arts is entirely distant from that of his teacher. In the *Poetics*, Aristotle outlines the major forms and functions of literary art (Aristotle, 1995: 2316–2340; Barnes, 1995). Unlike Plato, Aristotle does not see literature — drama and poetry principally — as dangers to Greek society but as a means of enriching it (Lebetter, 2001; Murray and Dorsch, 2000). Aristotle is similarly concerned with the effects of the arts upon a person, notably its emotional as well as intellectual effects (whether and how a work of literature 'works'), but he celebrates these in so far as it may contribute to a person's happiness and to the good of society. In so far as Aristotle's political and ethical philosophy is concerned with an understanding and facilitation of human happiness, in terms of his aesthetic philosophy, Aristotle's claim might well be that good literature contributes to human happiness while bad literature does not. Aristotle retains a paramount role in establishing an aesthetic philosophy promoting rather than denigrating the role of literature in social and political context. Aristotle is more concerned with understanding literature than with suppressing it. Where Plato would bar the poets from the Republic, for Aristotle a society without poets would be an impoverished place.

In the post-Platonic and Post-Aristotelian eras, after the political collapse of Greek political influence and the rise and eventual fall of the Roman Empire, Christianity was to draw upon the Platonic philosophic ideas in many ways. Not least here Christianity would take the view that this earthly realm was a poor imitation of a heavenly and ideal realm. Through the figure of Saint Augustine, Christianity (at this time and arguably until very modern times), would also adopt Plato's denigration of the poet rather than Aristotle's idealization. A great and still pervading philosophical and theological influence, well-versed in classical philosophy, Saint Augustine (354–430), at least after his conversion to Christianity, argued for the supremacy of Christian scriptural revelation over anything in Plato or Aristotle, to say nothing of more minor figures in Greek or later Roman or 'pagan' learning.

Plato's incalculable contribution to aesthetic, ethical and political philosophy, and nearly every other branch of western philosophy, as well as Christian theology, cannot obviously or simply be reduced to a typology of dissent — accommodation and repression — in regard to freedom of expression.

◆　See Appendix X　◆

A Typology of Dissent *and* A Typology for Interrogation of Dissent

PAGE 219

◆　It is a useful and instructive exercise to compare the statecraft represented

by the rights and freedoms in Appendices I through to IX with Plato's

polity in *The Republic*　◆

Yet Plato's views on freedom of expression reveal a whole statecraft, a totalitarian and intolerant one. Plato also reveals through his proposed repression of the poets, a worldview which stresses the rational over the artistic (and to Plato emotional and anti-rationalistic) and theological; as we have seen from Asmis, this is not simply a rejection of the artistic but an indirect rejection of the religious as a way of determining what we know about the world. And herein, from Plato's *Republic* onwards, were sowed the seeds of a dissent that was to foment for millennia. The influence of classical learning, after its decline alongside the rise of the Christian era, was not resurrected for a thousand years until the Renaissance and with this came the growth of humanism and an increasing emphasis upon individualism and reason, a momentum which carried on until the Reformation and the Enlightenment, by which time the influences of secular reasoning had come full circle, and reason came to re-establish its ascendancy over theology, a move that Plato had tried so hard to establish.

In all these contexts, the benchmark for defining freedom of expression remained (as arguably it does today) the perennial tension between a rationalistic model of statecraft without theology or a theology of statecraft. Freedom of expression is limited not only by political or theological worldview; in between the extremes of unrestricted liberalism and fierce repression there are the messy accommodations of democracies under threat from totalitarianism or its modern fundamentalist guises. Freedom of expression in all these instances thus serves as a barometer for wider worldviews, and the implications these have for human freedom — philosophical, political, and or religious. Many of the issues at stake in modern states are nevertheless similar to those confronted by ancient ones, and from a consideration of Plato we move to Saint Augustine, and the tension between classical worldview and Christian.

References

Appignnanesi, Richard (ed.) (2003) *The End of Everything: Postmodernism and the Vanishing of Everything; Lyotard, Haraway, Plato, Heidegger, Habermas, McLuhan*, foreword by Will Self, introduction by Stuart Sim. Cambridge: Icon.

Aristotle (1995) *Poetics*, 2316–2340, in Barnes, Jonathan (ed.) (1995) *The Complete Works of Aristotle*, revised Oxford translation.

Asmis, Elizabeth (1999) 'Plato on Poetic Creativity', 338–364, in Richard Kraut (ed.) *The Cambridge Companion to Plato*. Cambridge: Cambridge University Press.

Barasch, Moshe (2000) *Theories of Art*, three volumes, London and New York: Routledge.

Babonich, Christopher (2002) *Plato's Utopia Recast: His Later Ethics and Politics*. Oxford: Oxford University Press.

Barnes, Jonathan (1995) 'Rhetoric and Poetics', 259–285, in Jonathan Barnes (ed.) The Cambridge Companion to Aristotle. Cambridge: Cambridge University Press.

Barnes, Jonathan (ed.) (1995) *The Complete Works of Aristotle*, revised Oxford translation. Two volumes.

Brickhouse, Thomas C. and Smith, Nicholas D. (2004) *Routledge Philosophy Guidebook to Plato and the Trial of Socrates*. London Routledge.

Coleman, Janet (2000) *A History of Political Thought: From Ancient Greece to Early Christianity*. Oxford: Blackwell.

Ebenstein, William, Ebenstein, Alan (2000) *Great Political Thinkers: Plato to the Present*, 6th edition. Fort Worth, Texas: Harcourt College Publishers.

Eyres, Harry (2001) *Plato's The Republic: A Beginner's Guide*. London: Hodder & Stoughton.

Gracia, J.E., Reichberg, Gregory M., Schumacher, Bernard N. (eds.) (2003) *The Classics of Western Philosophy: A Reader's Guide*. Malden, MA; Oxford: Blackwell.

Haworth, Alan (2003) *Understanding Political Philosophers: From Plato to Rawls*. London: Routledge.

Heidegger, Martin (2002) *The Essence of Human Freedom: An Introduction to Philosophy*, trans. Ted Sadler. London: Continuum.

Jackson, Roy (2001) *Plato: A Beginner's Guide*. London: Hodder & Stoughton.

Kraut, R. (2003) *Plato*. Stanford Encyclopedia of Philosophy.

Lane, Melissa S. (2001) *Plato's Progeny: How Plato and Socrates Still Captivate the Modern Mind*. London: Duckworth.

Lebetter, Grace M. (2003) *Poetics Before Plato: Interpretation and Authority in Early Greek Theories of Poetry*. Princeton, NJ; Oxford: Princeton University Press.

Levin, Susan B. (2001) *The Ancient Quarrel Between Philosophy and Poetry Revisited: Plato and Greek Literary Tradition*. Oxford: Oxford University Press.

McCabe, Mary Margaret (2000) *Plato and his Predecessors: The Dramatisation of Reason*. Cambridge: Cambridge University Press.

Mitchell, Basil, and Lucas, J.R. (2003) *An Engagement with Plato's Republic: A Companion to The Republic*. Aldershot; Burlington, Vermont: Ashgate, 2003.

Monoson, Susan Sara (2000) *Plato's Democratic Entanglements: Athenian Politics and the Practice of Philosophy*. Princeton, NJ: Princeton University Press.

Murray, Penelope and Dorsch, T.S. (eds.) (2000) *Classical Literary Criticism*. London: Penguin.

Nadaff, Ramono (2003) *Exiling the Poets: The Production of Censorship in Plato's Republic*. Chicago: University of Chicago Press.

Pappas, Nickolas (2003) *Routledge Philosophy Guidebook to Plato and the Republic*, 2nd ed. London: Routledge.

Popper, Karl (1946) *The Open Society and Its Enemies*. Two volumes. London: Routledge.

Plato (1935) *Plato's Republic*, translated by A.D. Lindsay. London; New York: Everyman.

Rorty, Amelie Oksenberg (ed.) (2003) *The Many Faces of Philosophy: Reflections from Plato to Arendt*. Oxford: Oxford University Press.

Selected Electronic Sources

A number of websites offer hubs of philosophy resources such as:

CLASSICAL POLITICAL THEORY: WEB SITE LINKS
www.wiu.edu
(and follow links)

PHILOSOPHY RESOURCES ON THE INTERNET
www.epistemelink.com (and follow links)

THE INTERNET ENCYCLOPEDIA OF PHILOSOPHY
www.utm.edu/research (and follow links)

There are numerous websites containing primary source materials, including:

www.perseus.tufts.edu (and follow links)
www.netlibrary.com (and follow links)
www.gutenberg.org (and follow links)
www.classics.mit.edu (and follow links)
www.eawc.evanville.edu (and follow links)
www.4literature.net (and follow links)
www.socrates.clarke.edu (and follow links)
www.etext.library.virginia.edu (and follow links)
www.etext.library.adelaide.edu.au (and follow links)

These sites, in addition to containing the main texts (in English but occasionally in Greek) also have either linked reference sites or specific commentaries on the following works of Plato:

Alcibiades	*Gorgias*	*Meno*	*Symposium*
Apology	*Greater Hippias*	*Minos*	*Theaetetus*
Charmides	*Hipparchus*	*Parmenides*	*Timaeus*
Cratyl	*Ion*	*Phaedo*	
Critias	*Laches*	*Phaedrus*	
Crito	*Laws*	*Philebus*	
Epinomis	*Lesser Hippias*	*Protagoras*	
Eryxias	*Letters*	*Republic*	
Euthydemus	*Lysis*	*Sophist*	
Euthyphro	*Menexenus*	*Statesman*	

If you only visit one website on Plato, go to

The *Stanford Encyclopedia of Philosophy* http://plato.stanford.edu

The encyclopedia is authoritative and is a marvelously useful work for general reference in philosophy.

Saint Augustine (354 – 430)
Confessions

I wrote, I think, two or three books 'on the Beautiful and the Fitting'. You know, God. They have slipped my memory. I do not possess them now, and I do not know where they are gone.

I was led astray and I led others astray, deceived and deceiving in all manner of lusts, openly by so-called liberal teaching, privately under the false name of religion, now in pride, then in superstition, and in all things fruitless . . . seeking empty popularity, cheers in the theatre, poetic competitions, strife for straw crowns, trifles of stage shows, and undisciplined desires . . .

Saint Augustine's Confessions

In a present era where the processes of canonizations are begun soon after a person's death, Augustine early recognized as a towering intellectual giant and 'Doctor of the Church' — was not declared a saint until almost a thousand years after his death. This may in part have been the result of his autobiographical description of his spiritual quest. The *Confessions* is a work that remains, sixteen centuries after it was written, not simply a priceless insight into the declining early years of the Roman Empire but an enduringly popular book available in many translations, and unsurpassed as a story of a literary and spiritual genius (Quinn, 2002; Paffenroth and Kennedy, 2004). But as for immediate sainthood, Augustine's honesty reveals moral flaws — he admits to theft in childhood, he had a mistress and illegitimate child, was a member of a marginal religious cult, and was driven by much worldly ambition (Willis, 2001). It is these imperfections which portray both his flawed humanity and provide the basis for many of his insights into the human condition (Magadanz, 2004; Clark, 2005; Matthews, 2005) — philosophical, theological, even political insights — which some have argued are the foundations for modernity (Hanby, 2003).

In a world in which there were strictly defined limits to philosophical and religious orthodoxy — and indeed political compliance to a declining if still absolutist Roman governance — Augustine helped to enforce a strict orthodoxy whose influence was to continue upon the Christian world for two millennia (Cross, 1998; Knowles and Penkett, 2004). Augustine lived in an age of the great heresies which, by their extreme unorthodoxy, helped define orthodox Christian theology. In his support for orthodoxy Augustine helped to enforce a common notion at the time, that free expression of philosophical or theological ideas, outside boundaries established by episcopal authority, was not simply ill-advised but injurious, and injurious not only to the individual thus seeking expression but to the wider polity (Brinkman, 2003). Augustine's undoubted importance — in philosophy, politics, theology, and for our discussion of the development of freedom of expression as an idea — is in how he acted as a bridge between the 'pagan' philosophy of the ancient world (indeed its suppression) and the Christian theology that would form the basis of modernity (Gracia, Reichberg and Schumacher, 2003). Augustine thus sets the groundwork for theology in the late Roman Empire and for medieval theology until the Renaissance and the re-discovery of suppressed ancient learning. Augustine's writings are formative therefore not simply for the first millennia of the Christian era in which he lived but for the second millennia which, after conscious rejection of the heritage of Greece and Rome, began in the Renaissance to rediscover them. It is the Renaissance and the humanism which this engendered that was to become the basis for the Reformation and the modern world, with its individualism, its scepticism, and indeed its emphasis upon the individual right to dissent freely from any dominant religious or political system.

Augustine the Author

Augustine received his early education in Carthage. His mother was a Christian and his father a pagan. We know little about his father except this. It was his Christian mother, Monica, who was to be the dominant and enduring figure in his later life; though in his earliest years Augustine was not swayed by her religious creeds (Willis, 2001; Matthews, 2005). Indeed as a youth Augustine followed the heretical sect of the Manicheans who believed in a strict duality of good and evil, struggling in a great cosmic fight for dominance in the universe (Knowles and Penkett, 2004). Augustine is both criticized and admired by modern thinkers for his over-emphasis upon sin and death, and God's final judgment of good and evil. Augustine's thinking — much influenced by Saint Paul in the New Testament — seems also to incorporate a notion of predestination: that God in his omniscience has foreknowledge of the future of each individual soul that He created, including, logically whether the soul is destined for salvation or damnation; and indeed we see Augustine's influence on the Reformation reformers like Luther. Such rigid, deterministic thinking does not seem to fit in well with philosophical or modern ideas of individual autonomy or freedom (though in fact Augustine did retain the notion of individual freewill), yet they remain important philosophical problems.

After a North African childhood in Thagaste — idyllic apart from the theft of a pear from an orchard which seems to be a defining moment in Augustine's life, not only for its guilt but perhaps for the biblical resonances such a theft has from the Garden of Eden — Augustine resided in Carthage, until his mid-twenties. In Carthage he perfected his skills in rhetoric and knowledge of what Augustine defines as the liberal arts, essentially an introduction to the learning of the ancient world — especially of Greece but also of Rome, which of course at the time of Augustine was more modern than ancient.

Augustine travelled to Italy in search of more money and acclaim than Carthage, a small province of the Roman Empire, could provide. In Rome he had these opportunities, and also a concubine, with whom he had a son (a boy who would later die in his teenage years).

More professional opportunities arose outside Rome and Augustine travelled to Milan where he took up a post as professor of rhetoric. Augustine was later dismissive of his achievements there: 'I taught the art of rhetoric over these years. In zeal for a livelihood, I sold a triumphant wordiness. Yet, Lord, as you know, it was my preference to teach those accounted good. Without guile I taught them guile, not to use against the life of the inno-cent, though at times to save the life of the guilty.' And here, as throughout the *Confessions*, Augustine makes a close correlation between literary self-expression and its philosophical, even theological, dimensions. Theatre is not simply drama, plays, entertainment, but part of a wider divine ordinance and free expression here — 'freedom' is to Augustine only a travesty of liberty — it is equated with moral licence, even licentiousness, sinfulness, and therefore separation from God:

> I recollect an occasion, when I had in mind to enter a theatrical competition, and some sort of soothsayer asked me what fee I would pay him to win. I, however, detesting and abomi-nating such foul rites, replied that though the garland should be of indestructible gold, I would not permit a fly to be killed for my victory. In his sacrifices he was intending to kill living crea-tures, by such rites, it seemed, purposing to call on demonic support. But this evil I cast aside . . . Sighing for such fictions, does not the soul commit uncleanness against you, put trust in falsehood and feed the winds? (Augustine, 1987: 79)

It was in Milan that Augustine met Bishop Ambrose who was to start Augustine on the road to Christian conversion. Augustine had by now abandoned his mistress, the woman with whom he had had a child. It was around this period that his mother Monica arrived in Milan with plans for Augustine to marry a Christian girl. Monica's journey from North Africa to Italy indicates the strong rule of Roman law that would allow a woman travel-ling independently to make such a journey in safety and security. It was, however, a world increasingly unstable as each year passed — by the time of her son's death in 430, when he was Bishop of Hippo, Vandal hordes were at the gate of the city. Yet it was not barbarism but the rise of Christianity — of which Augustine was to play so pivotal a role — that would also in part undermine the Roman Empire. Around 386, Augustine suffered a deep personal crisis. A year later, at Easter 387, Augustine was baptized into the Christian faith.

In 388, Augustine returned to Africa. It was the year Monica died. Back in Thagaste he founded a monastic community. In 391 he was ordained priest in Hippo (an extinct city now but close to today's Annaba, Algeria). Augustine's sermons, more than 300 of which are extant, were legendary. Augustine had, like St Paul before him, the benefits of a clas-sical education which gave him added advantage in combating philosophical opponents; just as his own Manichean background gave him the ability to contest heresy on familiar ground. In 396 Augustine was made assistant bishop and when the serving bishop died there was a natural succession of the bishopric to Augustine. Augustine remained in the role of Bishop of Hippo until his death over thirty years later in August 430. As Bishop of Hippo, Augustine wrote not only against the Manicheans, but against the Pelagians and Donatists. The corpus of letters, books, papers and sermons by Saint Augustine is extra-ordinary. His major works include: *On Christian Doctrine* (397–426); *Confessions* (397–398); *The City of God* (c. 413–426); and *On the Trinity* (410–416).

Augustine, the *Confessions* and Freedom of Expression

The *Confessions* of Saint Augustine are an admission of an early life of grave personal, philosophical and theological error and waywardness, and the belated profession of a man converted mid-life to a profound new faith in Christianity. Saint Augustine and Plato are equally intolerant of literature, and for reasons which are not that dissimilar:

> The drama enthralled me, full of representations of my own miseries and fuel for my own fire. Why does a man make himself deliberately sad over grievous and tragic events which he would not wish to suffer himself? Yet he is willing as an onlooker to suffer grief from them, and the grief itself is what he enjoys. What is that but wretched lunacy? He is more stirred by them in proportion to his sanity. When he suffers personally it is commonly called misery. When he feels it for others it is called mercy. (Augustine, 1987: 59)

Plato despises the poets and theatre for making men weaker than they need be and unsuited for the utopian republic. Augustine also despises literary enterprise for the moral weakness that it engenders, but in Augustine it is separation from a state of a different nature and order than Plato's; Augustine's utopia is to be found in the *City of God*. It is a theological metaphysics that Augustine most simply expresses in the *Confessions* when he discusses his journey from waywardness to a return home in God, 'However long away our home falls not to ruin. It is your eternity' (Augustine, 1987: 98). Yet the Platonic influence remains apparent, for Augustine's vision presumes, like Plato's, that the world of forms cannot but mirror imperfectly the heavenly realm from which is derived all models of perfection. Although Plato's theory of forms does not amount to a theology, many Christian thinkers wrote as if it represented a pre-Christian precursor to such.

The theology of Augustine, however, shows no such reciprocal reverence to the learning of the Greeks — to Plato or to Aristotle. Indeed, the subtlety of Aristotelian thinking is dismissed fairly early in Augustine's *Confessions*. Augustine gives Aristotle credence for an undoubted intellectual sophistication. Yet the wider inheritance of classical learning is collectively condemned as in error, and no less in error for its cleverness. Indeed, in a rare instance of intellectual vanity, Augustine refers dismissively to his own intellectual abilities in grasping the subtleties of Plato, Aristotle and wider classical learning:

> Without great difficulty, and without a teacher, I grasped rhetoric, logic, geometry, music, mathematics, as you know, Lord God, because speed of understanding and acuteness of discernment are your gift. Yet I sacrificed none of it to you but for my destruction. Of what use therefore, my nimble wit, nimble in those disciplines, and of what use the unravelling of all those knotty volumes without the slightest help from man's instruction, while in the teaching of godliness, I wandered on disgracefully and amid impious uncleanness? (Augustine, 1987: 97–99)

Christianity, of course, is a religion not simply of a single book, the Bible, but a religion of literary as well as theological orthodoxy. The New Testament 'canon' of accepted books — four Gospels, the Acts of the Apostles, various letters, and the Book of Revelation. In the first centuries of the Christian Church accounts of his life and collections of Jesus' sayings circulated widely. Only some of these were to form the body of orthodox teaching and those outside were condemned; hence the accepted canon of twenty-seven New Testament books. Books and letters outside of these do not have the status of divine revelation. Professing such divine revelation was condemned as in error, and heretical (Cross, 1998).

Restricting theological expression to within the bounds of apostolic and ecclesiastical authority thus began early within Christianity through the process of establishing a literary and theological canon. At Ephesus (Acts 19: 19) new converts burn 'heretical' texts, with the approval of Saint Paul. A similar approval to such acts is given by St. Paul to Titus (3: 10). Yet for the first three centuries of its existence Christianity did not have the political power to systematically persecute those with whom it disagreed — on the contrary, the early years of Christianity are testimony to its own persecution, especially by Rome. We find notorious accounts of this from the first-century Roman historian Tacitus who tells how Christians were lit as human torches in the garden of the Emperor Nero. When Christianity became the official religion of the Roman Empire a few hundred years later, from 325 by decree of the Emperor Constantine, this marks the period of increasing confidence in condemnation of theological unorthodoxy by Christianity — if only because the condemnation of popes was from that time supported by that of Emperor. With this came the capacity to destroy not only heretical ideas but the books that contained such thinking. For example, it was not simply the heresy of Arius that was condemned at the Council of Nicea (325) — Arius emphasized Jesus' humanity over and above any divinity — but Arius' 'book' *Thalia*. The Emperor Constantine demanded that the writings of Arius everywhere be submitted to be burned. It is somewhat ironic that the Christian Church, once its status changed from that of persecuted religion to state religion — with the conversion of Emperor Constantine, from 325 — began its period of more active persecution. A decree of Pope Gelasius I (circa 496) against un-Christian books, for instance, has been described as the first Roman Index. It was a pattern set to continue throughout the medieval period which succeeded the fall of Rome. The paucity of books in the early Church and through the period of Augustine and onwards, until the advent of the printing press, meant however that direct prohibition of books written and circulated by means of handwritten copies was not such a difficult task. It meant, of course, that once destroyed the historical records of what these books contained was lost forever.

The age in which Augustine wrote his *Confessions* (the late 390s) was a period of transition from the hegemony of Roman rule. The temporal power of Rome was weakened by a heterogeneity of tribes, tribes Rome had formerly conquered and suppressed, but with whom it now shared the same spiritual outlook — that of Christianity. In North Africa Christianity was becoming an increasingly dominant worldview, but if it was the official religion of the Roman Empire it was not the religion of all the people. Indeed, one of the values of Augustine's *Confessions* is to historians as well as to theologians, and his account tells us of the diversity of 'pagan' learning, that is the classical traditions of Greece and Rome which had formed the young Augustine, which continued to thrive in his lifetime, and which so many of his post-conversion writings focused upon undermining. The seemingly unstoppable Christian hegemony was not threatened until the rise of Islam in the sixth and seventh centuries, and the clash did not turn to violence until the Crusades.

The majority of Augustine's writings, including the *Confessions*, are written not simply with the genius for language which he most certainly possessed but with the authority of a bishop. The power of argument he had learned from his training and professorial practice of rhetoric, but with ecclesiastical authority came the power of excommunication. The irreligious writings of pagans stood themselves in obvious condemnation but it was the theologians who claimed the religion of Christianity that the Church took most energy to combat. A challenge to doctrine was a challenge to authority, for the keys of the kingdom resided in the power of the Church to bestow or deny salvation. The early Church had introduced pervasive notions of eschatology and salvation history — the theological idea that God's eternal judgment hung over actions of seemingly minute earthly significance. The notion that the capacity of a person to freely express his or her views was an inherent good would have been regarded as anathema; indeed there is no Christian church, even today, that would place the value of literary or philosophical free expression above the message of the Gospels, nor present the freedom to blasphene or offend against religious belief as desirous.

Augustine gives immense insight into the thriving, if vapid, literary and theatrical life late in the Roman Empire: 'Stage plays also captivated me, with their sights full of the images of my own miseries: fuel for my own fire. Now, why does a man like to be made sad by viewing doleful and tragic scenes, which he himself could not by any means endure? Yet, as a spectator, he wishes to experience from them a sense of grief, and in this very sense of grief his pleasure consists. What is this but wretched madness?' (Augustine, 1987: 59). For his own literary and philosophical skills — and interestingly he links both classical philosophy and literature as equally in error — Augustine feels only disgust: 'I was led astray and I led others astray, deceived and deceiving in all manner of lusts, openly by so-called liberal teaching, privately under the false name of religion, now in pride, then in superstition, and in all things fruitless . . . seeking empty popularity, cheers in the theatre, poetic competitions, strife for straw crowns, trifles of stage shows, and undisciplined desires . . . ' (Augustine, 1987: 79). And he remarks on the question central to aesthetic philosophy today — the idea of the beautiful, its definition and expression — an idea commonly discussed and seen as not resolvable since Plato's *Phaedo*:

> I was going down into the abyss and saying to my friends, 'Do we love anything that is not beautiful? What is Beauty in its essence? What is it that draws and unites us to that which we love? For unless there is grace and splendour in it, in no way could they draw us to it.' And I marked and saw that in any given entity there was a beauty as it were of the whole, and something else which owed its beauty to a proper relationship to something else, as for example a part of the body to the whole body, a shoe to a foot, and such like. And this thought bubbled up into mind out of the depths of my heart and I wrote, I think two or three books 'on the Beautiful and the Fitting'. You know, God. They have slipped my memory. I do not possess them now, and I do not know where they are gone. (Augustine, 1987: 92)

It is this last inconsequential dismissal of his work within the field, probably works written as a philosopher of rhetoric at Milan, that is most striking. At one fell swoop he dismisses worldly ambition and its errors, in philosophy as well as literature. If the Christian Bible differentiated most clearly the Christian from the classical era, then this foundation remains the benchmark for the post-conversion Augustine.

Confessions: at a Glance

Book One	A North African childhood
Book Two	Secondary education at Maduara, theft of pear

Summary

Like Plato, Augustine's contribution to western philosophy and theology is immeasurable. From his youthful dissatisfaction of ancient Greek and Roman learning and Manichean heresy, his intellectually honest conversion to Christianity displayed philosophical and theological genius; as a convert he fought, with growing and ultimately insurmountable power, dissent on many fronts, directly against the philosophical ideologies of the classical world and against heresy within the Christian Church. To this extent Augustine's intellect was used — for good and ill — in subsequent centuries.

◆   See Appendix X   ◆

A Typology of Dissent

PAGE 219

◆   It is a useful and instructive exercise to compare the statecraft

represented by the rights and freedoms in Appendices II through to IX

with the worldview of Augustine's *Confessions*   ◆

It is ironic that when in the fourth century — around 325 — Christianity turned from a religion repressed to a faith of the state, it turned its attention almost immediately to the rigorous repression of heresy. There was no greater indicator of this trend than the Council of Nicea in 325, coinciding with the time Rome became the official religion of the Empire. The campaign against Arius was a major focus of Nicea. Arius had emphasized the humanity and downplayed the divinity of Jesus. With the rise of Christianity to the role of religion of the Roman Empire, the repression of the Arian heresy was given the weight of temporal as well as ecclesiastical authority.

The tension between religion and the literary arts is apparent throughout Augustine's struggle towards Christian conversion. Augustine's *early* life was characterized by a move *away* from Christianity and towards philosophy, rhetoric and the arts. It was an eventual and tortured return to Christianity, followed by the final stage of a maturation of that faith and writing upon Christian philosophy and theology which were incomparably to influence the future of Christianity itself.

The first four or five centuries of Christianity were marked by philosophical separation of the church from classical inheritance. Within the emergent Church was the struggle for its definition, often rigid, of its distinctive theological ideas — the demarcation of true doctrine, especially over the nature of God as Trinity, over the incarnation, about the human and divine aspects of God. The great age of heresy — in which such debates over heresy were prevalent — was clearly not quite over when Augustine was born. Augustine's age remains a period of fascination for Christian as well as classical historians, particularly for Augustine's portrayal of the relative calm of the last days of the Roman Empire, of Thagaste, Madura, Carthage, Rome, and of Hippo before the Vandal hordes approached the doors of the episcopal seat in the year of the saint's death.

A major mantle of succession between Augustine and the Middle Ages was Saint Aquinas. Aquinas' was an age struggling with similar tensions found in Augustine's is between the classical and the Christian. In Augustine's time the classical heritage of Greek and Roman civilization was still thriving but, with the rise of Christianity, about to be suppressed; in Aquinas' age such classical heritage was only just being re-discovered — the first stirrings of the Renaissance. Yet in Aquinas' time the Church's unassailable spiritual power was still matched by an equally unquestionable temporal power, made most terribly manifest in the Inquisition. The full force of theological purity was enforced here by the power of the state as well as the Church, the separation of which did not occur until the Reformation.

If the tortures and executions of the Inquisition are based upon the violent defence of ideas — their expression in texts, and their orthodoxy — we cannot reasonably link Augustine's cerebral disgust at his preoccupation with literature and rhetoric with the institutionalized intolerance and brutality of the later medieval period. But the two are not so distantly separated. There remains a relationship between freedom of expression and the rigours of its definition. Art, like all aspects of human life, is subject in Augustine to tests against theological ideals, and this reached its logical — brutal and violent — conclusion in the practices of the Inquisition. Saint Augustine gave up his own literary aspirations, and relinquished as empty and unworthy the pursuit of literary fame and glory:

> At that time, in my wretchedness, I loved to grieve; and I sought for things to grieve about. In another man's misery, even though it was feigned and impersonated on the stage, that performance of the actor pleased me best and attracted me most powerfully which moved me to tears. What marvel then was it that an unhappy sheep, straying from thy flock and impatient of thy care, I became infected with a foul disease? This is the reason for my love of griefs: that they would not probe into me too deeply (for I did not love to suffer in myself such things as I loved to look at), and they were the sort of grief which came from hearing those fictions, which affected only the surface of my emotion. Still, just as if they had been poisoned fingernails, their scratching was followed by inflammation, swelling, putrefaction, and corruption. Such was my life! But was it life, O my God? (Saint Augustine, 1987: 59)

As Saint Augustine became, and arguably remains, amongst the most influential Christian thinkers in the two millennia of theological history, his decision to abandon the literary life as empty and worthless had a profound influence on the Church's attitude to literary self-expression.

References

Augustine, Saint (1997) *Confessions*. London: Hodder & Stoughton

Augustine, Saint (2002) *De Civitate Dei: The City of God*, trans. P.G. Walsh. Oxford: Aris & Phillips.

Brinkman, M.E. (2003) *The Tragedy of Human Freedom: The Failure and Promise of the Christian Concept of Freedom in Western Culture*, trans. Harry Flecken and Henry Jansen. Amsterdam: Rodopi.

Clark, Gillian (2005) *Augustine: The Confessions*. Bristol: Phoenix Press.

Cross, F.L. (ed.) (1998) *A Dictionary of the Christian Church*, third edition. Oxford: Oxford University Press.

Gracia, J.E., Reichberg, Gregory M., Schumacher, Bernard N. (eds.) (2003) *The Classics of Western Philosophy: A Reader's Guide*. Malden, MA; Oxford: Blackwell.

Hanby, Michael (2003) *Augustine and Modernity*. London; New York: Routledge.

Knowles, Andrew and Penkett, Pachmios (2004) *Augustine and His World*. Oxford: Lion.

Magadanz, Stacy (2004) *St Augustine's Confessions*. New York; Chichester: Wiley.

Matthews, Gareth B. (2005) *Augustine*. Oxford: Blackwell.

O'Daly, Gerard J.P. *Augustine's City of God: A Reader's Guide*. Oxford: Oxford University Press.

Paffenroth, Kim and Kennedy, Robert P.(eds.) (2003) *A Reader's Companion to Augustine's Confessions*. Louiseville, Kentucky; London: Westminster John Knox Press.

Quinn, John M. (2002) *A Companion to the Confessions of St Augustine*. New York: P. Lang.

Willis, Gary (2001) *Saint Augustine's Childhood*. London: Continuum.

Selected Electronic Sources

CONFESSIONS OF AUGUSTINE: AN ELECTRONIC EDITION (COPYRIGHT 1992 JAMES J. O'DONNELL)
http://www.stoa.org (and follow links)

HISTORICAL, LITERARY AND THEOLOGICAL LINKS TO AUGUSTINE
http://ccat.sas.upenn.edu (and follow links)

ROMAN CATHOLICISM AND FREEDOM OF EXPRESSION
(and indeed an excellent resource on Roman Catholic Christianity in general)

Roman Catholic Encyclopedia at http://newadvent.org (and follow links)

See especially entries on:

- Counter Reformation
- Inquisition
- Index of Banned Books
- Reformation

ORIGINAL TEXTS OF THE INQUISITION
Visit the University of Notre Dame special collection on original manuscripts and scholarly commentaries as well as related materials, http://www.coins.nd.edu

Links here to:

- Manuals of instruction
- Banned Books
- Autos-de-fe
- Certificates
- Official Publications
- Early Works
- Secondary Works

If you only visit one website on Augustine, go to

The Christian Classics: Ethereal Library, Calvin College   http://www.ccel.org

Here you will find an excellent translation of the *Confessions of Saint Augustine* and a good reference section on Augustine, Saint (354–430), Bishop of Hippo and Doctor of the Church.

The following primary texts and commentaries are all at: http://www.ccel.org

Augustine — from *Encyclopedia Britannica* (9th ed.)
St. Augustine — *The New Schaff and Herzog Encyclopedia of Religious Knowledge*
St. Augustine — *Dictionary of Christian Biography*
Confessions of Augustine: An Electronic Edition
Dictionary of Christian Biography and Literature to the End of the Sixth Century — Wace, Henry (1836–1924)
Confessions and *Enchiridion*, newly translated and edited by Albert C. Outler
On Christian Doctrine, in Four Books
Handbook on Faith, Hope, and Love
The Confessions and Letters of St. Augustine, with a Sketch of his Life and Work
St. Augustine's City of God and *Christian Doctrine*
On the Holy Trinity; Doctrinal Treatises; Moral Treatises
Augustine: *The Writings Against the Manichaeans and Against the Donatists*
St. Augustine: *Anti-Pelagian Writings*
St. Augustine: *Sermon on the Mount; Harmony of the Gospels; Homilies on the Gospels*
Confessions of Saint Augustine
City of God

Martin Luther (1483 – 1546)
Ninety-Five Theses

3

> . . . it is just as impossible to separate faith and works as it is to separate heat and light from fire! Therefore, watch out for your own false ideas and guard against good-for-nothing gossips, who think they're smart enough to define faith and works, but really are the greatest of fools.
>
> Martin Luther, *Large Catechism*

The Protestant Reformation marks one of the most iconoclastic periods in Christian history. If, as is often said, the icons and images of the great medieval cathedrals were the books of an illiterate peasantry then the destruction of such can be considered the equivalent of a vast artistic censorship. And if the stained glass of the cathedral was the illiterate Christian peasant's Bible, then the destruction of these and the images of the saints of Catholic worship were the equivalent of a century's long period of book-burning. Of course the period also marked a time in which Catholic and Protestant Christians burned each other as well as their artefacts and their books.

The destruction of images by the Puritans was particularly virulent but the ransacking and levelling of entire monasteries had an equally if not more excessive violence about it (Chadwick, 1990, gives a classic account; also Chadwick, 2001). In England, the centuries of the post-Reformation period represented the eradication of vast swathes of medieval art — books, paintings, architecture which were thought to be mortally sinful or particular translations of Bible abhorrent (Ostrem, Fleischer and Holger, 2002).

We might also wish to consider, however, that in western art in the medieval period there was little or no art beyond the production of items of utility that was not associated with religion. In western context art was religious art — visual, musical, literary. Augustine had set a precedent which suggested that any artistic expression or philosophical speculation not in the service of God was at best unworthy activity and at worst dangerous profanity (Levi, 2002).

The Renaissance changed all of this — the rebirth of Greek and Roman learning contributed greatly to the growth of European humanism, an emphasis on the individual and much of the developments of the modern world, including cultural riches in which religion played a decreasing and, what in the future would become, an increasingly minor role (Chadwick, 2001; again, Levi, 2002). This remains the case today. Most art today is non-religious; the signs of religious art that do exist are remnants of an age when religion dominated the worldview and the culture of Europe (Tomlin, 2002).

In the period immediately prior to the Renaissance, which provided the groundwork for Luther, a number of key medieval heretics had trodden similar paths as the Augustinian monk. Peter Abelard (1079–1142), French theologian, criticized the excessive power of Rome, and suffered humiliating physical mutilation. John Wycliffe (1330–84), lecturer at Oxford (1361–82), blamed for the growth of revolutionary Lollards and the Peasant's Revolt 1381, attacked the theocracy of the medieval Church, particularly its wealth and power. Wycliffe also instituted the first English translation of the Bible. However, he attacked the doctrine of transubstantiation and this forced his retirement from Oxford. John Huss (1372–1414), Bohemian religious reformer at Prague University, a supporter of John Wycliffe, was excommunicated in 1411, and burned at the stake in 1414 (McEnhill and Newlands, 2004; for period 1000–1200, see Fichtenau, 1998).

Martin Luther the Author

Martin Luther was a German Protestant theologian and a pivotal figure within the Protestant Reformation that would reconfigure the face of Christianity and world history. From 1508 he taught at the University of Wittenberg, a place and a university to which his name was attached until the end of his life, and where he held the post of professor of scripture from 1512 to 1546. It was in 1517, and to great dramatic effect, that Luther nailed his ninety-five theses to the door of the church at Wittenberg. This single demonstrative act symbolized the Protestant Reformation that was to follow and made Luther — who held no great office of Church or state — not simply its first leader but its historical epitome (Chadwick, 1990; 2001; Bainton, 2002; Tomlin, 2002; Nestingen, 2003; Mullet, 2004). The response of the Roman Catholic Church was the Counter-Reformation, embodied in the Council of Trent (1545–1563/4), and the institution of an official body of the Roman Catholic Church that would monitor theological dissent — the Inquisition.

Protected by the German princes who resented the temporal power of the popes, Luther's books included major work on the translation of the Bible into the German vernacular. Luther's translation of the Bible into German, a translation which proceeded from 1522 to 1534, facilitated the progress of the Bible into vernacular languages around Europe. Through this, directly and indirectly, Luther's impact on the German language and literature was of major significance; in England the century which produced the English Bible also laid the foundations for Shakespeare and Milton (Vandiver, Keen and Frazel, 2002; Levi, 2002; Ostrem, Fleischer and Petersen, 2003).

Martin Luther, *Nine-Five Theses* and Freedom of Expression

Luther had long preached that salvation was by faith alone, and this re-introduced an ancient debate about freedom and predestination. By predestination is meant that a person is saved from the damnation which is his or her inevitable inheritance from original sin, the

Fall from God's grace in the Garden of Eden; that a person would accept or reject the salvation offered by God to the world through the incarnation, death and resurrection of his Son Jesus Christ was a matter of God's grace; that a person was open to such acceptance or rejection of God's grace was itself also a matter of God's grace. No amount of good works could open a person to God's salvation, only faith and God's grace could do this. Individual Christians might demonstrate their openness to God's grace and salvation by leading moral lives, but good works themselves were signs of God's grace and salvation, not a way of influencing it. Good works did not and could not affect God's will for the salvation of all humankind, but nor could they affect God's divine and eternal foreknowledge that some of His creatures would reject His will and would, through this rejection, open themselves to damnation. It was impossible that God — being omniscient — did not know who would choose the path to salvation and who would chose the path of damnation since before even the beginning of time.

Martin Luther found the major source for this belief in the writings of Saint Paul, especially in the latter's Letter to the Romans, upon which there is a profound and vast theological literature. Luther was also a monk of the Augustinian Order and it was in Saint Augustine's writings that Luther found some of the philosophical and theological reasoning that led him to the conclusions concerning salvation by faith alone.

At the time, the Roman Catholic Church taught — as it still teaches now — that salvation is always through God's grace, for nothing can be achieved without this, but it also taught that in this life on earth a person can show a change of heart for wrongdoing and can gain merit through good works. Roman Catholic teaching, in contrast to Luther's, presented the possibility of salvation by faith *and* good works. Roman Catholic theologians have always suggested that the Lutheran and wider Protestant doctrine of salvation by faith alone is a one-sided doctrine — the New Testament is full of instances of Jesus imploring disciples to a life of good works, and amongst the letters in the early Church it is the short New Testament Letter of Saint James which is most often cited as scriptural authority for salvation by faith and good works.

The doctrine of salvation by faith alone had considerable philosophical and theological implications for the understanding of human freedom. For if a person could in effect do nothing to enable his or her own salvation by good works, and God had divine and eternal foreknowledge of all the paths or their final outcome — to ultimate salvation or damnation — then good works, and more broadly all human actions, were simply a matter of show. We were predestined to our fate whatever our actions in this world. This doctrine of predestination and the implications for human freewill became a central debate throughout the Reformation years. The nature, extent and limitations to human freedom remain a critical issue for philosophy today, as well as new and emergent fields of enquiry throughout those sciences concerned with biological and environmental conditioning of human life and action.

Luther's teaching, contrary to orthodox Catholic theology, also had a major effect upon the ecclesiastical order of the Roman Catholic Church. If the philosophical and theological implications of salvation by faith were fundamental to the nature of human freedom, they inevitably posed a challenge to the Roman Catholic Church's teaching on indulgences. Indulgences were the remission of punishment in purgatory that the Christian would need to serve before his or her soul was sufficiently 'purged' of the effects of sin before entering the Kingdom of Heaven. In many regards it was an extension of the doctrine of salvation by good works, since a person could say a certain number of prayers or undertake a devotional act like pilgrimage, combined with charitable actions, which together could aid the path to salvation.

The abuse of indulgences in the Middle Ages came when they began to be offered for sale — a development justifiably interpreted as one of lazy convenience. If one had money and salvation could be bought, how much easier this would be than working for it through more challenging moral actions. Perhaps this issue was an early precursor of television evangelistic pleas for money. Most generously the donation of personal wealth to charity is integral to all Christian ethical teaching, and — just as not all English monasteries were corrupt — so too we have no way of knowing whether *all* purveyors of indulgences were exploitative or motivated simply by pecuniary gain. Indulgences, while looking like a superstitious medieval curiosity today, were integral to a sophisticated theological teaching in Catholic Christianity that wanted to hold in balance both divine omniscience and omnipotence with human freedom to affect human salvation through good actions. Good works could have an effect upon salvation: buying an indulgence was a way of doing a good act, akin to giving to charity.

In 1517, Luther's *Ninety-Five Theses* nailed to the door of the church at Wittenberg, were more than a complaint against the exploitation of indulgences but were an attack upon a Catholic theology and papal authority: Luther taught that salvation was by faith and not good works, and that indulgences were symptomatic of a flawed soteriology, or doctrine of salvation. It was the attack upon both this aspect of Catholic theology, and the ecclesiastical authority that propounded it, which had Martin Luther excommunicated in 1521 at the Diet of Worms, Luther famously declaring in his defence, 'Here I stand, I can do no other' (Bainton, 2001)

Martin Luther's *Ninety-Five Theses*, of all the documents of the period, most closely represent the foundational statement of the Protestant Reformation. It is ironic indeed that it was from within the *Augustinian* Order that a monk would arise who would challenge Rome, whose authority had been underpinned by the writings of Saint Augustine for over a thousand years. If it had not been for Martin Luther and the Protestant Reformation that ensued — and this may seem overly obvious — there would have been no Counter-Reformation and without the Counter-Reformation there would have been no revival of the Inquisition.

95 Theses: the Text

Out of love for the truth and the desire to bring it to light, the following propositions will be discussed at Wittenberg, under the presidency of the Reverend Father Martin Luther, Master of Arts and of Sacred Theology, and Lecturer in Ordinary on the same at that place. Wherefore he requests that those who are unable to be present and debate orally with us, may do so by letter.

In the Name our Lord Jesus Christ. Amen.

1. Our Lord and Master Jesus Christ, when willed that the whole life of believers should be repentance.
2. This word cannot be understood to mean sacramental penance, i.e., confession and satisfaction, which is administered by the priests.
3. Yet it means not inward repentance only; nay, there is no inward repentance which does not outwardly work divers mortifications of the flesh.
4. The penalty [of sin], therefore, continues so long as hatred of self continues; for this is the true inward repentance, and continues until our entrance into the kingdom of heaven.

5. The pope does not intend to remit, and cannot remit any penalties other than those which he has imposed either by his own authority or by that of the Canons.

6. The pope cannot remit any guilt, except by declaring that it has been remitted by God and by assenting to God's remission; though, to be sure, he may grant remission in cases reserved to his judgment. If his right to grant remission in such cases were despised, the guilt would remain entirely unforgiven.

7. God remits guilt to no one whom He does not, at the same time, humble in all things and bring into subjection to His vicar, the priest.

8. The penitential canons are imposed only on the living, and, according to them, nothing should be imposed on the dying.

9. Therefore the Holy Spirit in the pope is kind to us, because in his decrees he always makes exception of the article of death and of necessity.

10. Ignorant and wicked are the doings of those priests who, in the case of the dying, reserve canonical penances for purgatory.

11. This changing of the canonical penalty to the penalty of purgatory is quite evidently one of the tares that were sown while the bishops slept.

12. In former times the canonical penalties were imposed not after, but before absolution, as tests of true contrition.

13. The dying are freed by death from all penalties; they are already dead to canonical rules, and have a right to be released from them.

14. The imperfect health [of soul], that is to say, the imperfect love, of the dying brings with it, of necessity, great fear; and the smaller the love, the greater is the fear.

15. This fear and horror is sufficient of itself alone (to say nothing of other things) to constitute the penalty of purgatory, since it is very near to the horror of despair.

16. Hell, purgatory, and heaven seem to differ as do despair, almost-despair, and the assurance of safety.

17. With souls in purgatory it seems necessary that horror should grow less and love increase.

18. It seems unproved, either by reason or Scripture, that they are outside the state of merit, that is to say, of increasing love.

19. Again, it seems unproved that they, or at least that all of them, are certain or assured of their own blessedness, though we may be quite certain of it.

20. Therefore by 'full remission of all penalties' the pope means not actually 'of all,' but only of those imposed by himself.

21. Therefore those preachers of indulgences are in error, who say that by the pope's indulgences a man is freed from every penalty, and saved;

22. Whereas he remits to souls in purgatory no penalty which, according to the canons, they would have had to pay in this life.

23. If it is at all possible to grant to any one the remission of all penalties whatsoever, it is certain that this remission can be granted only to the most perfect, that is, to the very fewest.

24. It must needs be, therefore, that the greater part of the people are deceived by that indiscriminate and high sounding promise of release from penalty.

25. The power which the pope has, in a general way, over purgatory, is just like the power which any bishop or curate has, in a special way, within his own diocese or parish.

26. The pope does well when he grants remission to souls [in purgatory], not by the power of the keys (which he does not possess), but by way of intercession.

27. They preach man who say that so soon as the penny jingles into the money-box, the soul flies out [of purgatory].

28. It is certain that when the penny jingles into the money-box, gain and avarice can be increased, but the result of the intercession of the Church is in the power of God alone.

29. Who knows whether all the souls in purgatory wish to be bought out of it, as in the legend of Sts. Severinus and Paschal.

30. No one is sure that his own contrition is sincere; much less that he has attained full remission.

31. Rare as is the man that is truly penitent, so rare is also the man who truly buys indulgences, i.e., such men are most rare.

32. They will be condemned eternally, together with their teachers, who believe themselves sure of their salvation because they have letters of pardon.

33. Men must be on their guard against those who say that the pope's pardons are that inestimable gift of God by which man is reconciled to Him;

34. For these 'graces of pardon' concern only the penalties of sacramental satisfaction, and these are appointed by man.

35. They preach no Christian doctrine who teach that contrition is not necessary in those who intend to buy souls out of purgatory or to buy confessionalia.

36. Every truly repentant Christian has a right to full remission of penalty and guilt, even without letters of pardon.

37. Every true Christian, whether living or dead, has part in all the blessings of Christ and the Church; and this is granted him by God, even without letters of pardon.

38. Nevertheless, the remission and participation [in the blessings of the Church] which are granted by the pope are in no way to be despised, for they are, as I have said, the declaration of divine remission.

39. It is most difficult, even for the very keenest theologians, at one and the same time to commend to the people the abundance of pardons and [the need of] true contrition.

40. True contrition seeks and loves penalties, but liberal pardons only relax penalties and cause them to be hated, or at least, furnish an occasion [for hating them].

41. Apostolic pardons are to be preached with caution, lest the people may falsely think them preferable to other good works of love.

42. Christians are to be taught that the pope does not intend the buying of pardons to be compared in any way to works of mercy.

43. Christians are to be taught that he who gives to the poor or lends to the needy does a better work than buying pardons;

44. Because love grows by works of love, and man becomes better; but by pardons man does not grow better, only more free from penalty.

45. Christians are to be taught that he who sees a man in need, and passes him by, and gives [his money] for pardons, purchases not the indulgences of the pope, but the indignation of God.

46. Christians are to be taught that unless they have more than they need, they are bound to keep back what is necessary for their own families, and by no means to squander it on pardons.

47. Christians are to be taught that the buying of pardons is a matter of free will, and not of commandment.

48. Christians are to be taught that the pope, in granting pardons, needs, and therefore desires, their devout prayer for him more than the money they bring.

49. Christians are to be taught that the pope's pardons are useful, if they do not put their trust in them; but altogether harmful, if through them they lose their fear of God.

50. Christians are to be taught that if the pope knew the exactions of the pardon-preachers, he would rather that St. Peter's church should go to ashes, than that it should be built up with the skin, flesh and bones of his sheep.

51. Christians are to be taught that it would be the pope's wish, as it is his duty, to give of his own money to very many of those from whom certain hawkers of pardons cajole money, even though the church of St. Peter might have to be sold.

52. The assurance of salvation by letters of pardon is vain, even though the commissary, nay, even though the pope himself, were to stake his soul upon it.

53. They are enemies of Christ and of the pope, who bid the Word of God be altogether silent in some Churches, in order that pardons may be preached in others.

54. Injury is done the Word of God when, in the same sermon, an equal or a longer time is spent on pardons than on this Word.

55. It must be the intention of the pope that if pardons, which are a very small thing, are celebrated with one bell, with single processions and ceremonies, then the Gospel, which is the very greatest thing, should be preached with a hundred bells, a hundred processions, a hundred ceremonies.

56. The 'treasures of the Church,' out of which the pope grants indulgences, are not sufficiently named or known among the people of Christ.

57. That they are not temporal treasures is certainly evident, for many of the vendors do not pour out such treasures so easily, but only gather them.

58. Nor are they the merits of Christ and the Saints, for even without the pope, these always work grace for the inner man, and the cross, death, and hell for the outward man.

59. St. Lawrence said that the treasures of the Church were the Church's poor, but he spoke according to the usage of the word in his own time.

60. Without rashness we say that the keys of the Church, given by Christ's merit, are that treasure;

61. For it is clear that for the remission of penalties and of reserved cases, the power of the pope is of itself sufficient.

62. The true treasure of the Church is the Most Holy Gospel of the glory and the grace of God.

63. But this treasure is naturally most odious, for it makes the first to be last.

64. On the other hand, the treasure of indulgences is naturally most acceptable, for it makes the last to be first.

65. Therefore the treasures of the Gospel are nets with which they formerly were wont to fish for men of riches.

66. The treasures of the indulgences are nets with which they now fish for the riches of men.

67. The indulgences which the preachers cry as the 'greatest graces' are known to be truly such, in so far as they promote gain.

68. Yet they are in truth the very smallest graces compared with the grace of God and the piety of the Cross.

69. Bishops and curates are bound to admit the commissaries of apostolic pardons, with all reverence.

70. But still more are they bound to strain all their eyes and attend with all their ears, lest these men preach their own dreams instead of the commission of the pope.

71. He who speaks against the truth of apostolic pardons, let him be anathema and accursed!

72. But he who guards against the lust and license of the pardon-preachers, let him be blessed!

73. The pope justly thunders against those who, by any art, contrive the injury of the traffic in pardons.

74. But much more does he intend to thunder against those who use the pretext of pardons to contrive the injury of holy love and truth.

75. To think the papal pardons so great that they could absolve a man even if he had committed an impossible sin and violated the Mother of God — this is madness.

76. We say, on the contrary, that the papal pardons are not able to remove the very least of venial sins, so far as its guilt is concerned.

77. It is said that even St. Peter, if he were now Pope, could not bestow greater graces; this is blasphemy against St. Peter and against the pope.

78. We say, on the contrary, that even the present pope, and any pope at all, has greater graces at his disposal; to wit, the Gospel, powers, gifts of healing, etc., as it is written in I. Cor. xii.

79. To say that the cross, emblazoned with the papal arms, which is set up [by the preachers of indulgences], is of equal worth with the Cross of Christ, is blasphemy.

80. The bishops, curates and theologians who allow such talk to be spread among the people, will have an account to render.
81. This unbridled preaching of pardons makes it no easy matter, even for learned men, to rescue the reverence due to the pope from slander, or even from the shrewd questionings of the laity.
82. To wit: — 'Why does not the pope empty purgatory, for the sake of holy love and of the dire need of the souls that are there, if he redeems an infinite number of souls for the sake of miserable money with which to build a Church? The former reasons would be most just; the latter is most trivial.'
83. Again: — 'Why are mortuary and anniversary masses for the dead continued, and why does he not return or permit the withdrawal of the endowments founded on their behalf, since it is wrong to pray for the redeemed?'
84. Again: — 'What is this new piety of God and the pope, that for money they allow a man who is impious and their enemy to buy out of purgatory the pious soul of a friend of God, and do not rather, because of that pious and beloved soul's own need, free it for pure love's sake?'
85. Again: — 'Why are the penitential canons long since in actual fact and through disuse abrogated and dead, now satisfied by the granting of indulgences, as though they were still alive and in force?'
86. Again: — 'Why does not the pope, whose wealth is to-day greater than the riches of the richest, build just this one church of St. Peter with his own money, rather than with the money of poor believers?'
87. Again: — 'What is it that the pope remits, and what participation does he grant to those who, by perfect contrition, have a right to full remission and participation?'
88. Again: — 'What greater blessing could come to the Church than if the pope were to do a hundred times a day what he now does once, and bestow on every believer these remissions and participations?'
89. 'Since the pope, by his pardons, seeks the salvation of souls rather than money, why does he suspend the indulgences and pardons granted heretofore, since these have equal efficacy?'
90. To repress these arguments and scruples of the laity by force alone, and not to resolve them by giving reasons, is to expose the Church and the pope to the ridicule of their enemies, and to make Christians unhappy.
91. If, therefore, pardons were preached according to the spirit and mind of the pope, all these doubts would be readily resolved; nay, they would not exist.
92. Away, then, with all those prophets who say to the people of Christ, 'Peace, peace,' and there is no peace!
93. Blessed be all those prophets who say to the people of Christ, 'Cross, cross,' and there is no cross!
94. Christians are to be exhorted that they be diligent in following Christ, their Head, through penalties, deaths, and hell;
95. And thus be confident of entering into heaven rather through many tribulations, than through the assurance of peace.

In the context of its times the *Ninety-Five Theses* were, in short, a brief and concise attack upon the theology as well as the authority of Rome. Beyond theological stalwartness, the theses possess a vehemence akin to a political manifesto. In form if not in content the theses parallel a Thomas Paine pamphlet or a tract like the *Manifesto of the Communist Party* and, in point-for-point political summary, are similar to a document like the Universal Declaration of Human Rights written over four centuries later. Luther's combination of political and theological challenge was a stimulus against centuries of repression and counter-repression in terms of freedom of expression.

The Protestant Reformation which was to follow permanently divided Christianity; and the weapon most commonly used by both sides — Protestant and Catholic — was the theological censor, determining the extent or otherwise of orthodoxy or heterodoxy. The battle over theological orthodoxy became a battle over freedom of expression. Thus the Counter-Reformation and the formal establishment of the Inquisition which followed in the wake of the Reformation (Chadwick, 1990; 2001) were forever to define theological censorship and even epitomize a wider repression of freedom of expression.

The medieval Christian Church — as we have noted from the repression of Abelard, Wycliffe, and Huss — had become increasingly characterized by a brutality and violence in the face of theological dissent, and in a way not witnessed in the early Church when *it* challenged heresy. The Reformation and Counter-Reformation maintained this distinctly and violently intolerant approach to dissent. In Spain, Philip II had previously used an Inquisition of sorts to maintain spiritual and temporal authority, and yet this was arguably more in the nature of a national ruler maintaining control of a state. Philip II used the imposition of fear over religious orthodoxy to maintain his power in Spain but his 'Inquisition' — even when used against Jews or Muslims — was not responding to a real religious threat or motivated by a need to maintain orthodoxy against a serious rival to Roman Catholicism, as was the case in the Counter-Reformation. That said, the *Auto-da fe* (Portuguese for act of faith) was a radically imposed public execution by the Spanish Inquisition. Under Tomas de Torquemade in Seville, in 1481 alone around two thousand people suffered such a fate. Spaniards' repression of books extended beyond those identified by the Holy Office to include books by Muslims ('Moors') and Jews, astrological works and vernacular Bibles.

Prior to the Reformation too there had been papal decrees — by Alexander VI in 1501 and one by Leo X in 1515 which presented a major shift — in which demands were made that *all* publications were to be subject to approval by Church authorities, centrally in Rome and not simply on an *ad hoc* basis in individual Christian kingdoms. Yet it was during the height of the Counter-Reformation, at the Council of Trent (1545–1563/4), that the Catholic Church established a permanent institution to deal with censorship, an official body called the Congregation of the Inquisition. Pope Paul IV (1476–1559) oversaw the body of this 'Inquisition' from Rome. The Congregation of the Inquisition (*Congregatio Indicis Liborum Prohibitorum*) was charged with the compilation of a list of books likely to endanger faith or morals. *The Index of Banned Books* (1559) was the result of its efforts. In 1564 the *Tridentine Index* also contained the rules governing procedures for censorship for the banning of publications potentially harmful to faith and morals, including all heretical and superstitious writings, and all books deemed obscene. From the time of the *Tridentine Index* we can also note the development of a distinction between *censura praevia* — censorship before the printing or publication — and *censura repressive* — censorship after the printing or publishing, by repressing or prohibiting it. Other editions of the *Index* followed (around nineteen) until the final 1948 edition.

The following extract is from the last (1948), twentieth-century, edition of the *Index*, which could have been written in the sixteenth:

The Holy Church has through many centuries carried out immense persecutions, and the number of heroes who sealed the Christian faith with their blood, were multiplied. Today we face a struggle which is led by the Devil himself; it is founded on something both insincere and destructive: malicious publications. No other danger is greater, it threatens the faith and exercise of custom and integrity, therefore the Holy Church will increasingly point this out to the Christians, in that way enabling them to retreat before this threat. The Holy Church, which was appointed by God himself, could not proceed otherwise. It represents an infallible master who securely leads his believers. Thus, the Church is equipped with all necessary and useful means to prevent the infection of the herd of Jesus, by the erroneous and corrupt which will show itself irrespective of the mask it hides behind. Consequently the Holy Church has the duty, and hence the right, to pursue this aim.

One must not claim that the condemnation of harmful books is a violation of freedom or a war against the Light of Truth, and that the index of forbidden books is a permanent attack against the progress of science and literature. Irreligious and immoral books are written in a seductive manner, often with themes which deal with fleshly passion, or themes that deceive the pride of the soul. These books are carefully written to make an impression and aim at gaining ground in both the heart and mind of the incautious reader.

In addition, the necessity to suppress malicious publications for the well-being of the public, has particularly been proven lately, when even civil governments, have used preventive censorship to protect the judicial system and public order, with a rigidity unknown to the Church. This shows us how well it corresponds with the true liberty. No matter how much true literary and scientific values a book can possess, it cannot legitimate the distribution which opposes religion and good custom. On the contrary, the more subtle and seductive the evil is, the more it necessitates stronger and more efficient suppression of it.

These prohibited books were written to make an impression, and all this have been exposed to remove any doubt occurring among the Catholic believers. This explanation is intended for the devoted, good sons, who readily listen to the words of the good Shepherd Jesus, and to his representative on earth; the Pope. In short, this is intended for those who scrupulously comply with the rules, possibly with some exceptions arising from extreme conditions, where the Church grant exemptions for those who dissociate themselves from reading or owning the books which have been prohibited by the Holy Church. (For the full text of the final, 1948 Index, and a database of over 50,000 works banned in other contexts, go to www.beaconforfreedom.org, and follow links)

The *Index* and the Inquisition originated at the height of the Counter-Reformation to counteract the threats to Roman Catholic orthodoxy from the Protestant Reformation — and while it was dealing with these it saw fit to condemn the works of non-Christian, humanist and distinctly liberal-leaning works originating from the Renaissance. With documents like the nineteenth-century *Syllabus of Errors* (1864) and early twentieth-century pronouncements against 'Modernism', three and four hundred years later the Catholic Church would be maintaining prohibitions against modernity, which resulted from such late medieval Renaissance and humanistic developments in philosophy, theology and polity. For instance, the trend to repression of ideas is evident in the First Vatican Council (1870–71) which defined papal infallibility on matters of faith and morals, including a tight grip on freedom of expression through the *Index*. The Roman Catholic Church thereby reaffirmed an intransigent stance against the world, essentially separating the Catholic Church from modernity itself, and almost all developments of post-Enlightenment philosophy and politics — including notions of open and democratic governance, and the right to free speech and critique on which rested these latter notions of modern polity.

Pronouncements of papal infallibility at Vatican I occurred at a time when the Catholic

Church was already losing much of its temporal authority. Vatican I was the Catholic Church's attempt to retain absolute power in an area where it felt it could give no ground — the battle to repress ideas through an *Index* of banned and prohibited books was increasingly futile in the mid-nineteenth century. Indeed, with the printing press already well established in the sixteenth century the banning or suppressing of books during the Counter-Reformation — initially a defence against Luther and other Reformation leaders — was already increasingly difficult. By the twentieth century such censorship was an impossible task and at the end of the Vatican II (1962–65), a new era of relative openness to the modern world was to prevail.

Summary

In Luther's world — as in Augustine's — the limits to free expression were restricted primarily to the orthodoxy of religious belief. There was only one true view of the world — and the only real choice of human freewill was between eternal salvation or heaven and eternal damnation or hell. The notion that one would be ultimately free to express oneself into hell might have been an unpalatable choice to Luther — setting aside debates over predestination — but the choice was there. The notion that freedom of expression was an inalienable right however would have seemed peculiar. Salvation remained the predominant intellectual preoccupation of the day, as much as the individual's reflection of their fate in the light of God's Last Judgment preoccupied all souls. Yet the Renaissance had, by Luther's time, reacquainted Europe with the lost works of the ancient worlds of Greece and Rome, and the growth of such knowledge had produced a flourishing of philosophy and literature that would lead, via the Reformation and the Counter-Reformation, to the Enlightenment. It is noteworthy too, that the Reformation and Counter-Reformation, a period of such ferocious religiosity but the beginnings of a freedom from religious autocracy — the age of Luther — was to produce so much *non-religious* literary expression: foremost was Miguel de Cervantes' (1547–1616) *Don Quixote*, and the just emergent literary form of the novel, as well as the plays of William Shakespeare (1564–1616) and the other great European dramatists.

Luther's theological rebellion is, though, a good example of a religious divide in Christianity having profound consequences beyond Christian tradition, and it provoked responses from the Roman Catholic Church, in particular the Inquisition, that now epitomize repression in freedom of expression. We must recall that Protestantism itself became divided and the iconoclasm of its destruction of the supposedly idolatrous and the profane must not be forgotten — from Henry the Eighth's Dissolution of the monasteries, the general destruction of images of saints in European cathedrals, to the Puritan's repression of theatrical and all manner of literary arts. All these led to the irreplaceable loss of a vast medieval artistic, architectural, literary and wider cultural heritage.

◆ See Appendix X ◆

A Typology of Dissent

PAGE 219

◆ It is instructive to compare the rights and freedoms espoused by Luther's *Ninety-Five Theses* with those rights and freedoms outlined in Appendices II through to IX ◆

It was not until the Second Vatican Council (1962–65) that the Roman Catholic Church adopted a much more conciliatory approach to the modern world (Flannery, 1987). With regard to the *Index of Banned Books* (listing books that were a danger to faith and or morals, for reading of which Roman Catholics risked excommunication), the risk of excommunication was lifted by Pope Paul VI in 1966, and the *Index* itself relegated to a largely historical document. The Congregation of the Inquisition became the less threatening Congregation for the Doctrine of the Faith, once headed by Cardinal Ratzinger — now his Holiness Pope Benedict XVI. Roman Catholic theologians still require the mark of *Imprimatur* and *Nihil Obstat* as episcopal confirmations of theological orthodoxy but the tone is pastoral and conciliatory, rather than instantly condemnatory. And if the Congregation for the Doctrine of the Faith had, especially since the papacy of his predecessor Pope John Paul II, instigated a rigorous campaign to maintain doctrinal conformity amongst Roman Catholic theologians — including high profile cases like Leonardo Boff and Hans Kung — nevertheless relations with non-Christian world faiths, Protestant and other Christian denominations have improved dramatically. More widely, the modern-day accommodation of all Christian churches to secular and non-Christian literature, and indeed the fundamental protection of freedom of expression — even the right to dissent — are immeasurably beneficent compared with the Christian heritage of repression so marked from the Reformation onwards.

References

Bainton, Roland H. (2002) *Here I Stand: A Life of Martin Luther*. London: Penguin.

Chadwick, Owen (1990) *The Reformation*. Harmondsworth: Penguin.

Chadwick, Owen (2001) *The Early Reformation on the Continent*. Oxford: Oxford University Press.

Cross, F.L. (ed.) (1998) *A Dictionary of the Christian Church*, third edition. Oxford: Oxford University Press.

Fictenau, Heinrich (1998) *Heretics and Scholars in the High Middle Ages, 1000–1200*, translated by Denise A. Kaiser. University Park: Pennsylvania State University Press.

Flannery, A. (1982) *Vatican II: The Conciliar and Post-Conciliar Documents*. Dublin: Veritas.

Levi, A.H.T. (2002) *Renaissance and Reformation: The Intellectual Genesis*. New Haven; London: Yale University Press.

McEnhill, Peter and Newlands, George (2004) *Fifty Key Christian Thinkers*. London: Routledge.

Mullet, Michael A. (2004) *Martin Luther*. London: Routledge.

Nestingen, James Arne (2003) *Martin Luther: A Life*. Minneapolis: Augsburg.

Østrem, Eyolf, Fleischer, Jens and Petersen, Nils Holger (2003) *The Arts and Cultural Heritage of Martin Luther*. Copenhagen: Museum Tusculanum Press.

Tomlin, Graham (2002) *Luther and His World*. Oxford: Lion.

Vandiver, Elizabeth, Keen, Ralph, and Frazel, Thomas D. (2002) *Luther's Lives: Two Contemporary Accounts of Martin Luther (by Philip Melanchton and Johannes Cochaeus)*, translated and annotated by Elizabeth Vandiver Ralph Keen and Thomas D. Frazel. Manchester: Manchester University Press.

Selected Electronic Sources

If you only visit one website on Luther, go to

Project Wittenberg   wwww.lclnet.org (and follow links to Project Wittenberg)

There is an extraordinary range of historical, literary and theological links, and a full selection is provided below:

ABOUT LUTHER

- *Bible Commentaries.*
- *Famous Passages of Martin Luther.*
- *Selected Sermons from Martin Luther.*
- *Concerning Christian Liberty.*
- *Disputation On the Divinity and Humanity of Christ.*
- *The Last Written Words of Luther . . .*
- *Let Your Sins Be Strong.*
- *An Open Letter to The Christian Nobility.*
- *To Several Nuns.*
- *A Treatise on Good Works.*
- *On Translating.*
- *Prefaces from Luther's German Bible Version.*
- *Ninety-Five Theses.*
- *Luther's Larger Catechism.*
- *Luther's Smaller Catechism.*

CONTEMPORARY ACCOUNTS

A Christian Sermon Over the Body and At the Funeral of the Venerable Dr. Martin Luther, preached by Mr. Johann Bugenhagen Pomeranus (1546).

From the Pitts Theological Library, Emory University (Graphics of a German facsimilie at Pitts)

A History of the Life and Actions of the Very Reverend Dr. Martin Luther, Faithfully Written by Philip Melancthon. Wittemburg. 1549.

The History of the Life and Acts of Luther. 1548. Melanthon, Philip. Prepared by Dr. Steve Sohmer 1996. Translated by T. Frazel 1995.

BIBLE COMMENTARIES BY LUTHER

Galatians — Commentary on the Epistle to the Galatians (1535), by Martin Luther. Translated by Theodore Graebner (Grand Rapids, Michigan: Zondervan Publishing House, 1949).

FAMOUS PASSAGES FROM THE WRITINGS OF MARTIN LUTHER
Martin Luther's Definition of Faith.
Martin Luther on Quoting Martin Luther.
What is Your God? Devotional Thoughts of Martin Luther.
Martin Luther Discovers the Gospel: The Tower Experience.

SELECTED SERMONS FROM MARTIN LUTHER
Sermon on Threefold Righteousness by Martin Luther; from Philippians 2 (1518) Concerning
  Christian Liberty (1520):
  Part 1: Letter from Martin Luther to Pope Leo X
  Part 2: Beginning of the Treatise
  Part 3: Conclusion of the Treatise
Disputation on the Divinity and Humanity of Christ:
  Disputation on the Divinity and Humanity of Christ, February 27, 1540, conducted by Dr.
  Martin Luther, 1483–1546, translated from the Latin text, WA 39/2, 92–121, by Christopher
  B. Brown.
A Treatise on Good Works (1520):
  A Treatise on Good Works, Together with the Letter of Dedication by Dr. Martin Luther.
Let Your Sins Be Strong (1521):
  Let Your Sins Be Strong: A Letter from Luther to Melancthon. Letter no. 99, 1 August 1521
  From Wortburg (Segment). Translated by Erika bullman Flores. From Dr. Martin Luther's
  Saemmtliche Schriften. Dr. Johannes Georg Walch, Ed. (St. Louis: Concordia Publishing
  House, n.d.), Vol. 15, cols. 2585–2590.
An Open Letter to the Christian Nobility (1520): An Open Letter to the Christian Nobility of
  the German Nation Concerning the Reform of the Christian Estate, 1520, by Martin Luther.
  Introduction and Translation by C. M. Jacobs. *Works of Martin Luther With Introduction
  and Notes,* Vol. II. Philadelphia: A.J. Holman Co., 1915).
Translator's Introduction.
Luther's Cover Letters.
The Three Walls of the Romanists.
Abuses to Be Discussed in Councils.
Proposals for Reform I.
Proposals for Reform II.
Proposals for Reform III.
To Several Nuns (1524):
  To Several Nuns, by Martin Luther. From Wittenberg, 6 August 1524. Translated from Briefe
  aus dem Jahre 1524, No. 732–756. (Letters of the Year 1524, Nos. 733–756). Weimarer
  Ausgabe. Translated by Erika Bullman Flores.

ON TRANSLATING (1530)
Martin Luther's Classic tract *On Translating* is the foundation of the modern science of linguis-
  tics, of Bible translation and a classic of the German language.

THE PREFACES FROM MARTIN LUTHER'S GERMAN BIBLE VERSION
Preface to Hosea in German.
Preface to the Book of Romans in English (1522).
Preface to the Book of Romans in German (1522).

MARTIN LUTHER'S NINETY-FIVE THESES
Disputation of Doctor Martin Luther on the Power and Efficacy of Indulgences (1517).
Study Guide for the Disposition of Doctor Martin Luther on the Power and Efficacy of

Indulgences more commonly known as The Ninety-five Theses, prepared by Lyman Baker, Department of English, at Kansas State University.

MARTIN LUTHER'S LARGE CATECHISM (1530)
The Large Catechism, by Martin Luther. Translated by F. Bente and W.H.T. Dan. Published in: *Triglot Concordia: The Symbolical Books of the Ev. Lutheran Church* (St. Louis: Concordia Publishing House, 1921).

THE LAST WRITTEN WORDS OF LUTHER (1646)
The Last Written Words of Luther: Holy Ponderings of the Reverend Father Doctor Martin Luther, 16 February 1546, Dr. Martin Luthers Werke (Weimar: Hermann Boehlaus Nachfolger, 1909), Band 85 (TR 5), pp. 317–318. Translated by James A. Kellerman.

4   Thomas Paine (1737–1809)
Rights of Man

> While the Declaration of Rights was before the National Assembly, some of its members remarked, that if the Declaration of Rights was published, it should be accompanied by a Declaration of Duties. The observation discovered a mind that reflected, and it only erred by not reflecting far enough. A Declaration of Rights is, by reciprocity, a Declaration of Duties also. Whatever is my right as a man, is also the right of another; and it becomes my duty to guarantee, as well as to possess.
>
> Thomas Paine, *Rights of Man*

After much post-Reformation bloodshed over religious belief, the European Enlightenment, even in its own time, was termed the 'Age of Reason', defining the manner in which reason was supplanting theology as a way of interpreting the world. The high marks of the Enlightenment can be historically located in the eighteenth-century; its ideological and philosophical antecedents are identifiable centuries earlier, with the re-discovery of Greek and Roman philosophy during the Renaissance and the new humanism which this engendered. Humanism, as the term implies, centred the universe on man rather than — in theocentric terms — his Creator. This new post-Renaissance humanism encouraged individuals to think for themselves rather than be dependent upon priests and bishops and — the ultimate medieval authority in matters spiritual and temporal — the pope. In the wake of this humanism came the Reformation — a period of dissent against the established Roman Catholic Church — which emphasized the authority of individual Christians in matters of faith, in the reading of scriptures, and so forth. The effect of this, however, was to further the conditions for the individualism of the modern world, characterized by the Enlightenment's call to reason over theology. This post-Reformation period — thus characterized rightly as the Age of Reason — was marked therefore not only by a weakening of Roman Catholic authority but a wider decline of Christianity in Europe. Guided by the spirit of reason rather than theology, the Enlightenment also produced revolutionary calls — notably the 1789 French Revolution — to new forms of governance based on democracy and the 'rights of man' rather than on ecclesiastical or monarchical authority. In this new era freedom of speech and religion would prevail as key civic and political ideals. Thomas Paine was the author of some of the most notable tracts of the time, his *Rights of Man* and *The Age of Reason* placing him at the heart of an age he did so much to define.

    The politics and philosophy of the Enlightenment were to have worldwide effects. In politics the American Declaration of Independence (1776) and the French Revolution and the Declaration of Rights of Man (from 1789 onwards) are here pivotal; in philosophy Immanuel Kant's *Critique of Pure Reason* (1781), conceptualized not only the pre-eminence of reason but provided the rationalistic groundwork for the scientific, technological and industrial revolutions that were to follow. The political revolutions in America and France brought a separation of church and state, and the philosophy of Kant provided the philosophical grounds for an ascendancy of reason over theology. In political terms, the Enlightenment did not immediately bring power to the people — including their capacity to freely express critiques of both political and religious elites — but it brought its possibility. Wresting knowledge and power from theologians to politicians was a critical stage in the development of modern political governance. It was from this period that we can see developing the notion of a true 'freedom of expression'.

If the Enlightenment was, therefore, marked in both philosophical and political terms by liberation from the controlling autocratic and centralized powers of the Catholic Church in Rome, it was also characterized by increasing dissent from the authority of Christianity in general, including the now numerous Protestant denominations evident through Europe. Ironically, however, it is arguable that the Enlightenment's marginalization of Christianity in Europe gave impetus to Christian missionary zeal in new arenas of global imperialism and colonization. The wider irony is that European political powers that were encouraging the 'rights of man' at home were abusing them abroad. That aside, in the newly established colonies of both North and South America, religion in the seventeenth and eighteenth centuries had yet to relinquish its authority; in North America Protestant denominations prevailed still as bastions against Rome, while throughout Latin America the Roman Catholic Church retained a power more akin to that which it had possessed in the medieval times. Yet in both North and South America indigenous peoples were decimated by the new creeds as much as by the economic imperialism which was the main impetus behind such colonization. In Africa it was not until the nineteenth-century that Christianity accompanied the colonizer as it did in India and throughout Asia; but in Asia at least it was to resist the wholesale conversions witnessed in Africa. It was not until the twentieth-century in Asia and the Middle East that the resurgence of Islam provided a theological challenge to Christianity in former European colonies. In all these cases of European Christian colonization, declining powers of the Christian Church in Europe — from the post-Enlightenment period onwards — were compensated by extensions of ecclesiastical authority abroad (Hastings, 1999). The locus for the control of freedom of expression had shifted drastically in Europe away from the church to the state, and to secularity and rationality — a move that would, on the same continent, ultimately give rise not only to new freedoms but also to new extremes of repression, often militantly atheistic.

The European Enlightenment was, in short, a time of new political, philosophical and religious freedoms that would have been inconceivable during the worst excesses of Reformation repression. At the same time the Age of Reason was characterized not only by democratizing idealism but politically revolutionary excess (Fiero, 1998; Burns and Rayment-Pickard, 2004; Salerno, 2004). The immediate political aftermath of the French Revolution, for example, engendered not only the murder of royalty and aristocracy but the persecution of churchmen and clergy as well as 'ordinary' religious believers. This godless reign of terror was a direct result of the more militantly irreligious forms of pre- and post-Enlightenment rationalism — later engendering militant atheistic doctrines, from communism to fascism and Nazism (Royle, 2003; Ford, 2003; Foner, 2005). A number of political thinkers, celebrating the absence of a restraining Christianity and the new ideology of reason, adopted such freedoms into social agendas — figures such as Thomas Hobbes (1588–1679), John Locke (1632–1704), Jean-Jacques Rousseau (1712–1778), Thomas Paine (1737–1809) — and these characters and their ideas became pivotal to the new political liberalism, often centred to differing degrees on the challenges to monarchy and church (Simpson, 1823; Grisenthwaite, 1825; Conway, 1892; 1992a; Paine, 1996; Norfolk, 1979; Kelly and Masters, 1990; Keane, 1996; Kaye, 2000; Kaminski, 2003). These figures helped to prepare and define modernity in polity and governance particularly the emergent notion and rights and representative democracy, and to establish the foundational principle implied in and by the existence of all their writings — freedom of expression, and critically the freedom to express dissent.

The period had also in this regard a strong cultural dimension which allowed for new forms of aesthetic expression — and which, in large measure, went hand in hand with new political and religious freedoms. The literary and aesthetic equivalence of political revolutions in the Age of Reason was 'Romanticism' (Engell, 1999; Micale and Dietle, 2000). Romanticism was a Europe-wide movement which emphasized individual feeling in thought and mood, often in response to nature. Its antecedents can be seen in the dual influences of Roman and Greek classicism and, millennia later, the humanistic influences of a post-Renaissance individualism; but the radical freedom of expression we see in the Romantics would not have been possible without freedom from political and religious oppression brought by the Age of Reason. In the English literary tradition this found its strongest expression amongst the essayists, poets, and novelists; in poetry William Wordsworth (1770–1850), Samuel Taylor Coleridge (1772–1834) and George Gordon (Lord) Byron (1778–1824), Percy Bysshe Shelley (1792–1822), John Keats (1795–1821); in the novel, Mary Shelley (1797–1851), notably *Frankenstein* (1818), and Emily Bronte (1818–1848), classically *Wuthering Heights* (1847). Interestingly, given our consideration of the poets in Plato's *Republic*, once again it was the Romantic poets who showed the strongest inclination towards the new forms of political idealism brought about by the Enlightenment. Amongst these, were Coleridge and Wordsworth, both young enough to understand and be enthralled by the French Revolution as well as to inspire the Romanticism in English letters. Coleridge, however, was never influenced by politics to the extent that the slightly older Wordsworth was; he was perhaps more influenced by the older dilettante Thomas de Quincey, author of *Confessions of An English Opium Eater*, and wrote little poetry in his later years — concentrating more on philosophy and criticism — arguably down to this lassitude inducing influence. Wordsworth, by contrast, maintained a political interest throughout his life, as indeed his poetic powers declined, but became greatly disillusioned by the excesses of the revolutionary terror that followed in the wake of the liberating ideals of the French Revolution, and ended his days as a conservative Member of Parliament in Westminster.

If many Romantic writers combined an interest in free self expression with political activity, this is nowhere better personified than in the figure of Lord Byron. His brilliant early promise was shown by a phenomenon unusual in any age — bestselling poetry. Byron's *Childe Harold's Pilgrimage* (1812–18) was just that. He also had a renown for licentiousness, and in 1815 his wife left him — after Byron's alleged incestuous affair with his half-sister. Ostracized in much of English public life, Byron, disillusioned and in debt, left England, to stay for a while in Geneva with the poet Shelley before settling in Italy. Byron maintained early poetic genius with enduring literary popularity in further epic poems such as *Don Juan* (1819–24) but he remained a moral and literal exile from main-stream convention. Byron thus scandalized an age in almost equal measure to the manner in which he enthralled it. He epitomized the wild spirit of Romanticism that defined homage to unlimited freedom of expression, in personal morality as much as in art. In democratic and liberal politics, he also epitomized the political freedoms of the Age of Reason. Byron's tragically early death during the struggle for Greek Independence only served to impress this unity of the political and the aesthetic. Byron's aristocratic back-ground was appealingly combined with poetic genius and, despite the privileges of an aristocratic birth, he held a commitment to defend the besieged and the oppressed. In this light, Byron became altogether more legendary in that the oppressed were the Greeks and that Greece was land under siege — the birthplace of Homer and (Plato aside) democracy. If Byron had died a famous poet in England that might have been enough to secure his reputation as a representative of unbridled free expression, one to be modelled within his own generation and in all subsequent ones. Romanticism encapsulated freedom of expres-sion — untrammelled by convention or petty confining traditions — as an ideal and as a way of life, and, if their *political* views are less well known now, they remain today a para-digm for aesthetic, moral and existential freedom. The unrestricted freedom espoused by Romanticism — its emphasis upon the individual against overbearing traditions and conventions — had its political advocate and spokesperson in Thomas Paine. Amongst all political philosophers of the Enlightenment, Paine's was a life led — like the Romantics — not simply cerebrally, but in the full wake of revolutionary battle against the tyranny of repressive convention and tradition.

Thomas Paine the Author

Thomas Paine was born in 1737 in a sea-facing eastern county of England, in the town of Thetford, Norfolk. By the age of twelve he had already left school and by nineteen he had failed in his first career — as an apprentice corset-maker in his father's business. Thomas Paine went to sea in search of a life of adventure. By the 1760s he was a tax officer, but his early political consciousness was apparent even then; in 1768, as a tax officer, he campaigned for the rights of his fellow officers. Indeed, one of Paine's early works — not one high on many university reading lists — was a tract on the rights of tax officers. Paine's is a life of extraordinary networking — he seems to have met and been on close — in turns friendly and antagonistic — terms with all the great political figures of his day. By 1774 he had met the great polymath Benjamin Franklin (1706–90), discoverer of the theory of elec-tricity as well as a towering eighteenth-century American statesman. Thus began Paine's literal and intellectual journey to America, a journey which was to change his life and influ-ence the constitution of a country newly independent of its colonial ties with England (Keane, 1996). Less than two years after his arrival in America, in 1776, Paine published *Common Sense*, a defence of the cause of American independence, which influenced the emergent American Declaration of Independence (1776). Indeed — perhaps most strik-ingly little known outside America — it was Paine who helped suggest the name for the newly settled country, the United States of America (Foner, 2005).

Always physically and intellectually restless, Paine returned to Europe. In England over the years 1791–2 he wrote *Rights of Man*, a response to the criticism of the French Revolution by Edmund Burke, to whom many parts of the book are addressed directly with biting ironic humour. Publication of *Rights of Man* had been planned to coincide with the birthday of George Washington but was delayed due to pressure made upon the publisher by agents of the government. Paine then negotiated another publishing arrangement for *Rights of Man*. Written in reply to Edmund Burke's *Reflections on the Revolution in France* — a damning critique of the Revolution and the Terror portrayed as integral to it — Paine's passionate defence of French revolutionary principles was, in England, an inflammatory political tract that contained self-evident criticism of monarchy (Paine, 1996). By the time of his pamphlet's publication, however, Paine had already left England for Paris when he was charged, in absentia, for seditious libel.

In France, Paine was elected to the National Convention, the new revolutionary government in France. He refused to sanction the execution of Louis XVI, objecting on moral grounds to capital punishment and revenge killings in general. Revenge killings were an integral part of revolutionary justice in the Terror — as noted by Burke and fictionalized in accounts such as Charles Dickens' *A Tale of Two Cities*. Yet — somewhat ironically — after falling out with the revolutionaries he had sought so eloquently to defend, Paine was himself imprisoned, and even faced the guillotine, allegedly at the original orders of a leading French revolutionary, Robespierre (1758–94), a man responsible for much of the post-Revolutionary Terror.

In prison — convinced of impending execution — Paine wrote, and later, after a dramatic escape, published *The Age of Reason* (1794–96), a text which was emblematic of the Enlightenment and the declining influence of Christianity. *The Age of Reason* was a deist tract against organized religion that alienated him from an American public and administration so unshakeably fervent in their belief in God. This deist spirit is encapsulated in the following extract:

> The opinions I have advanced are the effect of the most clear and long-established conviction that the Bible and the Testament are impositions upon the world, that the fall of man, the account of Jesus Christ, and of his dying to appease the wrath of God, and of salvation by that strange means, are all fabulous inventions, dishonourable to the wisdom and power of the Almighty; that the only true religion is Deism, by which I then meant, and mean now, the belief of one God, and an imitation of his moral character, or the practice of what are called moral virtues — and that upon this only (so far as religion is concerned) that I rested all my hopes of happiness hereafter. So say I now — and so help me God. (Paine, 1996)

By a legendary and fateful error on the part of one of his gaolers, Paine managed to escape imprisonment and the threat of execution. He left France in 1802 and returned to America — at the invitation of Thomas Jefferson (1743–1823), principal drafter of the American Declaration of Independence, and third US President.

Following the melodrama of his escape from France, Paine's initial journey to America was full of hope and optimism and some powerful allies remained, at least in the early stages of his return. Once there, however, Paine's views on religion did not find him friends or political allies; indeed his views on religion arguably lost him the majority of both friends and political allies. Essentially, his anti-religious views were not well favoured in a country which, although founded on the principles of the separation of Church and state, were — and arguably are still today — more integrally founded upon fundamental Christian beliefs. The belief in liberty so emblematic of the Enlightenment was in Europe often accompanied by an increasing scepticism towards religion — not so in the United States, where separation of Church and state did not mean a declining fervour in religious belief.

Thomas Paine died in 1809. He was seventy-two years old, a largely isolated and lonely man in the emerging metropolis of New York City. Through his conceptualization of the 'rights of man' Thomas Paine had great political influence on the first President of the United States, George Washington (1732–99), as well as its third, Thomas Jefferson. Paine had been held in high esteem by leaders who came in the wake of a new post-Revolutionary era in France — including Napoleon Bonaparte (1769–1821). Yet, for someone held in such high esteem by the political elite of his day, history attests that only a handful of mourners attended his funeral (Kelly and Masters, 1990; Keane, 1996; Kaye, 2000; Kaminski, 2003).

Thomas Paine, the *Rights of Man* and Freedom of Expression

Revolutionary, radical, rights-focused, possessing a barely understated religious scepticism, encouraging of freedom in personal morality and liberalism in public life, Thomas Paine's *Rights of Man* is a political tract of immense historical significance. It is also an intensely insightful portrayal of the dawning a new political era whose influence shaped the modern world. It defined personal as well as political moral freedoms — especially those of expression and religion — barely conceivable during the Reformation and its most violent excesses.

In *Rights of Man* — as in much of Paine's other work — freedom of expression had a twofold focus: freedom of religion and freedom of speech. These freedoms are linked in Paine, as they were in the French constitution, as a *freedom of conscience*:

> The French constitution hath abolished or renounced toleration, and intolerance also, and hath established universal right of conscience.
>
> Toleration is not the opposite of Intolerance, but it is the counterfeit of it. Both are despotisms. The one presumes to itself the right of withholding Liberty of Conscience, and the other granting it. The one is the pope armed with fire and faggot, and the other is pope selling or granting indulgences. The former is church and state, and the latter is church and traffic.
>
> But toleration may be viewed in a much stronger light. Man worships not himself, but his maker; and the liberty of conscience which he claims, is not for the service of himself, but of his God. In this case, therefore, we must necessarily have the associated idea of two beings; the mortal who renders the worship, and the immortal being who is worshipped. Toleration, therefore places itself, not between man and man, nor between church and church, nor between one denomination of religion and another, but between God and Man; and by the same act of assumed authority by which it tolerates man to pay his worship, it presumptuously and blasphemously sets itself up to tolerate the Almighty to receive it. (Paine, 1985: 86)

It is this freedom of conscience that will form the basis of articles 18 (freedom of religion) and 19 (freedom of expression) in the United Nations *Universal Declaration of Human Rights* just over one hundred and fifty years later.

More broadly, we find in Paine an early elaboration of the idea of rights or entitlements of citizens, a concept later dismissed by thinkers such as Jeremy Bentham (1748–1832) as 'nonsense on sticks':

First, that every civil right grows out of a natural right; or, in other words, is a natural right exchanged.

Secondly, that civil power, properly considered as such, is made up of the aggregate of that class of the natural rights of man, which becomes defective in the individual in point of power, and answers not his purpose; but when collected to a focus, becomes competent to the purpose of every one.

Thirdly, that the power produced from the aggregate of natural rights, imperfect in power in the individual, cannot be applied to invade the natural rights which are retained in the individual, and in which case the power to execute is as perfect as the right itself.

We have now, in a few words, traced man from a natural individual to a member of society, and shown, or endeavoured to show, the quality of the natural rights retained and of those which are exchanged for civil rights. Let us now apply these principles to governments. (Paine, 1985: 69)

Paine thus elaborates simply a development of this notion — of rights in relation to the sources of governmental authority — as an evolutionary progression away from the tyranny of state and or church towards a model of government based upon (here borrowing from Rousseau) the social contract; that is, an agreement between the people and the representatives they have elected to represent them and in whose hands the people voluntarily provide their collective power, and the scope to remove such power from government as well as elect them to it.

Further to the notion of rights, the evolutionary progression of *government*, Paine identifies as: 'First, superstition. Secondly, power. Thirdly, the common interest of society, and the common of rights of man.' Paine subsequently elaborates the first as 'a government of priestcraft, the second of conquerors, and the third of reason':

When a set of artful men pretended, through the medium of oracles, to hold intercourse with the Deity, as familiarly as they now march up the back-stairs in European courts, the world was completely under the government of superstition. The oracles were consulted, and whatever they were made to say, became the law; and this set of government lasted as long as this sort of superstition lasted.

After these a race of conquerors arose, whose government, like that of William the Conqueror, was founded in power, and the sword assumed the name of a sceptre. Governments thus established lasted as long as the power to support them lasts; but that they might avail themselves of every engine in their favour, they united to fraud force, and set up an idol which they called Divine Right, and which, in imitation of the Pope, who affects to be spiritual and temporal, and in contradiction to the founder of the Christian religion, twisted itself afterwards into an idol of another shape, called Church and State. The key of St Peter, and the key of the Treasury, became quartered on one another, and the wondering cheated multitude worshipped the invention. (Paine, 1985: 69–70)

It is in response to these models of statecraft that the French Revolution arose, models which enraged Paine as much as they did the French revolutionaries: 'When I contemplate the natural dignity of man; when I feel (for Nature has not been kind enough to me to blunt my feelings) for the honour and happiness of its character, I become irritated at the attempt to govern mankind by force and fraud, as if they were all knaves and fools, and can scarcely avoid disgust at those who are thus imposed upon.'

Paine proceeds then to delineate historical forms of government, between 'the governments which arise out of society, in contradistinction to those which arose out of superstition and conquest':

It has been thought a considerable advance towards establishing the principles of Freedom, to say, that government is a compact between those who govern and those who are governed: but this cannot be true, because it is putting the effect before the cause; for as man must have existed before governments existed, there necessarily was a time when governments did not exist, and consequently there could originally exist no governors to form a compact with. The fact must therefore be that the individuals themselves, each in his own personal and sovereign right, entered into a compact with each other to produce a government: and this is the only mode in which governments have a right to arise, and the only principle on which they have a right to exist. (1985: 70)

Of the formal document of the *Declaration of the Rights of Man and of Citizens* before the National Assembly — the post-Revolutionary French government — Paine comments:

In the declaratory exordium which prefaces the Declaration of Rights, we see the solemn and majestic spectacle of a Nation opening its commission, under the auspices of its Creator, to establish a Government; a scene so new, and so transcendentally unequalled by anything in the European world, that the name of a Revolution is diminutive of its character, and it rises into a Regeneration of man. What are the present governments of Europe, but a scene of iniquity and oppression? (Paine, 1985: 114)

The foundational political statement of rights before the National Assembly — clearly not having entirely lost sight of the ancient relationship between the theological and the political — exhorts that it 'doth recognize and declare, in the presence of the Supreme Being, and with the hope of his blessing and favour, the following sacred rights of men and of citizens'. The following are the three foundational articles:

I   Men are born, and always continue, free, and equal in respect of their rights. Civil distinctions therefore, can be founded on public utility.
II   The end of all political associations, is, the preservation of the natural and imperceptible rights of man; and these rights are liberty, property, security, and resistance of oppression.
III The nation is essentially the source of all sovereignty; nor can any individual, or any body of men, be entitled to any authority which is not expressly derived from it.

In Paine's commentary, he notes that the 'first three articles comprehend in general terms, the whole of a Declaration of Rights: All the succeeding articles either originate from them, or follow as elucidations'. Articles IV, V, X and XI have particular relevance to freedom of expression, and demonstrate how foundational these were to a wider polity of rights and democratic governance:

IV   Political Liberty consists in the power of doing whatever does not injure another. The exercise of the natural rights of man, has no other limits than those which are necessary to secure to every other man the free exercise of the same rights; and these limits are determinable only by the law.
V   The law ought to prohibit only actions hurtful to society. What is not prohibited by the law should not be hindered; nor should any one be compelled to that which the law does not require.
X   No man ought to be molested on account of his opinions, not even on account of his religious opinions, provided his avowal of them does not disturb the public order established by the law.

XI   The unrestrained communication of thoughts and opinions being one of the most precious rights of man, every citizen may speak, write, and publish freely, provided he is
responsible for this liberty in cases determined by the law. (Paine, 1985: 110–112)

It is clear that in the French *Declaration of the Rights of Man and of Citizens* — from
article X especially — that freedom of expression is integral to freedom of religion. This is
the only area of the Declaration which seems to irritate Paine, his natural antipathy — a
hint of *The Age of Reason* — becoming evident: 'But it is questioned by some very good
people in France, as well as in other countries, whether the 10th article sufficiently guarantees the right it is accorded with: beside which, it takes off from the divine dignity of
religion, and weakens its operative force upon the mind, to make it a subject of human laws.
It then presents itself to Man, like light intercepted by a cloudy medium, in which the
source of it is obscured from his sight, and he sees nothing to reverence in the dusky ray'
(Paine, 1985: 113).

Summary

Numerous key thinkers are identifiable as playing a part in the philosophical and political
groundwork of the Age of Reason — Kant, Hobbes, Hume, Locke, Rousseau (Eisenbach,
2002; Levine, 2002). Thomas Paine was responsible not simply for elaborating and helping
disseminate notions of new political governance — the foundational importance of representative democracy, rights and freedom to critique authority — he was on the frontline
of revolutionary political change. To paraphrase Marx, Paine was committed not simply
to describing the world but changing it.

Arguably, no single author of the modern age has so influenced the present-day discus-

◆   See Appendix X   ◆

A Typology of Dissent

PAGE 219

◆   Paine, of all the case studies so far, exemplifies the modern notion and
interpretation of political dissent. It is instructive to compare the rights and
freedoms represented in Appendices II through to IX with Paine's *Rights of Man*,
to see how indebted — in terms of polity and democratic government —
the modern era is to Paine's writings.   ◆

sion of rights as Thomas Paine — a freedom of expression he paid for with personal and
political isolation in later life. Yet his influence remains, and will endure, not simply for the
content but also for the manner of his discourse, his accessible political tracts popularizing
consideration of key political ideas for a wide audience. Thomas Paine's writing, and the
brave polemical style which embodies the freedoms he espoused encapsulated not simply

the ideas of his own enlightened age but helped to define them, for the Age of Reason and for future generations.

References

Brown, Marshall (1997) *Turning Points: Essays in the History of Cultural Expressions*. Stanford, California: Stanford University Press.

Burns, Robert and Rayment-Pickard, Hugh (2004) *Philosophies of History: From Enlightenment to Post-Modernity*. Oxford; Beijing: Peking University Press; Blackwell.

Conway, Moncure Daniel (1892) *The Life of Thomas Paine*, two volumes. London: Routledge/ Thoemmes.

Conway, Moncure Daniel (1892) *The Writings of Thomas Paine*, two volumes, with a new introduction by Michael Foot. London: Routledge/ Thoemmes.

Eisenach, Elden J. (2002) *Narrative Power and Liberal Truth: Hobbes, Locke, Bentham, and Mill*. Lanham: Rowman & Littlefield Publishers.

Engell, James (1999) *The Creative Imagination: Enlightenment to Romanticism*. Cambridge, MA: Harvard University Press.

Fiero, Gloria K. (1998) *The Humanistic Tradition*, four volumes. Madison, Wisconsin; Dubuque, Iowa: WCB Brown and Benchmark.

Foner, Eric (2005) *Tom Paine and Revolutionary America*. New York; Oxford: Oxford University Press.

Ford, Karen (2001) *Property, Welfare and Freedom in the Thought of Thomas Paine: A Critical Edition*. Lewiston, N.Y.; Lampeter: Edwin Mellen Press.

Grisenthwaite, William (1825) *A Refutation of Every Argument Brought Against the Truth of Christianity, and Revealed Religion, by Thomas Paine: in the first part of his work called The Age of Reason. London*: G.B. Whittaker.

Hastings, Adrian (ed.) (1999) *A World History of Christianity*. London: Cassell.

Kaminski, John P. (ed.) *Citizen Paine: Thomas Paine's Thoughts on Man, Government, Society and Religion*. Oxford: Rowman & Littlefield.

Kaye, Harvey J. (2000) *Thomas Paine: Firebrand of the Revolution*. New York; Oxford: Oxford University Press.

Kelly, Christopher and Masters, Roger D. (1990) *The Collected Writings of Rousseau*, translated by Judith R. Bush, Christopher Kelly and Roger D. Masters. Hanover, NH; London: University Press of New England.

Keane, John (1996) *Tom Paine: A Political Life*. London: Bloomsbury.

Levine, Andrew (2002) *Engaging Political Philosophy: From Hobbes to Rawls*. Malden, MA: Blackwell.

Micale, Mark S. and Dietle Robert L. (eds.) (2000) *Enlightenment, Passion and Modernity: Historical essays in European Thought and Culture*. Stanford, California: Stanford University Press.

Norfolk County Library (1979) *The Thomas Paine Collection at Thetford: An Analytical Catalogue*. Norwich: Norfolk County Library.

Paine, Thomas (1985) *Rights of Man*. Harmondsworth: Penguin.

Paine, Thomas (1996) *Thomas Paine: Life and Works*, six volumes. London: Routledge.

Royle, Edward (2003) *Thomas Paine and Nineteenth Century Freethought*. Nottingham: Thomas Paine Society.

Salerno, Roger A. (2004) *Beyond the Enlightenment: Lives and Thoughts of Social Theorists*. Westport, Connecticut: Praeger.

Simpson, David (1812) *A Plea for Religion and the Sacred Writings: addressed to the disciples of Thomas Paine, and wavering Christians of every persuasion*. Liverpool: Nuttall, Fisher and Dixon.

Selected Electronic Sources

FROM REVOLUTION TO RECONSTRUCTION (DOCUMENTS) — PAINE: *RIGHTS OF MAN*

USA-project, documents-area, Thomas Paine's *Rights of Man* at odur.let.rug.nl (and follow links), a Netherlands based resource looking at revolutionary history.

US HISTORY

www.historyplace.com contains an immense range of primary documentation and related secondary commentary, providing superb contextualization of Thomas Paine within wider American history.

THOMAS PAINE AND THE RIGHTS OF MAN, WITH RELATED DOCUMENTS

www.library.adelaide.edu.au (and follow links). This is a useful generic site which contains e-library sources for a useful range of primary documents.

INFIDELS

There area a number of sites which celebrate Thomas Paine's religious skepticism and hold Paine as a hero of atheistic free thought. Paine was a deist; he was skeptical of organized religion, Christianity in particular, and the claims to divine revelation of the Bible, but he did hold to a minimal religious belief in a deity. The website www.infidels.org (and follow links) demonstrates this sort of context for Paine's thinking. America largely rejected his religious skepticism while accepting his political philosophy. The site contains a considerable range of important historical documents.

ARCHIVING EARLY AMERICA

http://earlyamerica.com

Links to the *Rights of Man* in the context of early American constitutional and political history.

ARCHIVING EARLY AMERICA

The Rights of Man. A Political Pamphlet by Thomas Paine. Published in 1791. Go to earlyamerica.com (and follow links).

THOMAS PAINE AND THE RIGHTS OF MAN

www.constitution.org

Links to the text of Thomas Paine's writings and his life, with wider connection to the US Constitution, historically and in contemporary context.

If you only visit one website on Thomas Paine, go to

http://www.thomaspaine.org
This site contains the majority of Thomas Paine's writings, including letters:
Common Sense (1776)
Rights of Man (1791–1792)
Age of Reason (1794, 1796)

Karl Marx (1818 – 1883) and Friedrich Engels (1820 – 1895)

Manifesto of the Communist Party

Freedom is so much the essence of man that even its opponents implement it while combating its reality; they want to appropriate for themselves as a most precious ornament what they have rejected as an ornament of nature. No man combats freedom; at most he combats the freedom of others. Hence every kind of freedom has always existed, only at one time as a special privilege, at another as a universal right.

Karl Marx's *On Freedom of the Press*

Lenin was fighting for the party, but at the same time he secluded himself in the library. It is needless to say that Marx is the favourite author of Lenin . . . Lenin knows his Marx and Engels from the first to the last letter . . .

Zinoviev, 'The Period of Emigration' (Lenin in Paris)

All animals are equal.
But some animals are more equal than others.

George Orwell's *Animal Farm*

George Orwell's *Animal Farm* (1945) is a political fable centred on the inequalities of a farmyard regime ruled by humans, and of the rise to power through revolution by a small group of intelligent animals — who happen to be pigs — against the human oppressors. At the end of the tale we learn that the pigs themselves become oppressive, even taking to imitating their human forebears, walking on hind legs, declaring that 'all animals are equal but that some animals are more equal than others'. *Animal Farm* famously satirizes not only Soviet oppression but what Orwell saw as the inevitable political irony of the end result of revolution. In Orwell's other great political novel, *Nineteen Eighty-Four*, he tells the story of Winston Smith's small efforts of rebellion against a large system — a love affair with Julia in a world where sex is allowed but love is not permitted; their simple struggle for a private life beyond the totalitarian state, the mythical 'Big Brother', and the ever-watchful eyes of the state's television monitors regarded as an act of rebellion. Winston Smith and Julia are both captured. Much of the book covers the interrogation and torture of Winston Smith. Big Brother intimidates Winston Smith into renouncing Julia; more than a symbol of all that is good and true in his life, Julia is its epitome, Julia is the person through whom Winston has found existential meaning. Yet Winston's life-negating renunciation of Julia is insufficient capitulation for the totalitarian state. It is not enough for Big Brother to break Winston Smith's spirit — Winston Smith must not simply *obey* but *love* Big Brother. Although the state has ostensibly won against a powerless citizen, Winston Smith is the moral victor. Orwell's message is that even totalitarian states never win entirely, so long as there are individuals who recognize and take opportunities for freedom. Orwell's stories narrate the struggle against totalitarianism in fiction — they also epitomize the struggle of Cold War realities, and were themselves banned throughout the Soviet Union.

Animal Farm and *Nineteen Eighty-Four* were written in the immediate aftermath of the Second World War. The 'Cold War' was only just beginning, the historical facts of Lenin's repressions following the 1917 Russian Revolution were known, Stalin's (1879–1953) later repressions after the death of Lenin (1870–1924) also known but downplayed. Stalin, after all — apart from a brief pact with Hitler — had been an important part of the Allied forces (Pipes, 2001). *Animal Farm* and *Nineteen Eighty-Four* were Orwell's attempt to expose the brutality of Marxist-Leninism and Stalinism. They were brave books written by a man who had seen and become disillusioned by revolutionary struggle in the Spanish Civil War — Orwell was there in 1936. Many on the political left at the time remained sympathetic to Stalin; for instance, notable writer compatriots such as H. G. Wells met Stalin in person in 1934. Orwell, in advance of most other writers and artists on the left, was critical of Stalin and Stalinism, both for the Soviet Communist experiment and for the totalitarianism upon which, for its political implementation, Marxism of necessity depended (Shaffer, 1994; Meyer, 2002).

Karl Marx and Friedrich Engels as Authors

Friederich Engels — a man whose considerable family fortune had come from the abundant opportunities for wealth created by the industrial revolution — donated the royalties of his book *The Condition of the Working Classes in England* (1844/5) to Karl Marx. Such sources of unearned income, and other monies Engels encouraged wealthy patrons to donate to the cause of early Marxist economic and political research, enabled Marx and his impoverished family to live in relative comfort in England, where he was resident from 1849, and whose system of governance he so despised. The unearned income from capital effectively enabled Marx to continue the life of scholarly research on class oppression and thereby undermine the bourgeoisie from whom he had benefited so much, cumulated in his life's *Das Kapital*.

Das Kapital epitomizes Marx's scholarly genius in politics, history and economic theory. It was born, however, of the fruits and of the industrial, dehumanizing capital he critiqued. The product of long years in the British Library, *Das Kapital* remains an immensely influential and scholarly work. The first volume, of what was to become a three volume work, appeared in 1867. Outstanding in their foresight of global capitalist economy — already evident in the economic motivations behind worldwide Victorian imperialism and colonialism — the subsequent volumes appeared in 1885 and 1894, and after Marx's death (1883) were published with the aid of Engels' often unsung patronage. *Das Kapital* outlines the progressive stages of society — ancient, feudal, capitalist — and how control and ownership of capital in a small number of interested classes created historical imbalances which would eventually lead to a revolutionary class struggle. The struggle, which would inevitably be won by the working classes — Lenin, Stalin and Mao all believed in Marx's notion of such historical inevitability — would lead to a necessarily *preliminary* 'dictatorship of the proletariat'. This would be followed by the state of communism, the eventual decline of the state and the creation of an ideal and classless social order. The entire process was given an earlier and pithier outline in the 1848 *Manifesto of the Communist Party* (Worsley, 2002; Wood, 2004). It is this text of around thirty pages that would form the basis for the massive repressions, when revolutionary ideology transformed into the realities of totalitarian state politics critiqued by Orwell.

Karl Marx was born in Prussia in 1818. His family converted from Judaism to Protestant Christianity in 1824. Religion, however, was never to have a pronounced effect on Marx — except for the antagonisms which it provoked in him. Marx read law at universities in Bonn and Berlin, drawing from the pre-Socratic philosophy of Epicurus. He was a follower of the dialectical philosophy of Georg Wilhelm Friedrich Hegel (1770–1831). In the *Science of Logic* (1812–1816) Hegel outlined a complex philosophy of history, a dialectical interaction or process determining the pattern of emergent ideas — a 'thesis' countered by 'anti-thesis' followed by a new 'thesis' — which had far reaching implications in political philosophy. Hegel drew upon the implicit notion of Enlightenment philosophy that reason would bring progress and ultimately human happiness, and his dialectical philosophy brought a new model of history to the process: human history is influenced and changed by a series of interacting ideas that bring cultural and political change. Marx would later reject Hegel's idealism and replace it with a strict economic materialism — it was not ideas that changed the world but economic conditions — in the interpretation of human history. But he would retain Hegel's notion of a dialectical process and an inevitable pattern of change in history, an economic materialism that also showed faith in an historical determinism — the revolution would occur by force of historical necessity. We know from those who took up the mantle of communism in the twentieth century, that Marx's revolutionary philosophy would lead to the totalitarian state.

Along with Hegel, Ludwig Feuerbach (1804–1872) had an equally important influence on the development of Marx's early thought. Feuerbach's notion that human beings project upon an indifferent universe their wishes and desires was influential not only on Marx but the sociologists Emile Durkheim (1858–1917) and Max Weber (1864–1920) as well as the psychoanalyst Sigmund Freud (1856–1939). Feuerbach's *The Essence of Christianity* (1841) characterized Judaeo-Christian tradition as a projection of humanity's deepest desire for meaning — a wish fulfilment projected upon an indifferent universe — and was an intellectually pioneering, brave and devastating attack upon it. Feuerbach's critique was perhaps the most openly daring one since Christianity's establishment as a state religion in the declining years of the Roman Empire, over fifteen centuries earlier. It was the thinking of Hegel and Feuerbach that combined in Marx's thought and lead to the brilliantly creative formulation of an historically deterministic, economically materialistic and militantly atheistic philosophy directed to a praxis of revolutionary social change (Wheen, 1999; Worsley, 2002; Wood, 2004).

Despite obtaining a doctorate, Marx found the climate unhelpful for developing an academic career, thus he opted for a political life instead. He became editor-in-chief of the radical newspaper *Rheinische Zeitung* and moved from Bonn to Cologne to take up this position. The paper was subject to considerable censorship as the new editor further radicalized the paper's thinking and in 1843 it was fully suppressed. In the same year he married a childhood friend and moved to Paris to found a journal, only one issue of which now published. His revolutionary credentials were already evident in his merciless critique of every philosophical and religious system; in politics, his was an open call to revolution with a more than implicit call to arms.

In 1844 Engels arrival in Paris led to a close and enduring relationship between the two radical Hegelians/ Feuerbachians. It was their collaboration in the writing of *The German Ideology* in which the foundations of Marxist analysis become fully apparent, firmly breaking with Hegelian idealism to form a firmly materialistic interpretation of history. Marx argued that it was not — as Hegel had proposed — ideas that changed history but the violent struggle against social injustice; that it was 'not criticism but revolution that is the driving force of history, also of religion, of philosophy and all other types of theory'. The famous quote from the beginning of *The German Ideology* — 'The philosophers have only interpreted the world in various ways, the point is to change it' — highlights the revolutionary spirit of this materialism. The effects of this were felt in the 1917 Revolution in Russia — in other words, most clearly felt in the century following the death of both Marx and Engels. In their own lives neither man saw much revolution.

Contemporary political authorities regarded Marx, especially, with suspicion. Perceived, no doubt rightly, as a subversive influence, Marx was banned from Paris in 1845. He travelled in exile to Belgium. Radicalized in exile, he joined the Communist League. It was at the League's Second Congress in 1847 that Marx and Engels drew up the *Manifesto of the Communist Party*, published the following year, in 1848. On his specific contribution to political and economic theory — in an often cited letter to his colleague Weydemeyer in March 1852 — Marx wrote:

> And now as to myself, no credit is due for discovering the existence of the classes in modern society or the struggle between them. Long before me bourgeois historians had described the historical development of this class struggle and bourgeois economists, the economic anatomy of classes. What I did that was new was to prove:
> (1) that the existence of classes is bound up with the particular, historical phases in the development of production
> (2) that the class struggle necessarily leads to the dictatorship of the proletariat.
> (3) That this dictatorship itself only constitutes the transition to the abolition of all classes and to a classless society. (Marxist Internet Archive, 2005: 1)

By sheer coincidence, 1848 was a year for notable revolutions. In Paris especially, the barricades on the streets and in the Communes symbolize, even today, failed revolutionary aspiration. Marx, though banned, returned to Paris to witness from the sidelines. From Paris he returned to Germany. By this point the authorities throughout Europe were getting the measure of Marx and he was soon banished from Germany also, finally settling in England in 1849, where Engels was already established. It was in England that Marx completed the majority of his great historical, political and economic treatise, *Das Kapital*. Marx would see only the first volume of it published in his lifetime — as we have noted — in 1867, the two others being published posthumously. Karl Marx remained in England until his death in 1883. Had it not been for the financial support of Friedrich Engels the poverty of Marx's family life would have been greatly accentuated and were it not for Engels the second two volumes of *Das Kapital* almost certainly would not have been published. Engels died in 1895 (Steger and Carver, 1999).

Marx, Engels, the *Manifesto of the Communist Party* and Freedom of Expression

The classical opening to the *Manifesto of the Communist Party* is also a summative statement of the synthesis of history, politics and economics in Marxist philosophy: 'The history of all hitherto existing society is the history of class struggles.' The *Manifesto of the Communist Party* begins with a swathe of history, from ancient through medieval to modern times, and the contemporary focus of the class struggle between the bourgeoisie and the proletariat:

> Freeman and slave, patrician and plebeian, lord and serf, guild-master and journeyman, in a word, oppressor and oppressed, stood in constant opposition to one another, carried on an uninterrupted, now hidden, now open fight, a fight that each time ended, either in a revolutionary reconstitution of society at large, or in the common ruin of the contending classes.
>
> In the earlier epochs of history, we find almost everywhere a complicated arrangement of society into various orders, a manifold gradation of social rank. In ancient Rome we have patricians, knights, plebeians, slaves; in the Middle Ages, feudal lords, vassals, guild-masters, journeymen, apprentices, serfs; in almost all of these classes, again, subordinate gradations.
>
> The modern bourgeois society that has sprouted from the ruins of feudal society has not done away with class antagonisms. It has but established new classes, new conditions of oppression, new forms of struggle in place of the old ones. Our epoch, the epoch of the bourgeoisie, possesses, however, this distinct feature: it has simplified class antagonisms. Society as a whole is more and more splitting up into two great hostile camps, into two great classes directly facing each other. *Bourgeoisie and Proletariat* (Marx [1848] 2005: 1)

Marx's analysis of the rise of industrialization, and the globalization of capital, placing money and wealth, as well as power, in the hands of an economic elite was new, and in its day unsurpassed.

The *Manifesto of the Communist Party* remains today as a work of considerable foresight on the power of capital in a globalized economy:

> The feudal system of industry, in which industrial production was monopolised by closed guilds, now no longer sufficed for the growing wants of the new markets. The manufacturing system took its place. The guild-masters were pushed on one side by the manufacturing middle class; division of labour between the different corporate guilds vanished in the face of division of labour in each single workshop.
>
> Meantime the markets kept ever growing, the demand ever rising. Even manufacturer no longer sufficed. Thereupon, steam and machinery revolutionized industrial production. The place of manufacture was taken by the giant, Modern Industry; the place of the industrial middle class by industrial millionaires, the leaders of the whole industrial armies, the modern bourgeois.

The early recognition of the economic predominance of America is especially notable:

> Modern industry has established the world market, for which the discovery of America paved the way. This market has given an immense development to commerce, to navigation, to

communication by land. This development has, in its turn, reacted on the extension of industry; and in proportion as industry, commerce, navigation, railways extended, in the same proportion the bourgeoisie developed, increased its capital, and pushed into the background every class handed down from the Middle Ages. (Marx [1848] 2005: 2)

Marx's awareness shows how colonization of the 'new world' provided not only new markets but the grounds for an economic globalization. The *Manifesto* reads surprisingly freshly even a century a it was first written; for example, in the 'need of a constantly expanding market for its products chases the bourgeoisie over the entire surface of the globe'; 'it must nestle everywhere, settle everywhere, establish connections everywhere'; and whereby the bourgeoisie 'has through its exploitation of the world market given a cosmopolitan character to production and consumption in every country'.

In the *Manifesto of the Communist Party* the 'bourgeoisie, historically, has played a most revolutionary part' and 'stripped of its halo every occupation hitherto honoured and looked up to with reverent awe. It has converted the physician, the lawyer, the priest, the poet, the man of science, into its paid wage labourers.' So:

The bourgeoisie cannot exist without constantly revolutionizing the instruments of produc-tion, and thereby the relations of production, and with them the whole relations of society. Conservation of the old modes of production in unaltered form, was, on the contrary, the first condition of existence for all earlier industrial classes. Constant revolutionizing of production, uninterrupted disturbance of all social conditions, everlasting uncertainty and agitation distinguish the bourgeois epoch from all earlier ones. All fixed, fast-frozen relations, with their train of ancient and venerable prejudices and opinions, are swept away, all new-formed ones become antiquated before they can ossify. All that is solid melts into air, all that is holy is profaned, and man is at last compelled to face with sober senses his, real conditions of life, and his relations with his kind. (Marx [1848] 2005: 3)

The *Manifesto* traces the changing pattern of liberty and its repression — across much of the same ground we have covered in discussion of Plato, Augustine, Luther and Paine — but this history is presented as only preparing the ground for the ultimate, class struggle:

When the ancient world was in its last throes, the ancient religions were overcome by Christianity. When Christian ideas succumbed in the 18th century to rationalist ideas, feudal society fought its death battle with the then revolutionary bourgeoisie. The ideas of religious liberty and freedom of conscience merely gave expression to the sway of free competition within the domain of knowledge. (Marx [1848] 2005: 11)

This state of affairs was to Marx necessarily revolutionary because once faced with such harsh political and economic realities the working classes would unite and rebel against the forces of capital that had conspired in their dehumanization.

Marx was astute in recognizing that a 'spectre is haunting Europe — the spectre of communism' and 'all the powers of old Europe have entered into a holy alliance to exor-cise this spectre', 'Pope and Tsar', 'French Radicals and German police-spies':

Where is the party in opposition that has not been decried as communistic by its opponents in power? Where is the opposition that has not hurled back the branding reproach of commu-nism, against the more advanced opposition parties, as well as against its reactionary adversaries? Two things result from this fact:

   I. Communism is already acknowledged by all European powers to be itself a power.

  II. It is high time that communists should openly, in the face of the whole world, publish their views, their aims, their tendencies, and meet this nursery tale of the spectre of communism with a manifesto of the party itself. (Marx [1848] 2005: 1)

The particular form of the struggle would materialize in the following policies and the programme adumbrated was as follows:

1. Abolition of property in land and application of all rents of land to public purposes.
2. A heavy progressive or graduated income tax.
3. Abolition of all rights of inheritance.
4. Confiscation of the property of all emigrants and rebels.
5. Centralization of credit in the banks of the state, by means of a national bank with State capital and an exclusive monopoly.
6. Centralization of the means of communication and transport in the hands of the State.
7. Extension of factories and instruments of production owned by the State; the bringing into cultivation of waste-lands, and the improvement of the soil generally in accordance with a common plan.
8. Equal liability of all to work. Establishment of industrial armies, especially for agriculture.
9. Combination of agriculture with manufacturing industries; gradual abolition of all the distinction between town and country by a more equable distribution of the populace over the country.
10. Free education for all children in public schools. Abolition of children's factory labour in its present form. Combination of education with industrial production, &c. (Marx [1848] 2005: 12)

Ideological objections are rejected in advance of their later appearance:

All objections urged against the Communistic mode of producing and appropriating material products, have, in the same way, been urged against the Communistic mode of producing and appropriating intellectual products. Just as, to the bourgeois, the disappearance of class property is the disappearance of production itself, so the disappearance of class culture is to him identical with the disappearance of all culture. That culture, the loss of which he laments, is, for the enormous majority, a mere training to act as a machine. (Marx [1848] 2005: 10)

Charges against Communism made 'from a religious, a philosophical and, generally, from an ideological standpoint' are dismissed as 'not deserving of serious examination':

Does it require deep intuition to comprehend that man's ideas, views, and conception, in one word, man's consciousness, changes with every change in the conditions of his material existence, in his social relations and in his social life?

What else does the history of ideas prove, than that intellectual production changes its character in proportion as material production is changed? The ruling ideas of each age have ever been the ideas of its ruling class.

When people speak of the ideas that revolutionize society, they do but express that fact that within the old society the elements of a new one have been created, and that the dissolution of the old ideas keeps even pace with the dissolution of the old conditions of existence. (Marx [1848] 2005: 10)

Marx further dismissed the claim that 'religious, moral, philosophical, and juridical ideas have been modified in the course of historical development' and constantly survived such historical vicissitudes, thereby showing their inherent worth:

> Communism abolishes eternal truths, it abolishes all religion, and all morality, instead of constituting them on a new basis; it therefore acts in contradiction to all past historical experience. The Communist revolution is the most radical rupture with traditional relations; no wonder that its development involved the most radical rupture with traditional ideas. (Marx, 2005: 11)

As religion and petite bourgeois morality — and the petite bourgeois love of money and property — seemed tenacious, those responsible for inculcating the revolution needed to impose strict systems of state repression. And this is what would happen from Vladimir Ilich Lenin (1870–1924) to Joseph Stalin (1879–1953). Marx, however, would not live to see the ideology operational at the level of the state. It was not until 1917 and the Russian Revolution that Marx would have seen the first full scale implementation of his economic theories and revolutionary class struggle — the beginning of the Soviet experiment that would end so ignominiously with the emblematic fall of the Berlin Wall, in 1989.

The former Union of Soviet Socialist Republics gave way to no freedom of expression whatsoever. The USSR experienced the largest, most successful period of censorship in the twentieth-century. Yet the Soviet experiment had not started out as a repressive regime, at least in terms of censorship. Censorship had been, in fact, one of the hated aspects of czarist imperial rule Lenin had sought to overthrow:

> The Russian empire, having a long tradition of strict censorship, was slow to undergo the changes that central European countries had passed a century before. Censorship reforms were started in a single decade of tolerance, from 1855 to 1865 during the reign of tsar Alexander II, when the transition was made from legislation on pre-censorship to the punitive system based on legal responsibility. During the decade, the press enjoyed greater freedom and more radical ideas were voiced, thus censorship laws were re-imposed in 1866, practically eliminating the basic ideas of the reform. Only half a century later, pre-censorship was abrogated in the law of 1905–1906. Finally, all censorship were abolished in the decrees dated April 27, 1917 issued by the Temporary Government.

Lenin had a love of the library equal to Marx and in the early days of the revolution at least had sworn to have a state of open and free expression. Yet the freedom was short-lived. The decrees of Lenin against censorship were only in force until October 1917:

> Then a new, long and extensive era of strict censorship began, now executed by the revolutionary rulers of the USSR, lasting until the end of the 1980s. Taking into account the long history of strict censorship during tsar-regimes, the Russian people have only been without formal censorship in the last decade of this millennium. (www.freedomforexpression.org, and follow USSR links)

Freedom of expression was seen as being tolerable so long as it supported not only the revolution:

> The new order of the USSR meant drastic political and economic changes, but also the areas of culture, education and religion were subject to revolutionary changes, all with the idealistic intentions of relieving the new Soviet citizen of the suppressive yokes of feudalism. Hence religion, regarded as gross and misleading superstition, was targeted only a few months after the revolution. In the spring of 1918, a decree was issued formally separating church from state, followed by strict prohibitions imposed on religious bodies along with nationalization of all church property. (www.beaconforfreedom.org, and follow USSR links)

With religion deemed by its nature counter-revolutionary, any political ideology or aesthetics not in serve of state communism was also soon deemed counter-revolutionary.

It was in 1922 that the central censorship office known as 'Glavlit' was established. This body had absolute authority to purge 'counter-revolutionary' art, music, literature, and — in the time before Internet and television — print media. Any initial tendency to support artistic and intellectual innovation — within the bounds of the terror of revolution — ended formally, however, with the rise to power of Stalin in 1924. Not only were internal publications strictly controlled but the USSR held a tradition of rigid control over the importation of any literature into the Soviet Union. The censorship was widespread and systematic, and integral to the maintenance of the State itself:

> Censorship in the USSR period: 1917–1988 The Russian State Library in Moscow, the former Lenin State Library, holds the largest collection of banned publications published after 1917 in Russia. The collection was kept in the Department of Special Storage, founded at the Lenin State Library in 1922 (Decree of December 14, 1921). Simultaneously, the central censorship office - Glavlit - attached to the Council of Ministers of the USSR., was established. The Department of Special Storage received publications directly from Glavlit, authorized to withdraw literature from open collections and from bookstores.
>
> Initially, the collection was modest, containing mainly religious, anti-Bolshevist and anti-Leninist publications. The collection soon grew, following internal party conflicts of the 20s and 30s and the Stalin purges. The majority of banned books were written by persons who were purged during the reign of Stalin. Also publications deemed to contain other 'defects'; such as a preface written by a purged political figure or a photograph of the same person, or quotations from his or her works. Also minute 'defects' in seemingly quite innocent books could be placed in the closed storage. After World War II, the Department of Special Storage began receiving foreign books and periodicals on a regular basis from Glavlit; social-economic and military publications, and all literature by Russian emigrant authors, irrespective of subjects. By 1988 when perestroika began, the Department of Special Storage was closed down. The collections then contained app. 27,000 Russian books, 250,000 foreign books, 572,000 issues of foreign magazines, app. 8,500 annual sets of foreign newspapers and 8,000 publications. (www.beaconforfreedom.org, and follow USSR links)

The Beacon for Freedom of Expression (www.beaconforfreedomofexpression.org) has a database listing such texts, both pre- and post-Revolutionary.

Two examples must suffice to illustrate the extreme censorship from within the Soviet Union. Arguably most notable are the works of the dissident writer Alexander Solzhenitsyn. Born in 1918, he was later imprisoned in 1945 for eight years for criticizing Stalin, spending another three years in internal Siberian exile in the 'Gulag' by way of State rehabilitation and reeducation. We could not look at the pre-revolutionary literature of Russia — from Pushkin to Tolstoy — and say that bourgeois life could produce only poor art. Yet repression proved for Solzhenitsyn, as for many other writers of the time, an impetus to artistic inspiration. Indeed, for Solzhenitsyn, censorship seemed to produce a lifetime of creativity. The Soviet authorities permitted publication of Solzhenitsyn's first novel *A Day in the Life of Ivan Denisovich* (1962) which described conditions in the Soviet labour camps. Given the international outcry and acclaim that the book received, the Soviet authorities were less willing to allow publication of any more of Solzhenitsyn's work. He was awarded the Nobel Prize in Literature 1970. His magnum opus, *The Gulag Archipelago* (1973), detailing Soviet oppression, and universal abuse of human rights, facilitated his deportation to a then divided Germany in 1974.

The other example of an all-embracing pattern of Soviet censorship is encapsulated in the biography of the more subtly dissident writer Boris Pasternak (1890–1960). His literary reputation was established as a poet and author of *My Sister, Life* (1922), and his revolutionary credentials led to his survival through the repressions of both Lenin and Stalin. It was in the 1930s that he began his epic work, *Dr Zhivago*, a love story which details the life of a Russian citizen around the time of the October Revolution, and the years beyond it. The novel outlines the life of an eponymous protagonist and the much altered, post-revolutionary circumstances of his country, from 1917 onwards. *Dr Zhivago* was banned in Soviet Union, and had to be published first in Italy. It was from foreign publication of this great work that Pasternak enjoyed international literary celebrity. A discrete testament to the intelligentsia in Russia and artistic and intellectual freedom everywhere, Boris Pasternak was awarded the Nobel Prize in Literature in 1958, but was later forced to renounce the Prize by the Soviet authorities (Karolides, Bald and Sova, 1999; Feldman, 2000).

The advent of liberalization (perestroika) and openness (glasnost) from 1988 led eventually to the decline and fall of the Soviet experiment (Pipes, 2001). In 1994 Alexander Solzhenitsyn returned to Russia from exile in the United States, but was disillusioned to find the new freedoms he had fought so hard to advocate squandered on the vigorous embrace of an intellectually vacuous capitalism (Shaffer, 1994; Scammel, 1995; Shentalinskii, 1995; Schwartz, 2000).

Summary

Marx, a great scholar, had studied for many years in the British Library, London. Here he developed his historical, political and economic analyses that would form the basis for revolutions in the following century. Lenin too was a great scholar; after the failed 1905 Revolution in Russia, he was exiled in Paris, and studied revolutionary theory, especially Marx (Gooding, 2001). As Zinoviev comments on Lenin's exile in Paris, such scholarly activity can be *revolutionary* activity, indeed scholarship is often the necessary basis for revolution (Emmanuel, 2001; Gracia, Reichberg, and Schumacher, 2003; Solomon and Sherman, 2003; Parry, 2004): 'Lenin was fighting for the party, but at the same time he secluded himself in the library.' It was a period in which Lenin carried out 'a tremendous piece of theoretical work':

> Those days were marked by a sort of literary spoliation of the dead, by an unprecedented literary demoralization. Attempts were made to smuggle, under the flag of Marxism, the rotted ideas of bourgeois philosophy into working class audiences. Lenin spent two years in the Paris National Library, and carried out such a mass of work that even bourgeois professors who attempted to sneer at the philosophical studies of Lenin, themselves admitted that they could not understand how one man contrived to read such a mass of books in the course of two years. How, indeed, could Lenin succeed in this domain when 'we', who had studied at our fathers' expense, who had spent thirty years in our scientific careers, who had worn out so many armchairs, who had perused such truck-loads of books, had understood nothing in them at all. (Zinoviev, 2005: 14)

Lenin saw the library as a key to political as well as general literacy, and education as a critical tool for the progress of the masses; yet after the cataclysmic 1917 Russian Revolution would begin, through his political leadership, a period of intense repression of all aspects of learning and free expression of ideas. The political movement that had suffered considerable censorship under the strict repressions of nineteenth century Czarist Russia itself instituted even more extreme and systematic censorship throughout much of the century that was to follow — the 1917 Revolution had intended to dispense with censorship but a temporary measure introduced at the time was not revoked until 1990. The repression of materials deemed counter-revolutionary has become legendary, and these included not only literary and political works — with Orwell high on the list — but all works associated with religion, the Bible noteworthy amongst these (Webb and Bell, 1997; Schwartz, 2000; Hermina, Anghelescu and Poulain, 2001; Bliss Eaton, 2002; Blyum, 2003; Shtromas, 2003).

The causal leap from ideology to revolution is startlingly rapid, from the *Manifesto of the Communist Party* in the 1840s to the 1917 Revolution. Only religious traditions can claim such immediate effects from their founding texts, the founding texts of Christianity and the early Church, for example, were similarly separated by comparatively little history. Marx's wider writings on economic if not political theory retain contemporary relevance — particularly analyses on the globalization of capital (Strahern, 2001; Antonio, 2003; Arnot, 2003; Wolff, 2003). In terms of dissent, Marx's ideological and revolutionary framework — as encapsulated by Lenin and Stalin — was brutally systematic in the extent of its suppressions.

◆   See Appendix X   ◆

A Typology of Dissent

PAGE 219

◆   Marx exemplifies the increasingly revolutionary and atheistic trend of post-Enlightenment political dissent. It is instructive to compare the statecraft that Marx advocated with the rights and freedoms in Appendices II through to IX to see how such freedoms might be enhanced, and how many infringed, by the ideology of the *Manifesto of the Communist Party*   ◆

The former Soviet Union was governed by the principles of Marx and Engels' *Manifesto of the Communist Party*. The fact remains that *no* communist system has exercised true freedom of expression for authors or artists opposed to the revolution, those who were seen as counter-revolutionary (Bliss Eaton, 2000; Blyum, 2002; Todd, 2002; Doherty, 2003; Overy, 2004). The post-Cold War period has led to an uncritical economic embrace of market capitalism and liberalization of literary free expression, though media, including television and newspapers, remain under watchful state supervision in many countries of the former Soviet Union (Hermina, Anghelescu and Poulain, 2001; Doherty, 2003; Brown, 2004). It has also led to resurgence of Islam as a form of trans-national identity in those States where Muslim belief and practice were formally repressed, and in those states where Christianity was part of an historical tradition going back millennia. In Georgia, the birthplace of Stalin, Orthodox Christianity is increasingly being seen as integral to national identity (Fawn and White, 2002). For all the present-day critique of twenty-first century politicized religious-inspired terror, in the twentieth century the worst excesses of violence and genocide were instigated by atheistic regimes. Yet it remains ironic that the freedoms of the Enlightenment which promised so much in the way of liberty, freedom and equality for all engendered so many totalitarian ideologies, and so much dictatorial repression.

References

Antonio, Robert J. (ed.) (2003) *Marx and Modernity: Key Readings and Commentary*. Malden, MA; Oxford: Blackwell.

Arnot, Bob (2003) *Understanding Change in Russia: The Contemporary Relevance of Marx's Thought*. Glasgow: Glasgow Caledonian University Research Collections.

Bliss Eaton, Katherine (ed.) (2002) *Enemies of the People: The Destruction of Soviet Literary, Theater, and Film Arts in the 1930s*. Evanston, Illinois: Northwestern University Press.

Blyum, Areln (2002) *The System and Functions of Soviet Censorship*, translated by Paul Foote. Oxford: European Humanities Research Centre.

Brown, Archie (ed.) (2004) *The Demise of Marxism-Leninism in Russia*. Houndmills: Palgrave Macmillan.

Doherty, Thomas Patrick (2003) *Cold War, Cool Medium*. New York: Columbia University Press.

Emmanuel, Steven M. (ed.) (2001) *The Blackwell Guide to the Modern Philosophers: From Descartes to Nietzsche*. Oxford: Blackwell.

Fawn, Rick and White, Stephen (eds.) (2002) *Russia after Communism*. London: Frank Cass.

Feldman, Burton (2000) *The Nobel Prize*. New York: Arcade.

Garrard, John (1990) *Inside the Soviet Writers' Union*. London: Tauris.

Gooding, John (2001) *Socialism in Russia: Lenin and His Legacy*. Basingstoke: Palgrave.

Gracia, J.E., Reichberg, Gregory M., Schumacher, Bernard N. (eds.) (2003) *The Classics of Western Philosophy: A Reader's Guide*. Malden, MA; Oxford: Blackwell.

Hermina, G.B., Anghelescu and Poulain, Martine (2001) *Books, Libraries, Reading and Publishing in the Cold War*. Washington, D.C.: Library of Congress, Center for the Book.

Karolides, Nicholas J., Margaret Bald and Dawn B. Sova (eds.) (1999) *100 Banned Books: Censorship Histories of World Literature*. Checkmark Books.

Kouvelakis, Stathis (2003) *Philosophy and Revolution: From Kant to Marx*, trans G.M. Goshgarian, preface Frederic Jameson. London: Verso.

Marx, Karl and Engels, Friedrich (2004) *The Manifesto of the Communist Party*, edited and translated by L.M. Findlay. Peterborough, Ontario; Plymouth: Broadview Press.

Meyer, Jeffrey (2000) *Orwell: Wintry Conscience of a Generation*. London and New York: W.W. Norton.

Orwell, George [1945] 1949 *Animal Farm*. Harmondsworth: Penguin.

Orwell, George [1949] 1951 *Nineteen Eighty-Four*. Harmondsworth: Penguin.

Overy, R.J. (2004) *The Dictators: Hitler's Germany and Stalin's Russia*. New York: W.W. Norton.

Parry, Geraint (ed.) (2004) *Karl Marx*. Political Thinkers, volume 4. London: Routledge.

Pasternak, Boris [1957] (2002) *Dr Zhivago*. London: Vintage.

Pipes, Richard (2001) *Communism*. New York: Modern Library.

Popper, Karl (1946) *The Open Society and Its Enemies*. Two volumes. London: Routledge.

Scammel, Michael (ed.) (1995) *The Solzhenitsyn Files: Secret Soviet Documents Reveal One Man's Fight Against the Monolith*, translated under the supervision of Catherine A. Fitzpatrick. Chicago: Edition q.

Schwartz, Stephen (2000) *Intellectuals and Assassins: Writings at the End of Soviet Communism*. London: Anthem.

Shaffer, E.S. (ed.) (1994) *Revolutions and Censorship*. Cambridge; New York: Cambridge University Press.

Shentalinsky, Vitaly (1995) *The KGB's Literary Archive*, translated, abridged and annotated by John Crowfoot, introduction by Robert Conquest.

Shtromas, Alexander (2003) *Totalitarianism and the Prospects for World Order: Closing the Door on the Twentieth Century*. Lanham: Lexington Books.

Steger, Manfred B. and Carver, Terrell (1999) *Engels after Marx*. Manchester: Manchester University Press.

Strahern, Paul (2001) *Marx in 90 Minutes*. Chicago: Ivan R. Dee.

Solzhenitsyn, Alexander (1962) *A Day in the Life of Ivan Denisovich*. London: Penguin.

Solzhenitsyn, Alexander (1973) *The Gulag Archipelago*. London: Penguin.

Solomon, Robert C. and Sherman, David (2003) *The Blackwell Guide to Continental Philosophy*. Oxford: Blackwell.

Todd, Alan (2002) *The European Dictatorships: Hitler, Stalin, Mussolini*. Cambridge: Cambridge University Press.

Toker, Leona (2000) *Return from the Archipelago: Narratives of Gulag Survivors*. Bloomington: Indiana University Press.

Webb, W.L. and Rose Bell (1997) *An Embarrassment of Tyrannies: Twenty-Five Years of Index on Censorship* (London: Victor Gollancz).

Wheen, Francis (1999) *Karl Marx* (London: Fourth Estate).

Wolff, Jonathon (2003) *Why Read Marx Today?* Oxford: Oxford University Press.

Wood, Allen W. (2004) *Karl Marx*, 2nd edition. New York: Routledge.

Worsley, Peter (2002) *Marx and Marxism*. (London: Routledge).

Zinoviev (2005) *Lenin*. Marxist Internet Archive.

Selected Electronic Sources

BEACON FOR FREEDOM OF EXPRESSION

www.beaconforfreedom.org offers an outstanding historical resource covering key critical periods, country-by-country, but also dealing with the most infamous and long-lasting ideological and theological forms of repressions — some may find offensive the conflation of the Roman Catholic Church, the former Soviet Union and Nazi Germany.

HISTORY GUIDE

www.historyguide.org contextualizes Marx in his time and for the present.

MARX AS PHILOSOPHER

www.philosophypages.com contains useful analysis of Marx as an economic and political philosopher.

If you only visit one website on Marx and Engels, go to

Marxists Internet Archive www.marxists.org

Marxists Internet Archive offers by far the most comprehensive resource on Marxism available electronically.

John Stuart Mill (1806 – 1873)
On Liberty

Religion and poetry address themselves, at least in one of their aspects, to the same part of the human constitution; they both supply the same want, that of ideal conceptions grander and more beautiful than we see realized in the prose of human life.
John Stuart Mill *Essay on Religion*

I look around me and ask what is the state of England? Is not every man able to say what he likes? I ask you whether the world over, or in past history, there is anything like it? Nothing. I pray that our unrivalled happiness may last.
Matthew Arnold *Culture and Anarchy*

In comparison with the revolutionary ethos of Marx and Engels, John Stuart Mill's philosophy and writing are characterized by a spirit of moderate, gentlemanly intellectual refinement. Mill's bourgeois, colonial lifestyle was one that Marx and Engels would have seen overturned. Born in London in 1806, Mill was a liberal philosopher and economist whose life was integrally connected to the support of the British Empire — he worked at the East India Company for a large portion of his life between 1823 and 1858. A man also of some small political authority in later years, Mill was a Member of Parliament between 1865 and 1868 (Capaldi, 2004; Emmanuel, 2001). There is little that is truly original in Mill's two most famous books — *Utilitarianism* (1859) and *On Liberty* (1861) — but they are immeasurably significant for their balanced conceptualisation of liberal philosophy and notions of freedom of expression within open democratic societies. Even in Mill's time such freedoms were taken much for granted — if not by the poor and working class, or an equally disenfranchised female population, then at least by a property owning Victorian male elite, with means and opportunity. If the Enlightenment — and the American and French revolutions that came in its wake — had established the notion of democracy, human rights and freedom of expression as integral to modern political governance, Mill was exercised less by the revolutionary problems of establishing such a polity than by issues posed as to the day-to-day maintenance of such freedoms. Fundamentally, Mill's question was: liberty of course is desirable but to what extent, and in what circumstances, should freedom be limited?

Mill's world was that of liberal ideas and politics, of thinking inclined to moderation rather than revolution. His political writings were designed to maximize accommodation of worldviews in a Victorian society increasingly beset by revolutionary ideas — in the natural sciences and theology as much as in politics. Mill's writings on freedom of expression in this context were particularly notable but especially relevant to contemporary open societies. Yet, ironically, in his life and writings, Mill — greatly influenced by convention and tradition and keen to uphold liberal moderation — practised secrecy and exercised self-censorship. In his private life his surreptitious relationship with a married woman — Mrs Harriet Taylor — acknowledges his adherence to an outwardly Christian personal morality. More significantly, Mill repressed those of his writings which expressed his radical and sceptical thoughts against organized religion, and Christianity in particular.

Mill, at heart, was a Feuerbachian, as were many Victorian intellectuals who saw themselves as 'enlightened'. Feuerbach — as we noted in our consideration of Marx — claimed that human beings project their hopes and desires and fears onto an indifferent universe, as a result creating a world of illusions. John Stuart Mill shared such views. Mill's lack of radicalism in this regard is self-evident: Mill was prepared to continue to live in accord with the hypothetical reality of religious truths that he did not remotely believe. Yet he did so for the very utilitarianism philosophy which we will shortly detail. In short, Mill attested — we find this only in his posthumous writings on religion — that we might act 'as if' there were a point and a design for the universe, and a good and intelligent Creator. He suggested this would be the best way for society to advance the majority interest. Here we see the pragmatic compromise of Mill's utilitarianism — moral actions governed by the principle of their utility — and the harm principle. A moral action was good only if it was good for the majority, and the state should interfere only if a private course of moral action was not in the interests of either the state or the individual. In terms of religion, it made practical sense — there was less harm done, less strife, less sense of psychological meaninglessness — if human beings were to act *as if* their lives were not, in an ultimate sense, pointless (Petheram, 2002; Parry, 2004). Mill was happy to defend not the illusion of religion but the benefits that such an illusion brought to society. Mill's thinking is a less of a travesty than we might suppose — and entirely symptomatic of his concern to cause the least possible harm and disruption to the moderate workings of the state.

Mill lived in the age of Charles Darwin (1809–1882) and the theory of evolution, ideas brought to fruition in *The Origin of Species* (1859). Darwin rocked the worldview of nineteenth-century intellectual life in a profoundly different way from other revolutionary rationalistic thinkers. Appealing intellectual theories of the supremacy of human reason over theology were, after all, not new. Such ideas formed the basis of the Enlightenment — in philosophy with Kant, in theology with Feuerbach, in political theory with Paine and later, Marx — and changed the shape of human societies across the world. Kant had so raised the status of reason against theology to such an extent that he had weakened the power of not only theology but the churches which espoused it; Paine helped conceptualize in plain pamphleteer language the causes of oppression and the need for freedom that made ordinary people change their societies; to many Victorians, Feuerbach convincingly argued that Christianity itself was simply a projection of wish fulfilment, which influenced not only political theory in Marx but also the sociology of Max Weber (1864–1920), Emile Durkheim (1858–1917) and the psychological theories of Sigmund Freud (1856–1939). Darwin was arguably more radical still.

Before Darwin, sceptical rationalist thinkers had dismissed Christianity's foundational text, the Bible; Darwin seemed to provide direct scientific evidence against it, presenting evidence of the evolutionary theory that human life had originated not as the Bible had taught in Genesis but in a struggle amongst the fittest of species and their adaptability to survive under new and changing environmental conditions. A simple study of the way in which finches changed and adapted according to their environment on the Galapagos Islands had profound implications for the way other species changed and adapted and had done so in the distant past. Man seemed no longer the pinnacle of God's creation — although Darwin was never so incautious as to lean publicly towards militant atheism — but an animal among animals, quintessentially more creative than other animals, but an animal nonetheless. If the foundational chapters of the Christian Bible were flawed, a mere myth, a pleasant story which no intellectual could hope to accept as fundamental truth, then perhaps the rest of the Bible might be equally questionable. Indeed such questioning proceeded at the time, however cautiously; we remember the alienation that Thomas Paine suffered for his views on religion. John Stuart Mill — the great defender of freedom of expression — had similarly deist views on religion but these he self-suppressed, his radical views being only published posthumously (Raeder, 2002; Sell, 2004). John Stuart Mill's beliefs on liberty and freedom of expression were not, therefore, so fully exercised in regard to his own writings, and especially in regard to his thinking on religion. He self-censored because he felt certain ideas would not be in the public interest, and therefore run counter to his utilitarian principles (Skorupski, 1998; Riley, 1998; Emmanuel, 2001).

John Stuart Mill the Author

John Stuart Mill, an English philosopher whose first major published works concerned the defence of empiricism, was entirely educated by his father, James Mill — an emotionally exhausting experience for the young Mill, as described in John Stuart Mill's *Autobiography*. John Stuart Mill's early reputation centred on his *System of Logic* (1843), Mill here influenced by Auguste Comte's pioneering work on positivism, *Cours de Philosophie Positive* (1830), itself of major importance in the development of scientific method. If Comte's work on positivism remains today regarded as a foundational work in the social sciences, Mill's *System of Logic* is less generally well remembered. A considerable intellect, John Stuart Mill published not only in moral and political philosophy but also in logic and economics. Thus if *System of Logic* was Mill's technical masterpiece, his lasting fame was to be based more firmly on his popular works of moral and political philosophy (Eisenbach, 2002; West, 2004). It was the principle of utility that gave intellectual coherence to this moral and political worldview. Borrowing heavily from the Utilitarianism that so influenced his father, Mill was to provide a summary of this philosophy of moral action — the idea should be guided by the use it has in promoting the greatest happiness for the greatest number of people. Mill's individual interpretation of Utilitarianism took into account the harm principle, whereby he argued that the state should not intervene in the private life of its citizens; privacy was paramount. Mill's close and intimate association with a married woman — Mrs Taylor — may or may not have affected his desire to heighten the importance of this privacy in his philosophical writings. Mrs Harriet Taylor is credited with being co-author of *On Liberty* but this does not extend to Mill crediting her on the title page, and indeed her influence is only really being given full credit in recent times. In 1851, following the death of her husband, Mill married her (Jacobs, 2002).

Philosophers, then, might be appreciative of Mill's *System of Logic*, but it is not a work for non-philosophers who, by contrast, are more likely to have heard of *On Liberty* (1859) and *Utilitarianism* (1861). The latter books defended Jeremy Bentham's original ethical theory that the greatest good is the happiness of the majority and that moral actions should be determined according to whether or not they will add to or detract from human happiness (Gracia, Reichberg and Schumacher, 2003; Mill, 2003). It is *On Liberty* that contains his reflections on freedom of expression, yet it is *Utilitarianism* that sets forth the principles for such freedoms (O' Rourke, 2001; Mill, 2003; West, 2004). No reading of Mill's philosophy can therefore be complete without reference to his elaboration of Bentham's theory of utility in *Utilitarianism*.

Utilitarianism is divided into five chapters. The first deals with the distinction between intuitive and inductive schools. The former (including Kant) suggests that moral good can be determined without reference to direct experience; the inductive school (including Mill) suggests that only through application to experience can one come to a true sense of moral guidance in personal, social or political realities. The second chapter involves an assessment of human happiness as the single determining feature of the moral life, happiness meaning both intellectual and sensual happiness. Mill retains a Platonic sense that the intellectual is of a higher order than the sensual and that there are second order moral principles, such as 'do not steal', 'do not lie', 'do not murder'. We order our lives by reason of these latter principles, but human happiness remains in the first order of moral principle, the unifying and governing principle for moral action. Chapter three concerns the motivation we have — selfishness or the common good — for determining our actions. If X is the only thing desired, then X is the only thing to be desired. Chapter four expands on the idea of general happiness as the predominating desire of human beings, general happiness as the major objective that ought to be sought in personal, social and political life. Chapter five concerns the connections between justice and utility. A major criticism of utilitarianism is that it is anti-foundationalist — human actions and moral decision-making are taken without reference to the existence of God or a belief in the fundamental right and wrong of certain actions at all times in all places (Kant's categorical imperative), or the idea of a universal justice.

For Mill the principle of human happiness is paramount, the foundational principle around which Mill's utilitarianism revolves. In terms of the rights of citizens within a social and political context, for Mill, such rights are 'claims against society to protect us'. Rights, then, are there to protect us and to ensure our happiness, but it is social utility, not the 'existence' of such rights that forms the basis of such a need for protection. Mill contends that if justice was truly foundational — if certain 'rights' for example existed everywhere — then justice would not be so contended or contested. We would not constantly need — for instance in the context of law — to argue about the rights and wrongs of a particular situation. Justice therefore needs to be based upon *utility* — particular personal, social and political circumstances. These are necessarily contingent and historical, and decisions affecting them pragmatic, matters only of law and judgment.

These principles of utility are applied to his arguments in *On Liberty* in a famous defence of freedom of expression. The defence, in simple terms, is that the sole justification for the intervention of the state in the liberty of individual citizens is self-protection. Self and society's interests merge here — freedom is allowed only up to the point that it is of no harm to the individual or the state. This harm principle that remains a perennial justification for state interventions in freedom and liberty, setting conditions under which restriction of freedom is warranted (Myerson, 2001; Mill, 2003; West, 2004). The defence is gently conversational in its tone, even leisurely, without the vehemence of a revolutionary and is in this regard certainly not only a work of its time but clearly the product of a specific class of learned, intellectual Victorian gentleman. Yet Mill's delineation of the limits of freedom, including the justification for its restriction, remains extremely relevant in open democratic societies today.

John Stuart Mill, *On Liberty* and Freedom of Expression

On Liberty is a general treatise on the protection of individual rights and freedoms against state intrusion and attempts to restrict the private actions of citizens and subjects. Mill opens discussion on freedom of expression (in chapter two of the volume) with the assumption that such freedom is integral to any modern system of government:

> The time, it is to be hoped, is gone by when any defence would be necessary of the liberty of the press as one of the securities against corrupt or tyrannical government. No argument, we may suppose, can now be needed, against permitting a legislature or an executive, not identified in interest with the people, to prescribe opinions to them, and determine what doctrines or what arguments they shall be allowed to hear. This aspect of the question, besides, has been so often and so triumphantly enforced by preceding writers, that it needs not be specially insisted on in this place. (Mill, 2003: 86)

Mill might not have envisaged the implications of a state so powerful as to control all aspects of cultural life and exercise complete control over free expression. Indeed, irony was not one of the literary strengths of John Stuart Mill so we might presume — from evidence of totalitarianism in the century that followed and the unquestioning imperialism in his own century — Mill was misguided in this optimism.

On Liberty at a Glance

I   Introductory
II   Of the Liberty of Thought and Discussion
III   Of Individuality, as One of the Elements of Well-Being
IV   Of the Limits of the Authority of Society over the Individual
V   Applications

Yet even in a state where 'government is entirely at one with the people and never thinks of exerting any power of coercion unless in agreement with what it conceives to be their voice', Mill still argues that the role of the latter should be systemically restricted:

> I deny the right of the people to exercise such coercion, either by themselves or by their government. The power itself is illegitimate. The best government has no more title to it than the worst. It is as noxious, or more noxious, when exerted in accordance with public opinion, than when in opposition to it. If all mankind minus one, were of one opinion, and only one person were of the contrary opinion, mankind would be no more justified in silencing that one person, than he, if he had the power, would be justified in silencing mankind. Were an

opinion a personal possession of no value except to the owner; if to be obstructed in the enjoyment of it were simply a private injury, it would make some difference whether the injury was inflicted only on a few persons or on many. But the peculiar evil of silencing the expression of an opinion is, that it is robbing the human race; posterity as well as the existing generation; those who dissent from the opinion, still more than those who hold it. If the opinion is right, they are deprived of the opportunity of exchanging error for truth: if wrong, they lose, what is almost as great a benefit, the clearer perception and livelier impression of truth, produced by its collision with error. (Mill, 2003: 87)

It was not only mentally disabled and children who were determined by Mill as in particular need of having a societal restriction, Mill also extended such paternalism to 'uncivilized' peoples. He was in this regard a man of his time. His contemporary Matthew Arnold, for instance, similarly presupposed European superiority in matters of culture as much as politics. Mill's was no less the age of Darwin than it was imperialism and colonial empire. Notions of evolutionary superiority were easily applied to cultures not ruling supreme across their own states, cultures that could benefit from the benign interference of more advanced peoples (Levin, 2004), what Matthew Arnold defined as 'the raw and unkindled masses of humanity'.

It was Mill's contemporary, Matthew Arnold (1822–1888), who recognized in *Culture and Anarchy* the power of culture in political life. (A hundred years later Edward Said satirizes this in his own book *Culture and Imperialism*.) In *Culture and Anarchy*, Arnold quotes and then proceeds to attack one Mr Frederic Harrison:

Perhaps the very silliest cant of the day is the cant about culture. Culture is a desirable quality in a critic of new books, and sits well on a professor of belles letters; but as applied to politics, it means simply a turn for small fault-finding, love of selfish ease, and indecision in action. The man of culture is in politics one of the poorest mortals alive. For simple pedantry and want of good sense no man is his equal. No assumption is too unreal, no end is too impractical for him. But the active exercise of politics requires common sense, sympathy, trust, resolution and enthusiasm, qualities which your man of culture has carefully rooted up, lest they damage the delicacy of his critical olfactories. Perhaps they are only class of responsible beings in the community who cannot with safety be entrusted with power. (Arnold [1859] 1976: 470)

Matthew Arnold most famously defined culture as the finest elements of creativity that human societies have produced. Though he condemns neither religious or political dogma and attempts to convert or persuade, he suggested 'culture works differently', for 'it does not teach down to the level of inferior classes; it does not try to win them for this or that sect of its own, with ready-made judgements and watchwords'. Indeed Arnold's talk of a classless society shows similar preoccupations to those of Marx. In non-revolutionary contrast though, and here is Arnold's renowned claim, culture 'seeks to do away with classes; to make the best that has been thought and known in the current world current everywhere; to make all men live in an atmosphere of sweetness and light, where they may use ideas, as it uses them itself, freely, nourished, and not bound by them' (Arnold, 1976: 473). Arnold presents an interesting and sad case, however, of a major English poet whose adopted 'political' role as an education inspector in later life indirectly led him to relinquish poetry; his 'Dover Beach', a melancholic, elegiac reflection on the receding 'sea of faith' — an intellectual's love poem — is barely rivalled in Victorian verse.

Yet Arnold — aware, like Mill, of the widely cautious state of England's populace at expressing contentious views — is able, despite the sad melancholy which one critic has called a 'gift imprisoned', to look brightly upon an England he loves for the freedom it provides: 'I look around me and ask what is the state of England? Is not every man able to say what he likes? I ask you whether the world over, or in past history, there is anything like it? Nothing. I pray that our unrivalled happiness may last' (Arnold, 1976: 491). In terms of religion, Arnold maintained an adherence to orthodox Christian tradition, mourning its decline — again, above all, in his famous 'Dover Beach' — unlike the more religiously sceptical Mill, who famously defined 'the present age' as one in:

> . . . which has been described as 'destitute of faith, but terrified at skepticism' — in which people feel sure, not so much that their opinions are true, as that they should not know what to do without them — the claims of an opinion to be protected from public attack are rested not so much on its truth, as on its importance to society. There are, it is alleged, certain beliefs, so useful, not to say indispensable to well-being, that it is as much the duty of governments to uphold those beliefs, as to protect any other of the interests of society. (Mill, 2003: 90–91)

In terms of the wider question of free speech, Mill advances two arguments in *On Liberty* which found wider democratic liberties upon freedom of expression, both centring on the idea that 'We can never be sure that the opinion we are endeavouring to stifle is a false opinion; and if we were sure, stifling it would be an evil still.' The first argument he states as follows:

> . . . the opinion which it is attempted to suppress by authority may possibly be true. Those who desire to suppress it, of course deny its truth; but they are not infallible. They have no authority to decide the question for all mankind, and exclude every other person from the means of judging. To refuse a hearing to an opinion, because they are sure that it is false, is to assume that their certainty is the same thing as absolute certainty. All silencing of discussion is an assumption of infallibility. Its condemnation may be allowed to rest on this common argument, not the worse for being common. (Mill, 2003: 88)

Dismissing 'the supposition that any of the received opinions may be false, let us assume them to be true, and examine into the worth of the manner in which they are likely to be held, when their truth is not freely and openly canvassed', the second argument was based upon the need to question opinions held even if they are presumed to be true, for 'however unwillingly a person who has a strong opinion may admit the possibility that his opinion may be false, he ought to be moved by the consideration that however true it may be, if it is not fully, frequently, and fearlessly discussed, it will be held as a dead dogma, not a living truth.' Thus:

> There is a class of persons (happily not quite so numerous as formerly) who think it enough if a person assents undoubtingly to what they think true, though he has no knowledge whatever of the grounds of the opinion, and could not make a tenable defence of it against the most superficial objections. Such persons, if they can once get their creed taught from authority, naturally think that no good, and some harm, comes of its being allowed to be questioned. Where their influence prevails, they make it nearly impossible for the received opinion to be rejected wisely and considerately, though it may still be rejected rashly and ignorantly; for to shut out discussion entirely is seldom possible, and when it once gets in, beliefs not grounded on conviction are apt to give way before the slightest semblance of an argument. Waiving, however, this possibility — assuming that the true opinion abides in the mind, but

abides as a prejudice, a belief independent of, and proof against, argument — this is not the way in which truth ought to be held by a rational being. This is not knowing the truth. Truth, thus held, is but one superstition the more, accidentally clinging to the words which enunciate a truth. (Mill, 2003: 103)

It was a heritage that Mill was quite right in recognizing: 'If the intellect and judgment of mankind ought to be cultivated, a thing which Protestants at least do not deny, on what can these faculties be more appropriately exercised by any one, than on the things which concern him so much that it is considered necessary for him to hold opinions on them?' For, even in religious belief, 'If the cultivation of the understanding consists in one thing more than in another, it is surely in learning the grounds of one's own opinions.'

Mill was not unaware of the nineteenth-century's foundations upon the preceding critical heritage of a pre-Christian age, nor was he unaware of how free expression remained dangerous, as it had in ancient times: 'Mankind can hardly be too often reminded, that there was once a man named Socrates . . . This acknowledged master of all the eminent thinkers . . . was put to death by his countrymen, after a judicial conviction, for impiety and immorality. Impiety, in denying the gods recognized by the state; indeed his accuser asserted (see the *Apologia*) that he believed in no gods at all. Immorality, in being, by his doctrines and instructions, a 'corrupter of youth': 'Of these charges the tribunal, there is every ground for believing, honestly found him guilty and condemned the man who probably of all then born had deserved best of mankind, to be put to death as a criminal' (Mill, 2003: 93–94). In closing, Mill concludes with four bases upon which we should allow free expression of thought:

First, if any opinion is compelled to silence, that opinion may, for aught we know, be true. To deny this is to assume our own infallibility. Second, though the silenced opinion be an error, it may, and very commonly does, contain a portion of truth; and since the general or prevailing opinion on any subject is rarely or never the whole truth, it is only by the collision of adverse opinions that the remainder of the truth has any chance of being supplied. Thirdly, even if the received opinion be not only true, but the whole truth; unless it is suffered to be, and actually is, vigorously and earnestly contested, it will, by most of those who receive it, be held, in the manner of a prejudice, with little comprehension or feeling of its rational grounds. And not only this, but, fourthly, the meaning of the doctrine itself will be in danger of being lost, or enfeebled, and deprived of its vital effect on the character and conduct . . . (Mill, 2003: 118)

Summary

As they had since the days of the French Revolution in Europe and Independence in the New World since Rousseau and Paine, freedom of expression issues in the nineteenth century centred upon the liberty of ideas in regard to religion as much as art and politics. Moral ideas were central here but there were many philosophers — political and other — who had not yet felt free to exercise true defiance in the face of a system of Christian belief, a system of Christian belief which still underpinned all of the institutions of the state even if the unquestioning adherence to belief which had been a feature of previous ages was beginning to wane (O'Rourke, 2001). In the twenty-first century, a post-industrial and post-modern age, it is the issue of religion which has again re-surfaced. Using Mill's harm principle — that human freedom should be largely left untrammelled so long as no harm is done to others — is here made more complex. Today's secularists regard unrestricted freedom of religion as harmful, certain groups of religious fundamentalists believe that a secular state should never fully be tolerated.

In terms of all historical, literary and political case studies presented here, John Stuart Mill's philosophical position on freedom of expression is one of considerable political moderation and accommodation more than revolutionary dissent. Yet he retained, with Matthew Arnold, a sense of pervading elitism as much as idealism. Indeed the idealism of the Victorian bourgeois intellectual is integrally bound up with a notion of elitism. Mill retained a notion that specialization of knowledge is bound up with freedom of expression — in other words, that there were wise persons in society best suited to judge whether an action be permissible, or whether a freedom be restricted; and this allowed him to support colonial attitudes of superiority to many peoples subjugated within the British Empire, just as Matthew Arnold thought that Western culture was a bastion against anarchy. It was a sort of intellectual elitism not so far from Plato's philosophically informed guardian who would look after interests of the state, or the idea of a philosopher-king. Mill maintained, like Plato, a view that the elitism of the intellectual is better than the elitism of the tyrant:

> Conceding to this view of the subject the utmost that can be claimed for it by those most easily satisfied with the amount of understanding of truth which ought to accompany the belief of it; even so, the argument for free discussion is no way weakened. For even this doctrine acknowledges that mankind ought to have a rational assurance that all objections have been satisfactorily answered; and how are they to be answered if that which requires to be answered is not spoken? Or how can the answer be known to be satisfactory, if the objectors have no opportunity of showing that it is unsatisfactory? If not the public, at least the philosophers and theologians who are to resolve the difficulties, must make themselves familiar with those difficulties in their most puzzling form; and this cannot be accomplished unless they are freely stated, and placed in the most advantageous light which they admit of. (Mill, 2003: 105–106)

Freedom in Mill is therefore integrally related to intellectual elitism. However, as history has taught, tyrant-intellectuals are by no means unknown. Yet Mill steps back a long way from giving the state supremacy over the individual, especially in matters of freedom of personal morality, conscience, belief, or expression (McMann, 2004).

◆   See Appendix X   ◆

A Typology of Dissent

PAGE 219

◆   It is a useful and instructive exercise to compare the statecraft represented by the rights and freedoms in Appendices II through to IX with Mill's *On Liberty*. The liberal, open and conciliatory tone of Mill has been a major influence on current debates on freedom of expression and related cultural rights, including freedom of religion or belief.   ◆

In practical terms, Mill's liberalism developed in the twentieth-century into a creed upon which wider freedoms of the individual over and above the state have prevailed. Mill outlined the need for an informed government but argued that the state should interfere as little as possible in the lives of individuals and their communities. As ever (Boyd, 2004), this raises the problem of where one places the limits of individual freedom against that of the interests of the state — what of those individuals who are bound together by interests and loyalties that are transnational, and perhaps religious? In common with many liberal and post-Enlightenment philosophers, Mill expected to see religion decline in influence, its marginalization to a privatized sphere of individual choice, one not affecting matters of wider polity or the governance of the state (Magee, 2002; Raeder, 2002; Sell, 2004; Scanlon, 2005; Peters, 2005). Mill was not likely to have foreseen the emergence of strongly transnational and often religiously-influenced political threats to freedom of expression in the twenty-first-century; nor was Mill likely to have foreseen the worst excesses of repression and the violent extremes of totalitarianism in the twentieth.

References

Arnold, Matthew [1869] (1980) *Culture and Anarchy*. The Portable Matthew Arnold, edited by Lionel Trilling. Harmondsworth: Penguin.

Boyd, Richard (2004) *Uncivil Society: The Perils of Pluralism and the Making of Modern Liberalism*. Lanham: Lexington Books.

Capaldi, Nicholas (2004) *John Stuart Mill: A Biography*. Cambridge: Cambridge University Press.

Darwin, Charles [1859] (1968) *The Origin of Species*. Harmondsworth: Penguin.

Eisenach, Elden J. (2002) *Narrative Power and Liberal Truth: Hobbes, Locke, Bentham, and Mill*. Lanham: Rowman & Littlefield Publishers.

Emmanuel, Steven M. (ed.) (2001) *The Blackwell Guide to the Modern Philosophers: From Descartes to Nietzsche*. Oxford: Blackwell.

Gracia, J.E., Reichberg, Gregory M., and Schumacher, Bernard N. (eds.) (2003) *The Classics of Western Philosophy: A Reader's Guide*. Malden, MA; Oxford: Blackwell.

Jacobs, Jo Ellen (2002) *The Voice of Harriet Taylor Mill*. Bloomington, Indiana: Indiana University Press.

Levine, Andrew (2002) *Engaging Political Philosophy: From Hobbes to Rawls*. Malden, MA: Blackwell.

Levin, Michael (2004) *J.S. Mill on Civilization and Barbarism*. London: Routledge.

Magee, James J. (2002) *Freedom of Expression*. Westport, Conn: Greenwood Press.

McMann, Charles R. (2004) *Individualism and the Social Order: The Social Element in Liberal Thought*. London: Routledge.

Mill, John Stuart [1859; 1861] (2003) *Utilitarianism; On Liberty: Including Mill's Essay on Bentham, and Selections from the Writings of Jeremy Bentham and John Austin*, edited with an introduction by Mary Warnock, second edition, Malden, MA; Oxford: Blackwell.

Myerson, George (2001) *Mill's On Liberty: A Beginner's Guide*. London: Hodder & Stoughton.

Parry, Geraint (ed.) (2004) *John Stuart Mill*: Political Thinkers volume 5. London: Routledge.

Peters, John Durham (2005) *Courting the Abyss: Free Speech and Liberal Tradition*. Chicago; London: University of Chicago Press.

Petheram, Michel (2002) *J.S. Mill: A Beginner's Guide*. London: Hodder & Stoughton.

O'Rourke, K.C. (2001) *John Stuart Mill and Freedom of Expression: The Genesis of a Theory*. London: Routledge.

Raeder, Linda C. (2002) *John Stuart Mill and the Religion of Humanity*. Columbia, MO: London: University of Missouri Press.

Riley, Jonathan (1998) *Routledge Philosophy Guidebook to Mill On Liberty*. London: Routledge.

Scanlon, Thomas (2005) *The Difficulty of Tolerance: Essay in Political Philosophy*. Cambridge: Cambridge University Press.

Sell, Alan P.F. (2004) *Mill on God: The Pervasiveness and Elusiveness of Mill's Religious Thought*. Aldershot: Ashgate.

Skorupski, John (ed.) (1998) *The Cambridge Companion to Mill*. Cambridge: Cambridge University Press.

West, Henry (2004) *An Introduction to Mill's Utilitarian Ethics*. Cambridge: Cambridge University Press.

Selected Electronic Sources

There are some key sites on John Stuart Mill which present access to original sources and www.cpm.11.echime-u.ac.jp provides a full range of primary text and commentary options.

If you only visit one website on John Stuart Mill, go to

Stanford Encyclopedia of Philosophy http://plato.stanford.edu

The encyclopedia is authoritative and is a marvelously useful work for general reference in philosophy.

Adolf Hitler (1889 – 1945)
Mein Kampf

I wanted to become a painter and no power in the world could make me a civil servant. Yet, strange as it may seem, with the passing years I became more and more interested in architecture . . . At that time I regarded this as a natural complement to my gift as a painter, and only rejoiced inwardly at the extension of my artistic scope. I did not suspect that things would turn out differently.

Adolf Hitler *Mein Kampf*

Language and literature are grown from the nation.
To-day there is a contradiction between literature and the German nation. This is a shameful state of things.
Purity of language and literature depends on you!
Our most dangerous opponent is the Jew.
The Jew can only think Jewish. If he writes German, he is lying. The German who writes German and thinks Jewish is a traitor.
We mean to put an end to this lie, we mean to brand this treachery.
We mean to treat the Jew as a foreigner, and we mean to take the nation seriously. We therefore demand from the censorship the following: Jewish works must be published in Hebrew. If published in German, they must be described as translations. Only Germans have the right to write in German. The un-German spirit must be eradicated from the public libraries . . .

The German Student Organisation, from 'The Twelve
Theses against the Un-German Spirit',
posted Berlin University, 13th April 1933

Adolf Hitler was not well known for his liberal views on freedom of expression and the era of the Third Reich (1933–1945) was not renowned for its toleration of dissent. It is clear, however, that the Nazis considered the burning of both books and people as a purgative exercise, cleansing the German nation of cultural and racial contamination (McCarthy and von der Ohe, 1995). Hitler shares with all totalitarians and dictators utter intolerance to opposition and any freedom of expression under the Nazis was ruthlessly suppressed, whether of aesthetic or ideological or religious form, and in any media. Such control of press, radio, and all aspects of culture furthered Nazism's broader racialist aims (Weikart,

2004). Hitler's propaganda chief Joseph Goebbels (1893–1945) has often been cited as declaring: 'From these ashes will rise the phoenix of the new spirit.'

Austrian born in 1889, German Chancellor, the Führer and dictator of Germany (1933–1945) had long recognized the centrality of propaganda in the winning of military and political strategy. Germany's humiliating defeat in the First World War was arguably followed by a more humiliating peace after the Treaty of Versailles, with territory withdrawn, armaments forbidden and a state of economic, military and political powerlessness. Hitler, in hospital as a wounded corporal in the First World War, was astounded and ashamed by the absence of patriotism amongst the wounded German troops, and dismayed at the excuses they made not to be sent back to the Front; his desire — which was fulfilled — was that upon recovery he be returned to battle. It was this spirit of defeat and defeatism, even amongst German soldiers — this general absence of national pride, and expansionist military and political ambition — that Hitler came to witness in post-First World War Germany. It was a spirit he saw as being embodied in and generated by the liberal, avant-garde, cultural attitudes and political impotence of the Weimar Republic.

In contrast to the materialism of Marx, who saw material or economic conditions as more determinant of social conditions than cultural ideas, it was the *idea* that Hitler regarded as paramount. And the central idea for Hitler was that of a patriotic and proud Germany, one that demanded the materiality of the land, a greater Germany, extending through Slavic countries to the east and into Russia and purified of those elements that had contributed to its cultural and racial degeneration. Hitler and his idea ended ingloriously with a bullet in the mouth, with death in a bunker outside Berlin as Soviet and Allied troops attacked the city. Hugh Trevor Roper's (1995) *The Last Days of Hitler* recounts in detail the narrative of a vision that had begun so expansively yet ended so claustrophobically (Kershaw, 2000; Overy, 2004).

Founder of the National Socialist Workers' Party (later the Nazi Party), Hitler was imprisoned in 1923 after an unsuccessful *putsch* in Munich. During this period Hitler wrote *Mein Kampf*. It was his powers of oratory that gained him prominence, and even in *Mein Kampf* he declares how he would prefer the power of speech-making to book-writing. In 1933, by democratic means, aided by the power of his oratory, with ruthless intimidation of opponents and skilful political manoeuvring, he supplanted the Weimar Republic. The totalitarian Third Reich Hitler came to construct was a regime successfully consolidated by the joint forces of propaganda (the work of Goebbels) and fear (the organizational responsibility of Himmler, Head of SS, 1929–1945; Head of Gestapo, 1936–1945). In the real political aftermath of *Mein Kampf*'s vision for a greater Germany, we see the realization of a totalitarianism about which Plato could only speculate. All western philosophy is said to be no more than a footnote to Plato: yet if Plato had implemented any portion of his political perspectives in a systematic fashion his influence might today be less esteemed. Whereas with Plato we have a man whose dream of a utopia remained ideological rather than enacted, in the figure of Hitler we have a man with the power to implement his extremism.

There are further curious stylistic as well as ideological comparisons between Plato and Hitler. It goes without saying that Plato is considerably more accomplished than Hitler in terms of literary style and the ability to engage the reader dramatically with an idea. There is no comparison between *Mein Kampf* and the *Republic*. Interestingly, though, Hitler's lifelong preference for oratory over written language parallels Plato's choice of dialogue as the literary form of choice; not being a politician, dramatic dialogue was the closest Plato could get, beyond teaching, to public oratory. Hitler's preference for the spoken word — its dramatic effect, its directness — was powerfully demonstrated at Nazi rallies. To perpetuate the influence of the spoken word — once spoken it is gone — Hitler used the new technologies of radio, cinema and film. Such emergent electronic media were used extensively by the Nazis not simply for propaganda documentaries but for the systematic recording of, for example, the death camp atrocities of which the Third Reich was so proud; however, much of this evidence was destroyed as the Nazis and Axis powers began to lose the Second World War. In terms of its political philosophy, *Mein Kampf* is not considerably less extreme than Plato's *Republic*; and in terms of the indirect link between the revered ancient works of Plato and totalitarianism was raised, much to the shock and outrage of classical scholars. Karl Popper (1946) raised this issue indirectly with his publication of *The Open Society and Its Enemies*, the first volume of which he outlines the totalitarian features of Plato's political philosophy.

Adolf Hitler the Author

Plato's dislike of the poets was integral to his antipathy for democracy, but the drama of Socrates' engagement with his interlocutors is raised to the level of poetry by the sophistication with which his intolerance is broached. Hitler's cramped worldview, by contrast, more than simply reflects his imprisonment and the antagonism of sharing a cell with Rudolf Hess during the writing of *Mein Kampf*. The absence of a sophisticated educational background becomes apparent when one reads the book. Hitler's writing is a peculiar mix of rambling political autobiography — from embittered childhood to as yet untold political visions — and a single-minded vision of an idealized political state. In *Mein Kampf* Hitler is a man without particular cultural refinement who seems inadvertently to expose his own vulnerability. In *Mein Kampf* he portrays a devoted mother and small-minded bureaucrat father with low aspirations for his son. Hitler tells us 'my father I honoured' (which biographers say he did not) but 'my mother I loved' (which biographers tell us he did). These accounts of growing up in small town Austria, always conceived as Germanic, are intertwined with a highly romantic and romanticized, indeed openly sentimental, vision of Teutonic patriotism and nationalism. The political agenda is unsophisticated. It concerns the need for the imminent expansion of the German State and long-term future expansion of countries to the East, a move which will inevitably involve war, bloodshed and the displacement or at least subjugation of 'Slavic' races and the elimination of all Jewish cultural, economic and political influence in a greatly enlarged Germany.

Hitler has none of the broad economic theory of Karl Marx, or the system of philosophic advancement of Plato. *Mein Kampf* is almost anti-intellectual. It espouses honest working-class virtues of hard work and simple adherence to authority, and dedication to the furtherance of the German nation. The other major difference is that Plato's early political aspirations — remember the great influences in Plato's childhood and early manhood were his oligarchic relatives and Socrates — were not fulfilled. Any aspirations Plato had for power were finally realized not in personal political office or in the formation of any ideal Republic, but in the development of the Academy. This early, arguably first 'university' has served as a model for intellectual engagement for twenty-five centuries, beside which the compensation of short-term temporal power seems inconsequential. By contrast, Hitler had no great intellectual aspirations; his were largely political — that said, we know from *Hitler's Table Talk* (four volumes of informal 'conversation' collected by Hugh Trevor-Roper) that Hitler's intellectual interests were wide ranging, albeit beyond his capacity for informed, reasoned engagement.

Mein Kampf is probably the most influential of all poorly written books. Yet while it is customary to mock the repetitive literary style and the absence of philosophical finesse, its influence cannot be underestimated, not least for its part in the determination of Nazi policies of physical as well as cultural extermination. The loathing of Jews is as resounding in *Mein Kampf* as Marx's hatred of the bourgeoisie is in the *Manifesto of the Communist Party*. Hitler's worldview shares with communism a hatred of liberals or at least the forces of the Weimar that imprisoned him after the failed 1923 Munich *putsch*. But prison gave Hitler time to reflect and like many influential political tracts, *Mein Kampf* was written in this time of imprisonment. If a sense of despair and ruin are conceivably natural states of mind for the imprisoned, then for the rare person it leads to empowerment and utopian dreams — Thomas Moore's learned and sophisticated *Utopia* was so constructed centuries earlier at the height of the Reformation. In prison, dictating the thoughts of his struggle to Rudolf Hess, Hitler's absence of higher level education is clearly evident. A paucity of education is almost certainly more dangerous than an excess of it. Hitler's sweeping historical visions are based less upon scholarly erudition than a deep ingrained sense of social injustice at the suffering of the vanquished German State post-(1919) Versailles. It was a sense that Hitler felt personally through the failures of his own life — yet his poverty in Vienna as a struggling artist and his undertaking of manual labour gave him a sympathy for the working person; as he states early on in *Mein Kampf*, 'honest labour disgraces no one . . . ' (Hitler, 1992: 24).

The cultural and the artistic were central to Hitler's development as a politician, though his time as a politician was marked by strikingly intolerant attitudes to art and culture. He mentions how at the age of twelve he saw *Wilhelm Tell* for the first time and a few months later his first opera — provincial artistic experiences that were to intensify his feelings for the simple, patriotic and sentimental in art. Hitler's tastes were to remain in favour of the sentimental. His artistic patriotism combined with a desire to follow the life of a painter and a distaste for the future that his father had selected for him as a civil servant: 'I wanted to become a painter and no power in the world could make a civil servant'. And the chilling '[y]et, strange as it may seem, with the passing years I became more and more interested in architecture' is combined with the casual vanity of '[a]t that time I regarded this as a natural complement to my gift as a painter, and only rejoiced inwardly at the extension of my artistic scope' (Hitler, 1992: 20). Given that he wrote these words before the pre-Third Reich had come to power, the statement, 'I did not suspect that things would turn out differently', has a surprisingly prophetic resonance.

Adolf Hitler, *Mein Kampf* and Freedom of Expression

Adolf Hitler did not become a famous artist. If he was a failure in cultural and artistic terms, Hitler's real genius was for totalitarianism; ironically, later, he was in absolute control of all forms of cultural expression in the German State. Indeed the burning of Jewish books, perceived as cultural purification, was a priority for Nazism and integral to its scheme of mass death. The burning of books was the first of many totalitarian acts committed by the Nazis.

Mein Kampf by Adolf Hitler

At a Glance
Foreword from Landsberg Am Lech, Fortress Prison

Volume One: A Reckoning
In the House of My Parents
Years of Study and Suffering in Vienna
General Political Considerations Based on MY Vienna Period
Munich
The World War
War Propaganda
The Revolution
The Beginning of My Political Activity
The 'German Workers' Party'
Causes of the Collapse
Nation and Race
The First Period of Development of the National Socialist German Workers' Party

Volume Two: The National Socialist Movement
Philosophy and Party
The State
Subjects and Citizens
Personality and the Conception of the Folkish State
Philosophy and Organization
The Struggle of the Early Period — the Significance of the Spoken Word
The Struggle with the Red Front
The Strong Man is Mightiest Alone
Basic Ideas Regarding the Meaning and Organization of the SA
Federalism as a Mask
Propaganda and Organization
The Trade-Union Question
German Alliance policy after the War
Eastern Orientation or Eastern Policy
The Right of Emergency Defense
Conclusion

Go to www.hitler.org (and follow links)

Early artistic experiences led Hitler to a theory of politics that could not separate a hatred of culture from those peoples and contexts from which culture arose:

All these views have their deepest root in the knowledge that the forces which create culture and values are based essentially on racial elements and that the state must, therefore, in the light of reason, regard its highest task as the preservation and intensification of the race, this fundamental condition of all human cultural development.

> It was the Jew, Karl Marx, who was able to draw the extreme inference from those false conceptions and view concerning the nature and purpose of state; by detaching the state concept from racial obligations without being able to arrive at any other equally acknowledged formulation, the bourgeois world even paved the way for a doctrine that denied the state as such. (Hitler, 1992: 396)

(For English readers this has rather odd resonances with Margaret Thatcher's famous and famously contentious declaration in the 1980s that 'there is no such thing as society'.)

Although Hitlerite ideology was originally declared as 'national socialism' Hitler was concerned with working people, but not in terms of a class struggle as Marx was. In contrast to the revolutionary and international perspective of Marx — the communist rallying cry for workers to unite is a call across continents and beyond the narrow interest of nation states — Hitler was strictly nationalistic, and the interests of the worker and the German State were integral. Hitler shares with Marx a certain sympathy for the manual labourer suggesting that there is no inherent reason one might see that a 'brainless columnist just because he works with his pen is superior to a mechanic'. Hitler's early ideology is directly opposed both to Marx (not simply because of the latter's Jewish origins) and the bourgeois enemies of Marx, the weak, liberal bourgeois state that the Weimar has engendered in Germany:

> Even in this field, therefore, the struggle of the bourgeois world against the Marxist international must fail completely. It long since sacrificed the foundations which would have been indispensably necessary for the support of its own ideological world. Their shrewd foe recognized the weaknesses of their own structure and is now storming it with weapons which they themselves, even if involuntarily, provided. (Hitler, 1992: 396)

The struggle against liberal bourgeois indifference and dilettantism, together with the Marxist inspired communism which exploits such weakness, cannot be obtained without further struggle; 'this should be the concern of the National Socialist movement: pushing aside all philistinism, to gather and organize from the ranks of our nation those forces capable of becoming the vanguard fighters for a new philosophy of life'. Interestingly, both Hitler and Marx share the notion of conflict as fundamental to human nature, a fashionable nineteenth-century notion heightened by Charles Darwin's idea of the survival of the fittest. *Mein Kampf* was, after all, written in a time of great social and political upheaval in Germany and throughout Europe, in the immediate 1920s aftermath of the October 1917 Russian Revolution.

Hitler saw Marx, his philosophy of revolutionary communism, and the Russian Revolution which this inspired, as perverse 'Jewish' philosophies. Unlike Marx, Hitler's ideology stressed that it was not so much the material conditions of the worker that mattered but the patriotic ideal of nationalism and the German State. In many ways this intense nationalistic fervour was itself a product of the Enlightenment, as much as Enlightenment tendencies towards rationalism and irreligious attitudes in philosophy. For Hitler, it was not a revolutionary materialism that was of the utmost importance but patriotic idealism. As Hitler states in *Mein Kampf*, 'care must be taken not to underestimate the force of an idea'. And again, for Hitler the great idea is love of the German State.

Integrally related to this patriotism, Hitler's simple idea was to blame one section of the German State for its ills, including defeat in war and the difficult peace:

> And so the Jew today is the great agitator for the complete destruction of Germany.

Wherever in the world we read of attacks against Germany, Jews are their fabricators, just as in peacetime and during the War the press of the Jewish stock exchange and Marxists systematically stirred up hatred against Germany until state after state abandoned neutrality and, renouncing the true interests of the peoples, entered the service of the World War coalition. (Hitler, 1992: 569)

Hitler achieved political success in a way that cannot be credited simply to Nazi thuggery. He knew that only by crushing all dissent from such ideas could the Nazis achieve supremacy. Hitler's idealism was thus rooted in the practicalities of propaganda from the outset. In 1921, Hitler's key political chance came in the German Worker's Party when he became responsible for the management of propaganda. He suggests in *Mein Kampf* that 'it was less important to rack one's brains over organizational questions than to transmit the idea itself to a larger number of people'. Against over organization in the early development of a movement, he states: 'Ideas which have gripped a certain number of people will always strive for a greater order, and a great value must be attributed to this inner moulding' (Hitler, 1992: 527).

Always with an eye to the leadership he suggests that 'It would be absolutely mistaken to regard a wealth of theoretical knowledge as characteristic proof for the qualities and abilities of a leader . . . For leading means: being able to move the masses' (Hitler, 1992: 528). For Hitler, it was the relationship between leadership and vision with domination in political power and in ideas about the repression of dissent that were important qualities which when combined made an extraordinary leader. In his propaganda strategy, he distinguished between two large groups — supporters and members. The function of propaganda was to attract supporters, the function of organization to win members:

A supporter of a movement is one who declares himself to be in agreement with its aims, a member is one who fights for them . . . Propaganda tries to force a doctrine on the whole people; the organisation embraces within its scope only those who do not threaten on psychological grounds to become a break on the further dissemination of the idea . . . Propaganda works on the general public from the standpoint of an idea and makes them ripe for the victory of the idea while the organization achieves victory by persistent, organic, and militant union of those supporters who seem willing and able to carry on the fight for victory. The victory of an idea will be possible the sooner, the more comprehensively propaganda has prepared people as a whole and the more exclusive, rigid, and firm the organization which carries out the fight in practice. (Hitler, 1992: 529)

The propaganda strategy Hitler outlined in *Mein Kampf* in the early 1920s allowed him to make absolute, totalitarian, political power a reality a decade later:

The first task of propaganda is to win people for subsequent organisation; the first task of organisation is to win men for the continuation of propaganda. The second task of propaganda is the disruption of the existing state of affairs and permeation of this state of affairs with the new doctrine, while the second task of organisation must be the struggle for power, thus to achieve the final success of the doctrine. All great movements, whether of a religious or a political nature, must attribute their mighty successes only to the recognition and application of these principles, and all lasting successes in particular are not even thinkable without consideration of these laws. (Hitler, 1992: 530)

The evidence of what the Nazis were capable of — extreme cruelty combined with an equally ruthless and industrial efficiency — was apparent within the year that Hitler was declared Führer. In 1933 a left-wing radical and at the time far from mainstream publisher, Victor Gollancz, published a range of journalistic accounts of terror and oppression on a scale barely seen in a modern European country in peace time. The book, prepared by the World Committee for the Victims of German Fascism, was called *The Brown Book of Hitler Terror and the Burning of the Reichstag*. Its President was one Albert Einstein. In addition to the violent suppression of all political opponents, their imprisonment, systematic torture and the extrajudicial execution of many, the book details how 'Hitler and Goebbels are also waging war against the best sections of the German intelligentsia. Nazi boots trample on the life of the most prominent scientists and artists. In the literal sense they trample on the brutally treated bodies of many intellectuals, who are hated by the Nazis on account of their independence, their progressive and liberal outlook ... Goebbels commands the Brown inquisitors, who think that they can turn back the wheel of history to long before the French Revolution' (Marley, 1933: 160).

The Brown Book details the persecution of scientists amongst the wider cultural decimation:

> The flower of German science driven out. The best known case is that of Albert Einstein, whose reputation as a physicist is world-wide. Albert Einstein, a Swiss subject, member of the Prussian Academy of Sciences, has incurred the hatred of the Nazis for his left-democratic political views, his active interest in the Jewish question and his world-renowned scientific achievements. Einstein's scientific worlds were burnt in the bonfire at the University of Berlin, amid the delighted howls of the Nazis. This act alone is enough to make Hitler's Germany a laughing-stock in the world of modern science. (Marley, 1933: 162)

It is with journalistic precision that the scene of an early Spring day in Berlin is drawn:

> On May 10th the square in front of the Berlin opera house, opposite the university, was aglow with the flames of a great bonfire. The whole square was cordoned off with brown and black detachments of the storm troops and protective corps. Lorries brought in gigantic heaps of books. Bands played, orders rang out, the Minister of Propaganda, Goebbels, rushed up in a car. In the year 1933 this extraordinary spectacle of the burning of books took place, to the sound of Deutschland songs. (Marley, 1933: 171)

Written in 1933 — as the Nazi programme was only commencing — *The Brown Book* remains in some respects amongst the most prophetic books of the time. We noted above in the citation of the opening of this chapter, the German Student Organisation, from 'The Twelve Theses against the Un-German Spirit', posted Berlin University, 13th April 1933 — a citation often given as an example of the wide sympathy of Hitler's ideas amongst the populace. Scientists, poets, music, theatre, painting, films, education, the press, all were repressed if they were not in line with Hitler's ideology. At a time without television the eradication of printed mass media was systematic:

> It is not possible to enumerate all the prohibitions and warnings which have been directed against bourgeois papers and periodicals. The campaign of 'bringing into conformity' led to a dictatorial transformation of the whole of the German press services. Readers of the newspapers which still appear in Germany are hermetically sealed off from all reliable foreign news. Over 250 foreign newspapers are forbidden in Germany, from the following countries: United States 9, Argentine 2, Belgium 7, Canada, 2, Danzig 3, Great Britain 5, France 31, Holland 9, Lithuania 2, Latvia 1, Luxemburg 5, Austria 37, Poland 24, Rumania 1, Saar Territory 4, Sweden 1, Switzerland 26, Soviet Union 9, Spain 2, Czecho-Slovakia 66. (Marley, 1933: 193)

As the author of *The Brown Book* points out, Goebbels was also a writer and in his novel *Michael: A German Destiny in Diary Form*, Michael, the yearning German, has visions of the evil Ivan, a Russian, who entices him to Bolshevism. The victorious struggle is described thus:

> But I am stronger than he.
> Now I have him by the throat
> Now I hurl him to the ground.
> There he lies.
> The death rattle in his throat, and bloodshot eyes.
> Perish, carrion! I trample on his brains.
> And now I am free! (Marley, 1933: 177–178)

As Jonathan Rose writes of the Holocaust and its relationship to the book, 'the story of the Six Million is also the story of the One Hundred Million. This is the toll of books destroyed by the Nazis throughout Europe in just twelve years ...' Acknowledging that estimates might vary 'we can begin with a terrible certainty: the mass slaughter of Jews was accompanied by the most devastating literary holocaust of all time':

> Historians of the book all share the working premise that, in literate societies, script and print are the primary means of preserving memory, disseminating information, inculcating ideologies, distributing wealth, and exercising power. The first question they ask about any civilization is how it saved, used, and destroyed documents. From the culture of the New England Puritanism to the causes of the French Revolution to the implosion of the Soviet Union, this new approach to history has compelled us to think how the past worked. It can also, in the case of the Nazi Holocaust, help us to comprehend the incomprehensible. Film documentaries of the Hitler era open with the book burnings of 1933 and fade out with the death camps. That has become the standard narrative frame, the first and final chapters of the Third Reich. (Rose, 2000: 1)

Heinrich Heine had rightly predicted: 'There where one burns books, one in the end burns men.'

There were two manifestos from April 1933, the 'Twelve Theses against the Un-German Spirit' (resonances here with the Lutheran association of the thesis and a protest against the prevailing order) and *Feuersprüche* (Fire Incantations), the latter two manifestos read and chanted at the burnings as exemplary distillations of the Nazis' viewpoint. Leonidas Hill summarizes the cultural perspective of the Nazis:

> Romanticism, nationalism, racism, social Darwinianism, and antimodernism were the pillars of National Socialist cultural policy. From romanticism came the conviction that peoples expressed their special Geist (spirit or genius) in their language, literature and customs. Early nineteenth century conservative romanticism rejected Enlightenment cosmopolitanism and the egalitarian ideas of 1789. The wars of German unification and the First World War provided an infusion of militarism and chauvinism. . . . Nazi antimodernism espoused the romantic stereotypes of sturdy, unalienated, racially pure 'Nordic' peasants engaged in healthy agricultural labour and producing 'Aryan' children in an idealized countryside. It condemned the supposed licence, decadence, and abstract intellectualism of city dwellers living unhealthy, alienated, soulless, infertile lives in high rises surrounded by asphalt. Nazis preached an idealized vision of the human soul and fulminated against the elevation of the 'base drives' by modern psychology and psychoanalysis, against eroticism and homosexuality in practice as well as in literature, theatre, and the arts. They denounced modern music and architecture,

especially the 'Bolshevik' Bauhaus, and promoted 'traditional', 'pure', 'German' styles. They despised 'un-German, 'corrupt', 'materialistic' American culture, sometimes applying the term 'nigger culture' to Jews as well as blacks. (Hill, 2003: 10–11)

Until the mid-1930s, however, censorship in Germany lacked systematic effectiveness as responsibilities fell to individual German states. The imposition of censorship was nevertheless bloody (Marley, 1933). The Propaganda Ministry compiled the first official 'Index' of authors and books to be banned or suppressed, and the Gestapo and *Sicherheirsdienst* (the Nazi Party espionage service) periodically purged forbidden volumes on the Index from second-hand bookstores and lending libraries throughout Germany. The Index was made applicable throughout Germany, however its impact remained limited as it was sent to a restricted number of officials. After the promulgation of the Nuremberg Laws against the Jews during a September 1935 party rally, Goebbels obtained Hitler's approval for tougher measures against publishers and bookstores and, from April 1935, Goebbels, as head of the Reich Chamber of Literature, obtained supreme censorship. The initial repressions that had up until then been relatively sporadic, mob-led and centred on region-based bureaucratic restrictions gave way to a much more intense period of cultural repression (Barron, 1991; McCarthy and von der Ohe, 1995; Childs, 1997; London, 2000).

From 1935, and the passing of the Nuremberg Laws, there followed an increasingly systematic 'cleansing' action until a peculiar lacuna in the repression for the 1936 Olympic Games. Wary still of world opinion as to its anti-Semitic policies, the 1936 games — both the winter games held in Garmisch Pattenkirchen and the summer games held in Berlin — produced a reverse sort of censorship: anti-Semitic literature was restricted and signs banning Jews were removed from town and city centres. Heinrich Himmler's appointment in 1936 as head of the SS and chief of German police centralized police power, which facilitated censorship operations and wider cultural repressions. The groundwork for this had been facilitated by the Nuremberg racial laws, which Aryanized business and commerce and prevented Jewish ownership in these spheres, including the world of publishing and scholarship. The opportunities for writers antagonistic to Nazism were nil, and many writers and their publishers, liberal in view but not strictly antagonistic to the regime, benefited by default (Raven, 2003).

In May 1941 Martin Bormann, head of the Party Chancellery, succeeded Rudolf Hess as Secretary to the Führer after Hess was imprisoned in England. Fifteen or so years earlier it was Rudolf Hess who had been imprisoned with Hitler in the Bavarian fortress at Landsberg and who, during their incarnation, had recorded the narrative of Hitler's struggle, the text of which was to become *Mein Kampf*. Now it was Bormann, Hitler's new 'Secretary', who instructed that the secret conversations at Hitler's headquarters were to be recorded, from July 1941 to November 1944. *Hitler's Table Talk* was the result. Hitler had earlier refused all such attempts for his conversation to be so recorded, but the hubris of 1941, a time of seeming invincibility — though England had not been defeated, America had at least not joined the War, and Russia was looking vulnerable and the Eastern Front strong — led Hitler to accede, if not for simple vanity then as a record for posterity of the Führer. *Hitler's Table Talk* is especially important as an insight into Hitler's psyche, not as a man speaking to the masses at a party rally or to Allied adversaries, but to close friends and Nazi colleagues.

Bormann, in Hitler's headquarters in East Prussia (Ukraine), would also order the recording of the Führer's political, philosophical and other reflections. Heinrich Heim, one of Bormann's staff, was to take the role of scribe. There was an interlude of duties for four months from March 1942 when Dr Henry Picker deputized. (Therein lay a complicated publishing history which Hugh Trevor-Roper relates in *Hitler's Table Talk*. After the War, Picker contested the published rights of his sections of Hitler diaries. This delayed German publication considerably, but it allowed Trevor-Roper's English language copyrighted edition to appear decades before a fuller account of the conversation in German.) Trevor-Roper neatly summarizes the tone and content of the four volumes of what came to be known as *Hitler's Table Talk*:

> England, America, India, art, music, architecture, the Aryan Jesus, the Bolshevik St Paul, the Maccabbees, Julian the Apostate, King Farouk, Viking vegetarianism, the Ptolemaic system, the Ice Age, Shinto, prehistoric dogs, Spartan soup — there was no subject in which, however ignorant, Hitler was not prepared to dogmatize, and it is often difficult to see, through the utter rubbish which surrounds it, the vulgarity with which it is expressed, and the disgusting cruelty which enflames it, the hard kernel of Hitler's personal thought. Nevertheless, I think, that hard kernel is there, and can be defined as I have defined it here; and who can say that it has not, in spite of all its hideous and vulgar features, a terrible cohesion, a grim correspondency with the reality it almost created. (Trevor-Roper, 2000: xxxi)

A good example of the tone and content that Trevor-Roper describes is revealed in Hitler's pronouncements on the origins of Christianity and its relationship to revolutionary Bolshevism. The following entries are from '21 October 1941, midday':

> Originally, Christianity was merely an incarnation of Bolshevism the destroyer. Nevertheless, the Galilean, who later was called the Christ, intended something quite different. He must be regarded as a popular leader who took up His position against Jewry. Galilee was a colony where the Romans had probably installed Gallic legionaries, and it's certain that Jesus was not a Jew. The Jews, by the way, regarded Him as the son of a whore — of a whore and a Roman soldier.
>
> The decisive falsification of Jesus' doctrine was the work of St. Paul. He gave himself to this work with subtlety and for purposes of personal exploitation. For the Galilean's object was to liberate His country from Jewish oppression. He set himself against Jewish capitalism, and that's why the Jews liquidated Him.
>
> Paul of Tarsus (his name was Saul, before the road to Damascus) was one of those who persecuted Jesus most savagely. When he learnt that Jesus' supporters let their throats be cut for His ideas, he realized that, by making intelligent use of the Galilean's teaching, it would be possible to overthrow this Roman . . . Think of it, the Romans were daring to confiscate the most sacred thing the Jews possessed, the gold piled up in their temples! At that time, as now, money was their god.
>
> The religious ideas of the Romans are common to all Aryan peoples. The Jew, on the other hand, worshipped and continues to worship, then and now, nothing but the golden calf. The Jewish religion is devoid of all metaphysics and has no foundation but the most repulsive materialism. It was only later, under the influence of the Germanic spirit, that Christianity gradually lost its openly Bolshevistic character. It became, to a certain degree, tolerable. To-day, when Christianity is tottering, the Jew restores to pride of place Christianity in its Bolshevistic form. (Hitler, 2000: 136–137)

In this passage Hitler elaborates on the Bolshevistic threat — that is Soviet Communism — as a universal menace, destructive not only of civilized values but also cultural creations of the highest order. Although of course such early hatred of revolutionary communism did not prevent the alliance between Hitler and Stalin (Overy, 2004). He relates, for example, the destruction of the artefacts of Greece and the Roman Empire with the cultural destruction that followed the October Revolution: 'In the old days, as now, destruction of art and civilization. The Bolsheviks of their day, what didn't they destroy in Rome, in Greece and elsewhere? They've behaved in the same way amongst us and in Russia.' Hitler talks too with some irony of 'the destruction of the libraries', suggesting 'Isn't that what happened in Russia? The result: a frightful leveling-down' (Hitler, 2000: 137). On this same evening, Hitler unfavorably compares the 'art and civilization' of the Romans with the cultural poverty of the early Christians, described as 'the abject rabble of the catacombs'. Hitler recoils not so much at the methods but at the message of the Inquisition, 'the same old system of martyrs, tortures, faggots?' Again there is the illogical link between Christianity and Bolshevism, 'Of old it was in the name of Christianity. To-day, it's in the name of Bolshevism' (Hitler, 2000: 139).

Summary

There is no greater symbol, nor industrially efficient 'model' for repression, than the gas chamber. Yet the burning of cultural artefacts alone was never going to be enough for Hitler. Ironically, as Germany's defeat in 1918 led to the abortive founding of the soon-to-fail League of Nations, Adolf Hitler's totalitarianism was a major impetus to the founding of the United Nations. The cataclysmic violence which Hitler managed to engender between 1933 and 1945 was largely responsible for the foundational statements of the Universal Declaration of Human Rights in 1948 which arose from the great cultural silencing of genocide.

    Hitler's *Mein Kampf* was a book that was to be widely banned after the War, and

◆   See Appendix X   ◆

A Typology of Dissent

PAGE 219

◆   Hitler and the Nazi regime is arguably directly responsible for the subsequent internationalization of vast swathes of liberal legislation, including the protection of cultural freedom represented in Appendices II through to IX. It is instructive to ponder on what form the international framework of laws, with respect to freedom of expression, would be today if the Nazis had succeeded in their goal of dominating Western Europe and beyond.   ◆

notably from the newly created State of Israel. The rise of far right political extremists in Europe who idealize such works as *Mein Kampf* (Merkl and Weinberg, 2003), and the growth of politically militant religious fundamentalism globally is evidence of newly emergent issues about freedom of expression and liberty. *Mein Kampf*'s extremist content therefore remains as a present-day warning but also presents a perennial issue of liberty within the restraint of law (familiar since Mill's articulation of it), one that is acutely evident in contemporary societies: to what extent do open democratic societies tolerate the voice of political, or indeed as so often today, religious extremism?

One of the great critiques of totalitarianism is Popper's *The Open Society and Its Enemies* (to which we referred earlier) written by a philosopher who was also a refugee from Nazi Germany. Karl Popper was a Viennese Jew who took refuge from Nazism in New Zealand before eventually settling in England. Published in 1946, it is not Hitler who is the target for his critique of totalitarianism in his book *The Open Society and Its Enemies*, but Plato and Marx. Yet the argument holds against all dictatorial regimes: Popper's major point is that an open society needs to maintain a permanent guard upon those forces which might foreclose the openness of thought and other basic freedoms, whether these are from philosophical, political, ideological or theological sources. An authoritative critic of Popper puts it well: 'the maximum possible tolerance or freedom is an optimum, not an absolute, for it has to be restricted if it is to exist at all . . . the price of freedom is eternal vigilance' (Magee, 1985: 81).

References

Arendt, Hannah [1951] (1966) *The Origins of Totalitarianism*. New York: Harcourt, Brace and World.

Arendt, Hannah (2000) *The Portable Hannah Arendt*. New York; London: Penguin.

Barron, Stephanie (ed.) (1991) *Degenerate Art: The Fate of the Avante-Garde in Nazi Germany*. Los Angeles, California: Los Angeles County Museum of Art.

Childs, Elizabeth C. (ed.) (1997) *Suspended License: Censorship and the Visual Arts*. Seattle: University of Washington Press.

Hill, Leonidas E. Hill (2003) 'The Nazi Attack on "Un-German" Literature, 1933–1945' in Rose (2003), 7–46.

Hitler, Adolf (192) *Mein Kampf*.

Hitler, Adolf [1953] (2000) *Hitler's Table Talk, 1941–1944*, third edition, edited with introduction by Hugh Trevor-Roper. London: Phoenix Press.

Kershaw, Ian (2001) *Hitler*. London: Penguin.

London, John (eds.) (2000) *Theatre Under the Nazis*. Manchester: Manchester University Press.

Magee, Bryan (1985) *Karl Popper*. New York: Viking.

Marley, Lord (1933) *The Brown Book of Hitler Terror and the Burning of the Reichstag*. Prepared by the World Committee for the Victims of German Fascism — President Einstein. London: Victor Gollancz.

McCarthy, John A. and von der Ohe, Werner (1995) *Censorship and Culture: From Weimar Classicism to Weimar Republic and Beyond*. Tubingen: M. Niemeyer.

Merkl, Peter H. and Weinberg, Leonard (eds.) (2003) *Right-Wing Extremism in the Twenty-First Century*. London; Portland, Oregon: Frank Cass.

Overy, R.J. (2004) *The Dictators: Hitler's Germany and Stalin's Russia*. New York: W.W. Norton.

Popper, Karl [1946] (1978) *The Open Society and Its Enemies*. Two volumes. London: Routledge.

Raven, James (2004) *Lost Libraries: The Destruction of Great Book Collections Since Antiquity* (Basingstoke: Palgrave Macmillan).

Rose, Jonathan (eds.) (2003) *The Holocaust and the Book*. Amhert: University of Massachusetts Press.

Shavit, David (1997) *Hunger for the Written Word: Books and Libraries in the Jewish Ghettos of Nazi Occupied Europe*. Jefferson, N.C.: McFarland.

Trevor-Roper, Hugh [1947] (1995) *The Last Days of Hitler*. London: Macmillan.

Trevor-Roper, Hugh (eds.) [1953] (2000) 'Introduction', *Hitler's Table Talk*.

Weikart, Richard (2004) *From Darwin to Hitler: Evolutionary Ethics, Eugenics, and Racism in Germany*. New York; Basingstoke: Palgrave Macmillan.

Selected Electronic Sources

BEACON FOR FREEDOM

www.beaconforfreedom.org offers an outstanding historical resource covering key critical periods, country-by-country, but also dealing with the most infamous and long-lasting ideological and theological forms of repressions — some may find offensive the conflation of the Roman Catholic Church, the former Soviet Union and Nazi Germany.

CHURCHILL

www.churchillspeeches.com is an excellent resource for the speeches of a man who arguably surpassed Hitler in the power of oratory, and, with the Nobel Prize in Literature awarded in 1953, certainly did excel Hitler in terms of literary ability.

HIROSHIMA

www.theenolagay.com contains a relatively dispassionate account of the bombing mission leading to the dropping of the nuclear device that destroyed Hiroshima in August 1945.

HITLER.ORG

www.hitler.org contains materials relating to Hitler — speeches, photographs, and the text of *Mein Kampf* — and while claiming history should be taught neutrally, tends to suggest that Hitler and Nazism is generally represented unfairly, or one-sidedly.

Holocaust Museum and Resource

www.bethshalom is a significant resource associated with the Beth Shalom Holocaust Museum in Nottingham, England.

IMPERIAL WAR MUSEUM

www.iwm.org.uk offers a world class resource based in both London and Manchester, England, on the history of human conflict and a harrowing museum of the holocaust.

WORLD WAR TWO ESPIONAGE

www.bletchleypark.org.uk presents a number of authoritative insights into the world of Bletchley Park, important for deciphering a number of German secret codes.

If you only visit one website on Hitler and Nazism, go to

www.eyewitnesshistory.com (and follow links)

This website presents a useful historical resource, not only on Hitler and Nazism but related facets of twentieth-century history.

Chairman Mao (1893 – 1976)

'Little Red Book'

Quotations from Chairman Mao

In the world today all culture, all literature and art belong to definite classes and are geared to definite political lines. There is in fact no such thing as art for art's sake, art that stands above classes, art that is detached from or independent of politics. Proletarian literature and art are part of the whole proletarian revolutionary cause; they are, as Lenin said, cogs and wheels in the whole revolutionary machine.

'Talks at the Yenan Forum on Literature and Art' (May 1942), *Selected Works*

In our great motherland, a new era is emerging in which the workers, peasants and soldiers are grasping Marxism-Leninism. Once Mao Tse-tung's thought is grasped by the broad masses, it becomes an inexhaustible source of strength and a spiritual atom bomb of infinite power.

Lin Piao, 1966 Foreword, second edition of *Quotations from Chairman Mao*

The *Little Red Book* of Chairman Mao follows a distinct literary tradition within Chinese cultural history, its precedent set in collections of sayings by ancient Chinese sages — such as Lao Tzu and Confucius — and their traditional, aphoristic style. Furthermore, these Chinese traditions have tended to downplay theistic or metaphysical speculation — the sort we find in western theology and philosophy — for instance, while Lao Tzu emphasized harmony with nature, Confucius stressed ethical and political conformity. If Marx similarly dismissed religious and metaphysical objections to communist economic theory and materialist worldview as not even worth considering — the Marxist influence on Mao is self-evident, including an atheistic materialism, and not so out of line with a materialistic-leaning Chinese philosophy. Yet, apart from his adoption of a European philosophical and political analysis (that of Marx), Mao is *distinguishable* from the traditions of Chinese ethical and spiritual philosophy — emphasizing both harmony with nature and conformity to the state — through his *revolutionary* intentions and methods. We might in fact expect this as Mao, for all his indigenous Chinese credentials, had imported an essentially European (that is Marxist) philosophy — to which he added an Asian synthesis and style — to China (Cohen, 2002; Chan, 2003; Cheek, 2002). It was a synthesis — ultimately resulting in the present-day blend of capitalism and state communism in the world's most populace nation — that ultimately opened China to external political, cultural and economic influences that it had consciously resisted for previous millennia (Mitter, 2003; Grasso, Corrin and Kort, 2004; Kornberg and Faust, 2005).

Mao's intolerance of dissent was absolute and, over decades of Chinese history, relentless. His repression of opposition in any form was ruthlessly systematic. There was no freedom of expression in Mao's China except that which served the interests of the revolution; religious freedom of expression was, by its nature counter-revolutionary; aesthetic and ideological freedoms were strictly controlled and monitored. Even in a more liberal economic environment, such a legacy of state monitoring and control, including restrictions of freedom of expression at every level — aesthetic, political, religious — continues in present-day China (Chang, 2005).

Mao Tse Tung the Author

Mao Tse Tung (often seen now transliterated as Mao Zedong) was born the son of a peasant farmer who rose to become one of the most powerful and ruthless leaders the world has seen. An early life of obscurity changed through involvement with the Soviet-influenced Communist Party and its opposition to the traditionally and narrowly nationalistic politics of China. At 27 Mao attended the 1921 Chinese Communist Congress in Shanghai, and was elected two years later to its Central Committee. In 1931 Mao established the Chinese Soviet Republic in the South East of the country, until attacks by the nationalist government of Chiang Kai-shek forced it to end (Fenby, 2004).

Mao's political career can be simply and broadly defined by five major historical periods, each arguably, successively more repressive than the other. *First*, Mao's rapid rise to power within the Russian-backed Communist movement led to a brief if dramatic military success against nationalist forces, and the eventual founding of the — albeit short-lived — Chinese Soviet Republic (1931). *Secondly*, the superficially low point of the 'Long March' (1934) marked defeat for the Chinese Soviet Republic and the period of withdrawal from the overpowering forces of Chiang Kai-shek; yet it was a period of ideological regrouping and guerilla warfare consolidation of Communist forces. This period included the time when China was weakened by the Japanese occupation, from 1937, and, from 1939–1945, the Second World War. *Thirdly*, after fifteen years of strategic military and intellectual advancement — with Soviet backing and with Joseph Stalin literally at his side — Mao established the People's Republic of China (1949), with Communism as the dominant, indeed the only legitimate political ideology. *Fourth*, the Great Leap Forward (1958–60) was a period of economic re-structuring, which arose from Mao's recognition that China's development lagged in this regard behind the rest of the world — Marx's analysis had shown after all how the bourgeoisie had created the conditions for the most successful revolutions and China was arguably still a *feudal* society. The attempted acceleration of economic progress in China, including a vast shift to rural and peasant life intended to give China independence from its Soviet neighbour, was also a period of estrangement from the USSR. Further, Mao's Great Leap Forward was successful in ways unanticipated by the Chinese leader, since he succeeded in creating a bourgeoisie — or its Communist equivalent amongst Party leaders and intelligentsia — who subsequently became a threat not only to Party orthodoxy, but to Mao himself. *Fifth*, the Cultural

Revolution (its marked high point between 1965–68) was a period covering the most famous revolutionary event in Mao's last years — his attempt, with the aid of 'Red Guards', to reassert Communist ideology in the face of a growing class of intellectuals and a still bourgeoning 'bourgeoisie' potentially opposed to Mao.

All five periods were marked by repressive measures against any aesthetic, ideological or religious thinking or activity seemingly opposed to Communist orthodoxy. As much as the image of the red flag and the visage of Mao himself, Mao's *Little Red Book* — a famous icon of the Cultural Revolution — details the full extent of Mao's considerable ideological influence over a significant portion of twentieth-century Chinese history. Mao's writings in this book — as we have noted — essentially follow the aphoristic tradition of much Chinese spiritual and political literature. The 'book' is really a collection of key quotations culled from the period of revolutionary preparation in the 1920s to the height of Communist Party power that came with the establishment of the People's Republic of China (Lawrence, 2001; Chan 2003).

Mao Tse Tung, the *Little Red Book* and Freedom of Expression

The first period of initial revolutionary struggle marks Mao as a disciplined and ascetic figure fighting an ideological war which had already, seemingly, been won by his Communist neighours during the 1917 Revolution in Russia. The period marks Mao's initial stages of Communist Party involvement — indeed, not so long after the success of the 1917 Revolution — and, from 1921 onwards, Mao would be indispensable to its future in China. In the *Little Red Book*, in Mao's writings from this early period, we see Mao's collectivist Party tendencies condemn those in the Red Army 'whose individualism finds expression in pleasure seeking'. In an extract from the 1929 'On Correcting Mistaken Ideas in the Party' we read: 'They always hope that their unit will march into big cities. They want to go there not to work but to enjoy themselves. The last thing they want is to work in the Red areas where life is hard.' The Party was discouraging of all aspects of individual life and self-expression, and these early lines from Mao provide an inkling of the extent of later repression when he had political influence beyond the army and the Party — indeed totalitarian control of all aspects of life in the state in China.

At this revolutionary period, what Mao termed the 'People's War of Liberation', Mao, ironically, recognized the need for democratic openness and justice within the army. Thus, from a 1928 piece relating to 'The Struggle in the Chingkang Mountains', we read:

> Apart from the role played by the Party, the reason why the Red Army has been able to carry on in spite of such poor material conditions and such frequent engagements is its practice of democracy. The officers do not beat the men; officers and men receive equal treatment; soldiers are free to hold meetings and to speak out; trivial formalities have been done away with; and the accounts are open for all to inspect . . . . In China the army needs democracy as much as the people do. Democracy in our army is an important weapon for undermining the feudal mercenary army. (Mao, 1966: Section 24)

This emphasis upon democracy, fairness and listening constructively to dissent — all as a means of uniting against genuine counter-revolutionary opposition — demonstrates a predominant theme which permeates Mao's later speeches and writings, when his sphere of influence would extend beyond the army and Party to the state as a whole. When in power, Mao would thus also encourage openness as a means of uncovering dissent.

The limits of toleration and openness were, however, only ever acceptable in so far as they were in line with the struggle against liberalism, individualism and 'ultra-democracy' of the bourgeoisie; as this 1929 extract from 'On Correcting Mistaken Ideas in the Party' indicates:

> In the sphere of theory, destroy the roots of ultra-democracy. First, it should be pointed out that the danger of ultra-democracy lies in the fact that it damages or even completely wrecks the Party organization and weakens or even completely undermines the Party's fighting capacity, rendering the Party incapable of fulfilling its fighting tasks and thereby causing the defeat of the revolution. Next, it should be pointed out that the source of ultra-democracy consists in the petty bourgeoisie's individualistic aversion to discipline. When this character-istic is brought into the Party, it develops into ultra-democratic ideas politically and organizationally. These ideas are utterly incompatible with the fighting tasks of the proletariat. (Mao, 1966: Section 24)

Throughout the *Little Red Book,* Mao's military background is evident via an almost constant battle readiness in defending ideological unorthodoxy; in defeat he admonishes weakness, in victory he declaims against complacency. There are some human touches to the story of Mao — for he is a political and military man who never seems to have left his peasant origins. In 'Get Organized', for instance, an admonishment from 1943, he speaks directly to the peasantry: 'We must not become complacent over any success. We should check our complacency and constantly criticize our shortcomings, just as we should wash our faces or sweep the floor every day to remove the dirt and keep them clean.'

In the period prior to the establishment of the People's Republic of China, around 1948, 'The Democratic Movement in the Army', the 'three check-ups' and the 'three improve-ments' highlight the major foci for ideological control in the People's War of Liberation. The three check-ups varied between civilian and military Party members; for the former the three check-ups were verification of class origin, ideology and commitment to work; while in the army they were verification of class origin, performance of military duty and the will to combat. The three improvements, building on the foundations of the check-ups, were organizational consolidation, ideological education and conforming to the 'style of work' to Party lines. Openness is seen as needing to be constantly consultative, as in 'regard to military democracy, in periods of training there must be mutual instruction as between officers and soldiers and among the soldiers themselves; and in periods of fighting the companies at the front must hold big and small meetings of various kinds. It has been proved that the practice can only do good and can do no harm whatsoever' (Mao, 1966: Section 24). Chang (2005) has pointed out that Mao's strategy of apparent openness, and his stated emphasis of allowing freedom of expression, was a brilliant strategic ruse to iden-tify dissent.

Some years earlier, in a 1938 piece on 'The Role of the Chinese Communist Party in the National War', openness and democracy are seen as the foundations not only for military victory but the basis for Party life, where 'only in an atmosphere of democracy can large numbers of able people be brought forward'. In 'On Coalition Government' (April 1945) — when Mao is already contemplating power with the defeat of Japan and Germany imminent — he writes of the need for self-criticism as 'still another hallmark distinguishing our Party from all other political parties'. Similarly, he relates Communist ideology to Chinese tradition, citing the maxim, 'Say all you know and say it without reserve', 'Blame not the speaker but be warned by his words' and 'Correct mistakes if you have committed them and guard against them if you have not'. In 'The Task for 1945', from December 1944, he suggests:

> Anyone should be allowed to speak out, whoever he may be, so long as he is not a hostile element and does not make malicious attacks, and it does not matter if he says something wrong. Leaders at all levels have the duty to listen to others. Two principles must be observed: (1) Say all you know and say it without reserve; (2) Don't blame the speaker but take his words as a warning. Unless the principle of 'Don't blame the speaker' is observed genuinely and not falsely, the result will not be 'Say all you know and say it without reserve.' (Mao: 1966: Section 24)

The 'Long March' (1934), military conquest, the period of Japanese occupation (from 1937), and the period out of power (until 1949), were a time when reflections on culture and art became central to the development of a distinctive ideology. Often, as here in a 1940 extract 'On New Democracy' — it is culture always in service of revolution: 'Revolutionary culture is a powerful revolutionary weapon for the broad masses of the people. It prepares the ground ideologically before the revolution comes and is an important, indeed essential, fighting front in the general revolutionary front during the revolution.' When Mao possessed full and absolute power, however, from 1949, all aspects of cultural life were placed in the service of the state. Free expression was to be permitted so long as it was in the service of revolutionary ideology.

Mao therefore emphasized that all literature and art is for the masses — for the workers, peasants and soldiers. The following extract is from Mao's 'Talks at the Yenan Forum on Literature and Art' (May 1942):

> Our literary and art workers must accomplish this task and shift their stand; they must gradually move their feet over to the side of the workers, peasants and soldiers, to the side of the proletariat, through the process of going into their very midst and into the thick of practical struggles and through the process of studying Marxism and society. Only in this way can we have a literature and art that are truly for the workers, peasants and soldiers, a truly proletarian literature and art. (Mao, 1966: Section 32)

Mao defines the purpose of the Party in relation to creative expression, subsuming the latter to the needs to the former; the ideal is 'to ensure that literature and art fit well into the whole revolutionary machine as a component part, that they operate as powerful weapons for uniting and educating the people and for attacking and destroying the enemy, and that they help the people fight the enemy with one heart and one mind'. The following extract, from 'The United Front in Cultural Work' (October 1944), supports this integral relationship between the aesthetic and the ideological:

> In literary and art criticism there are two criteria, the political and the artistic . . . There is the political criterion and there is the artistic criterion; what is the relationship between the two? Politics cannot be equated with art, nor can a general world outlook be equated with a method of artistic creation and criticism. We deny not only that there is an abstract and absolutely unchangeable political criterion, but also that there is an abstract and absolutely unchangeable artistic criterion; each class in every class society has its own political and artistic

criteria. But all classes in all class societies invariably put the political criterion first and the artistic criterion second . . . What we demand is the unity of politics and art, the unity of content and form, the unity of revolutionary political content and the highest possible perfection of artistic form. Works of art which lack artistic quality have no force, however progressive they are politically. Therefore, we oppose both works of art with a wrong political viewpoint and the tendency towards the 'poster and slogan style' which is correct in political viewpoint but lacking in artistic power. On questions of literature and art we must carry on a struggle on two fronts. (Mao, 1966: Section 32)

Such was the cultural groundwork for the People's Republic of China (1949), and the establishment of Communism as the dominant ideology.

As Marx had anticipated, however, the dictatorship of the proletariat was a necessary stage before a classless communistic society. This Mao makes plain in the exuberant 1949 'On the People's Democratic Dictatorship' — but it required a systematic programme of ideological education:

The people's state protects the people. Only when the people have such a state can they educate and re-mould themselves by democratic methods on a country-wide scale, with everyone taking part, and shake off the influence of domestic and foreign reactionaries (which is still very strong, will survive for a long time and cannot be quickly destroyed), rid themselves of the bad habits and ideas acquired in the old society, not allow themselves to be led astray by the reactionaries, and continue to advance - to advance towards a socialist and communist society. (Mao, 1966: Section 24)

Within such an educative framework — or state-led indoctrinatory process — Mao allowed criticism, at least in theory and so long as it was of the kind of criticism that constructively contributed to the advance of the revolution. As Mao's *Speech at the Chinese Communist Party's National Conference on Propaganda Work* (March 1957) makes plain, the 'Communist Party does not fear criticism because we are Marxists, the truth is on our side, and the basic masses, the workers and peasants, are on our side'.

After ten years in power, Mao's growing confidence in this regard is reflected in *On the Correct Handling of Contradictions Among the People* (February 1957):

Letting a hundred flowers blossom and a hundred schools of thought contend is the policy for promoting the progress of the arts and the sciences and a flourishing socialist culture in our land. Different forms and styles in art should develop freely and different schools in science should contend freely. We think that it is harmful to the growth of art and science if administrative measures are used to impose one particular style of art or school of thought and to ban another. Questions of right and wrong in the arts and sciences should be settled through free discussion in artistic and scientific circles and through practical work in these fields. They should not be settled in summary fashion. (Mao, 1966: Section 32)

As ever in Maoist China, the words belied the realities. The Great Leap Forward, from which this extract is drawn, was to be a false dawn of openness before the less subtle repressions of the Cultural Revolution.

The Great Leap Forward (1958–60) — the attempted acceleration of economic progress in China, including a vast shift to rural and peasant life — was intended to give China independence from its Soviet neighbour. It did, but the economic progress also led to political estrangement between China and the USSR. Further, the economic progress of China in this period benefited a small group within the society — a professional and business class but also intellectuals — who not only spearheaded Mao's Great Leap Forward but who also fully took on board Mao's encouraging remarks about intellectual freedom. Mao, as we have seen, had encouraged freedom of expression in the People's War of Liberation, and he had espoused this viewpoint in his writings on art and culture in the immediate and exhilarating aftermath of 1949. In the Great Leap Forward, however, Mao's strategy seemed to have had unintentional results: Mao had created a free-thinking bourgeoisie, and a class of free-thinking intellectuals. Comfortable and confident, the developing elite had also become increasingly powerful — those made successful by the Great Leap Forward had *too* successfully followed Mao's dictates. The notorious Cultural Revolution (1965–68) that followed was Mao's attempt — with the aid of young 'Red Guards' — to reassert Communist Party orthodoxy in the face of a 'bourgeoisie' growing in confidence. Most dangerously for Mao, this economically affluent body spawned a class of free-thinking intellectuals — who embraced the economic liberalism and freedom of expression they had been encouraged to develop — and they were, for their pains, deemed to be a 'counter-revolutionary' threat to the ideological supremacy of Mao and Communist Party (Pietrusza, 1997; Cheek, 2002; Lubell, 2002; Law, 2003; Xing, 2004). Today's economic prosperity in China may yet bring similarly 'counter-revolutionary' results, and arguably did so in Tiananmen Square.

Quotations from Chairman Mao Tse-tung
The *Little Red Book* at a Glance

Study Chairman Mao's writings, follow his teachings and act according to his instructions. *Lin Piao*

CONTENTS

Go to http://art-bin.com (and follow links)

The foreword to the second edition of The *Little Red Book* epitomizes the Cultural Revolution. Here Lin Pio states that 'the most fundamental task in our Party's political and ideological work' is 'at all times to hold high the great red banner of Mao Tse-tung's thought, to arm the minds of the people throughout the country with it and to persist in using it to command every field of activity'. Drawn from late 1966, the foreword embodies the personality cult around the now elderly Mao. The quotations themselves, in thirty-three chapters, are drawn from across speeches and writings of Mao's long political life and — with their devoted and consistently pure ideological stance — show Mao to be the great Marxist-Leninist survivor: 'Mao Tse-tung's thought is Marxism-Leninism of the era in which imperialism is heading for total collapse and socialism is advancing to world-wide victory. It is a powerful ideological weapon for opposing imperialism and for opposing revisionism and dogmatism. Mao Tse-tung's thought is the guiding principle for all the work of the Party, the army and the country.' The historical materialism of Marx — the utopian hopes of a classless, communistic world — was ever-hopeful:

> In our great motherland, a new era is emerging in which the workers, peasants and soldiers are grasping Marxism-Leninism, Mao Tse-tung's thought. Once Mao Tse-tung's thought is grasped by the broad masses, it becomes an inexhaustible source of strength and a spiritual atom bomb of infinite power. The large-scale publication of *Quotations from Chairman Mao Tse-tung* is a vital measure for enabling the broad masses to grasp Mao Tse-tung's thought and for promoting the revolutionization (sic) of our people's thinking. It is our hope that all comrades will learn earnestly and diligently, bring about a new nation-wide high tide in the creative study and application of Chairman Mao's works and, under the great red banner of Mao Tse-tung's thought, strive to build our country into a great socialist state with modern agriculture, modern industry, modern science and culture and modern national defence! (Lin Pao, 1966: 1)

For the many, indeed innumerable, victims of Maoist interpretations of Marxist-Leninist philosophy — unknown 'dissidents' and 'counter-revolutionaries' in China and Tibet — there has emerged only a small number of high profile figures whose status and international profile has enabled them to highlight the plight of those denied rights to free expression, in culture, in religion or political dissent. The Dalai Lama has, for instance, since 1949, been a paramount, non-violent critique of the militantly atheistic Chinese Communist authorities, and an international symbol in his exile of rights to wider aesthetic, ideological and religious freedom of expression.

At the end of the Cold War — when relations thawed between the USA and the Soviet Union — hopes rose that China's totalitarian regime might also develop enhanced democratic openness, and indeed, increased trade links and a developing capitalist economy seemed positive indicators. The Tiananmen Square massacre and the repressive backlash in early 1990s China demonstrated the limits to Communist Party acceptance of an open society. China's huge and emergent economic power has meant that the world has had little option not to exclude China from the world community — it has always been a key member of the UN Security Council — but pressure on China for its persecutions in Tibet, for instance, has been light. Awarding China the honour of hosting the 2008 Olympic Games has arguably shown international policy on challenging human rights abuses at its most compromised.

Other agencies, especially cultural ones, have encouraged an ongoing critique of the repressive aspects of Chinese society. Indeed, it is perhaps not surprising that it is those aesthetic, ideological and religious groups most affected by political repression in China that have been most vociferous in opposition in dissent. In 2003 the Nobel Prize in Literature was awarded to a Chinese dissident, Gao Xingjian. Xingjian was born January 4, 1940 in Ganzhou, in Jiangxi province, in eastern China. Xingjian is today a French citizen. A writer in prose and drama, as well as translator, critic and artist, the Nobel organization narrates, 'Gao Xingjian grew up during the aftermath of the Japanese invasion, his father was a bank official and his mother an amateur actress who stimulated the young Gao's interest in the theatre and writing'. The Nobel organization highlights Xingjian's early career and the life story of his struggle against Chinese repression as follows:

> He received his basic education in the schools of the People's Republic and took a degree in French in 1962 at the Department of Foreign Languages in Beijing. During the Cultural Revolution (1966–76) he was sent to a re-education camp and felt it necessary to burn a suitcase full of manuscripts. Not until 1979 could he publish his work and travel abroad, to France and Italy. During the period 1980–87 he published short stories, essays and dramas in literary magazines in China and also four books: *Premier essai sur les techniques du roman moderne/A Preliminary Discussion of the Art of Modern Fiction* (1981) which gave rise to a violent polemic on modernism, the narrative *A Pigeon Called Red Beak* (1985), *Collected Plays* (1985) and *In Search of a Modern Form of Dramatic Representation* (1987). Several of his experimental and pioneering plays — inspired in part by Brecht, Artaud and Beckett — were produced at the Theatre of Popular Art in Beijing: his theatrical debut with *Signal d'alarme/Signal Alarm* (1982) was a tempestuous success, and the absurd drama which established his reputation *Arrêt de bus/Bus Stop* (1983) was condemned during the campaign against 'intellectual pollution' (described by one eminent member of the party as the most pernicious piece of writing since the foundation of the People's Republic); *L'Homme sauvage/Wild Man* (1985) also gave rise to heated domestic polemic and international attention.

The story of repression continued until 1986 when *L'autre rive/The Other Shore* was banned, from which time none of his plays have been performed in China:

> In order to avoid harassment he undertook a ten-month walking-tour of the forest and mountain regions of Sichuan Province, tracing the course of the Yangzi river from its source to the coast. In 1987 he left China and settled down a year later in Paris as a political refugee. After the massacre on the Square of Heavenly Peace in 1989 he left the Chinese Communist Party. After publication of La fuite/Fugitives, which takes place against the background of this massacre, he was declared persona non grata by the regime and his works were banned. In the summer of 1982, Gao Xingjian had already started working on his prodigious novel La Montagne de l'Âme/Soul Mountain, in which — by means of an odyssey in time and space

through the Chinese countryside — he enacts an individual's search for roots, inner peace and liberty. (www.nobelprize.org/literature)

Summary

Mao was an intensely private yet ruthlessly ambitious man (Li, 1996). In China — certainly from 1949 — Mao was politically all powerful for decades. Interpretations are inevitably contested as to Mao's role, successful or otherwise, in mid- to late twentieth-century Chinese history — totalitarian and tyrant or national hero — as are arguments over Mao's more than vestigial influence in the twenty-first; accounts of Mao's life and these debates currently proliferating (Short, 1999; Terril, 1999; Guo, 2000; Spence, 2000; Cheek, 2002; Lynch, 2003 Chang, 2004; Chang and Halliday, 2005).

◆   See Appendix X   ◆
A Typology of Dissent
PAGE 219

◆   Mao's legacy, amongst all modern dictators, is arguably the most enduring in present-day international politics, as expressed through the Chinese Communist Party. As an important member of the Security Council, established by the Charter of the United Nations (see Appendix I), China has a long tradition of balancing a Communist ideology with the liberal polity based on universal human rights as established by the Charter and subsequent international legislation (Appendices II through to IX). China raises the difficult question of how far the international community should intervene in the sovereign affairs of a nation-state in response to infringements of human rights — particularly in a world where supposedly universal rights are so rarely universal. It is often down to NGOs to exert pressure on a miscreant state when the international community is seen not to respond vigorously enough. A full list of freedom of expression issues is listed in Appendix VIII.   ◆

Chang's (2005) incisive interpretation of Mao's apparent periods of liberalism and freedom of expression — characterized by the famous phrase, 'let a thousand flowers bloom' — was that Mao used encouragement to openness cleverly in order to expose ideological dissent. Mao's periodic declarations in favour of freedom of expression were not the totalitarian's confident lightening of the reigns of power but a tightening of tyrannical control:

Terrorization had always been Mao's panacea whenever he wanted to achieve anything. But in 1956, after Khrushchev condemned Stalin's use of terror, Mao had to lower the rate of arrests and killings. On 29 February, as soon as he learned about Khrushchev's speech, Mao had ordered his police chief to revise established plans: 'This year the number of arrests must be greatly reduced from last year . . . The number of executions especially must be fewer . . . ' (Chang, 2005: 434)

This apparent 'liberalism' was a strategic preface to the terror of ideological conformity that followed in the Cultural Revolution. Speaking of dissent in Eastern Europe — that which would follow with the Soviet crushing of the Hungarian uprising, ending hopes of any premature conclusion to the Cold War — Mao criticized the Soviet authorities for not rooting out and eliminating dissent more fully: 'The basic problem with some Eastern European countries is that they didn't eliminate those counter-revolutionaries . . . Now they are eating their own bitter fruit'. Eastern Europe 'did kill on a grand scale'. Mao declared: 'We must kill. And we say it's good to kill.' (Chang, 2005: 434). Recent estimates have placed the number of deaths for which Mao and Mao's policies — economic, military, cultural — can be attributed at 'around' seventy million (Chang, 2005), arguably more than Hitler and Stalin combined. Today's People Republic of China is not that of Mao's. Yet, despite economic liberalization, politically-inspired ideological repression continues unabated. Religious practice and belief — personal and public — is still considered as 'counter-revolutionary'. According to some sources, repression against religious groups — amongst all forms of freedom of expression denied in China — is indiscriminate and harsh, whether Christian or Muslim; since 1949, in Buddhist Tibet, such repression has arguably become genocidal (Marshall, 2000; also Knuth, 2003).

References

Chan, Adrian (2003) *Chinese Marxism*. London; New York: Continuum.

Chang, Jung (2004) *Wild Swans: Three Daughters of China*. London: Perennial.

Chang, Jung and Halliday, Jon (2005) *Mao: The Unknown Story*. London: Jonathan Cape

Cheek, Timothy (2002) *Mao Zedong and China's Revolutions: A Brief History with Documents*. Boston, MA: Bedford/ St. Martin's.

Cheek, Timothy (1997) *Propaganda and Culture in Mao's China: Deng Tuo and the Intelligentsia*. Oxford: Clarendon Press.

Cohen, Martin (2001) *Political Philosophy: From Plato to Mao*. London: Pluto.

Fenby, Jonathan (2004) *Generalissimo: Chiang Kai-shek and the China He Lost*. London: Free Press.

Grasso, June M., Corrin, Jay, and Kort, Michael (2004) *Modernization and Revolution in China: From the Opium Wars to World Power*. Armonk, N.Y.; London: M. E. Sharpe.

Guo, Sujian (2000) *Post-Mao China: From Totalitarianism to Authoritarianism?* Westport, Conn: Praeger.

Knuth, Rebecca K. 'China's Destruction of the Libraries of Tibet'. In Raven (2003), 247–256.

Kornberg, Judith F., and Faust, John R. (2005) *China in World Politics: Policies, Processes, Prospects*. Boulder, Colorado; London: Lynne Reinner Publishers.

Law, Kam-yee (2003) *The Chinese Cultural Revolution Reconsidered: Beyond Purge and Holocaust*. Basingstoke: Palgrave Macmillan.

Lawrance, Alan (ed.) *China Since 1919: Revolution and Reform; A Sourcebook*. London, New York: Routledge.

Li, Zhisui (1996) *The Private Life of Chairman Mao*. London: Arrow.

Lubell, Pamela (2002) *The Chinese Communist Party and the Cultural Revolution*. Basingstoke: Palgrave.

Lynch, Michael (2003) *Mao*. London: Routledge.

Marshall, Paul (ed.) (2000) *Religious Freedom in the World: A Global Report on Freedom and Persecution*. London: Broadman and Holman.

Mitter, Rana (2004) *A Bitter Revolution: China's Struggle with the Modern World*. Oxford: Oxford University Press.

Pietrusza, David (1997) *The Chinese Cultural Revolution*. San Diego, California: Lucent Books.

Raven, James (2004) *Lost Libraries: The Destruction of Great Book Collections Since Antiquity*. Basingstoke: Palgrave Macmillan.

Spence, Jonathan D. (2000) *Mao*. London; Phoenix.

Short, Philip (1999) *Mao: A Life*. London: Hodder & Stoughton.

Terril, Ross (1999) *Mao: A Biography*. Stanford, California: Stanford University Press.

Xing, Lu (2004) *Rhetoric of the Chinese Cultural Revolution: The Impact on Chinese Thought, Culture and Communication*. Columbia: University of South Carolina Press.

Selected Electronic Sources

MEDIA AND MAO

www.washtimes.com/world contains a good, populist range of materials on Mao and Communist China.

QUOTATIONS OF CHAIRMAN MAO (THE *LITTLE RED BOOK*)

http://art-bin.com (and follow links) contains the work in translation. The Marxists Internet Archive holds an unsurpassed range of texts and data.

If you only visit one website on Mao, go to

Marxists Internet Archive www.marxists.org

This website offers by far the most comprehensive resource on Marxism available electronically.

www.marxists.org contains an excellent reference archive with:

Biography of Mao
Selected works by date, volume and pdf files of the majority of Mao
Major speeches and diktats.
Poetry of Mao
Images of Mao

The United Nations (1945–)
Universal Declaration of Human Rights

> Whereas disregard and contempt for human rights have resulted in barbarous acts which have outraged the conscience of mankind, and the advent of a world in which human beings shall enjoy freedom of speech and belief and freedom from fear and want has been proclaimed as the highest aspiration of the common people . . .
>
> Preamble to the *Universal Declaration of Human Rights*

It was totalitarianism and genocide that were on the mind of the newly formed United Nations (UN) when the UN General Assembly — established by its founding 1945 Charter — instituted a Universal Declaration of Human Rights in thirty articles, on 10 December 1948. Only the day before the UN General Assembly had made the Convention on the Prevention of Genocide. Arguably, because of this juxtaposition of declarations, totalitarianism and genocide define the subsequent contours of the UN mandate in all others areas of its operation (Ryan, 2000). The Universal Declaration of Human Rights arose from, or as a direct reaction to, the extreme denigration of freedoms by totalitarianism and the violence of two world wars. It was a world of the unprecedented systematization of violence brought about by new science and technologies — the industrialization of death witnessed in Nazi-genocide, carpet-bombing of European (Axis and Allied) cities, the detonation of atomic bombs in Japan. The repressions of totalitarianism and the violence of genocide are foundational motivations behind all modern-day international human rights legislation.

Democracy and human rights in governance underpinned by freedom of expression — particularly the capacity of citizens to exercise free and open critique of government and state — were, in the post-Enlightenment era, political principles that founded the French and American constitutions. The same political principles formed the basis for the UN and universal human rights two centuries later, when the world was subject to the indirect product of reason's supremacy — totalitarian repression and violence. The UN, and universal human rights enshrined in international law evolved as a corrective to political extremism and as a foundation for legal and universal moral principle as a result of the historically contingent. The principle of democracy and universal human rights — founded on freedom of expression in the widest possible sense — came now to be universalized in the UN era. The UN era is also, integrally, the era of globalization.

Studies abound of the United Nations, sixty years or so after its creation (Ryan, 1996;

Forsythe, 2000; Schlesinger, 2003; Baratta, 2004; Bowles, 2004; Fasulo, 2004; Krasno, 2004; Weiss, Forsythe and Coate, 2004). These studies review the successes and failures of the UN from its inception when the world was a smaller place to a time when the notion of globalization has become a worn cliché. Arguably the UN has been preeminent amongst bureaucratic inter-governmental structures which have, along with advances in communications and other technologies, made the world smaller. The First and Second World Wars were indicative of the global reach of technology demonstrated by world war and the impetus for a global inter-governmental system based on common values ('universal human rights') that would determine and maintain, at least in theory, the peace. More peculiarly, the First and Second World Wars demonstrated not only the worst possibilities of globalization but became, through the UN, also the impetus for the bureaucracy of world peace.

Freedom of expression was pivotal in all these historical and contemporary contexts — from the French Declaration of Rights of Man and of Citizens and the American Declaration of Independence to the Universal Declaration of Human Rights in the UN era. What began after the Reformation as freedom to express one's religious beliefs subsequently allowed for considerable aesthetic as well as political liberty; freedom of expression is undoubtedly centred on these elements of civic and cultural life — the aesthetic, the political and the religious. There is a perennial tension in the history of freedom of expression and human rights between these elements, from Plato to the modern-day. In world history just prior to the formation of the UN, we need only recall that the first act of Nazism in power was the burning of books in order to remind ourselves that the destruction of free expression will always be the first act of the dictator and the totalitarian state. Its second was the systematic eradication of cultural and religious minorities. Freedom of expression is not only a condition of liberty but also its foundation; if no open society is possible without aesthetic or religious freedoms, in polity there can be no open governance without the right to free critique of government.

The United Nations as Author

It is a sign of the times — we might reserve judgment on whether this is good or not — that the Universal Declaration of Human Rights, the most famous piece of writing on modern human rights, is neither a philosophical treatise nor a work of theology nor a piece of great literature but a statement comprised of thirty articles on justice and equality, democratic governance and moral principles written by a *committee*. As with any statement of political idealism, the times of such statements are often fraught with moral ambiguities: in France, the Revolution was followed by the Terror; in the American Declaration of Independence, slavery was to exist into the nineteenth-century. In early August 1945, Hiroshima and Nagasaki were decimated by nuclear bombs, in an alliance of the same powers who had signed the UN Charter only weeks earlier in June 1945. The major signatories of the Universal Declaration of Human Rights in 1948 still maintained considerable colonial empires. The contradictions and moral ambiguities in the development of universal human rights have been an integral feature of the development of the UN itself when we look at a timeline of its history.

Timeline of UN History and
Key Human Rights Documents

1940s
26 June 1945
Signing of the Charter of the United Nations (signed in San Francisco, USA)

9 December 1945
Convention on the Prevention and Punishment of the Crime of Genocide

10 December 1945
Universal Declaration of Human Rights

1950s
4 November 1950
European Convention on Human Rights (Council of Europe)

28 July 1951
Convention relating to the Status of Refugees

20 December 1952
Convention on the Political Rights of Women

23 October 1953
Protocol amending the Slavery Convention (originally signed in Geneva, Switzerland, 25) September 1926

28 September 1954
Convention relating to the Status of Stateless Persons

7 September 1956
Convention on the Abolition of Slavery, the Slave Trade, and Institutions and Practices Similar to Slavery

25 June 1957
Convention on the Abolition of Forced Labour

20 November 1959
Declaration of the Rights of the Child

1960s
14 December 1960
Declaration on the Granting of Independence to Colonial Countries and Peoples

20 November 1963
Declaration on the Elimination of All Forms of Racial Discrimination

21 December 1965
International Convention on the Elimination of All Forms of Racial Discrimination
– Committee on the Elimination of All Forms of Racial Discrimination established

16 December 1966
International Covenant on Civil and Political Rights
International Covenant on Economic, Social and Cultural Rights
– Human Rights Committee established

7 November 1967
Declaration on the Elimination of Discrimination against Women
Proclamation of Teheran — International Conference on Human Rights

26 November 1968
Convention on the Non-Applicability of Statutory Limitations to War Crimes Against Humanity

1970s
30 November 1973
International Convention on the Suppression and Punishment of the Crime of Apartheid

9 December 1975
Declaration on the Protection of All Persons from being Subjected to Torture and Other Cruel,
Inhuman or Degrading Treatment or Punishment

18 December 1979
Convention on the Elimination of All Forms of Discrimination against Women
– Committee on the Elimination of All Forms of Discrimination against Women established thereby

1980s
27 June 1981
African Charter on Human and Peoples' Rights (Organization of African Unity)

25 November 1981
Declaration on the Elimination of All Forms of Intolerance and of Discrimination Based on Religion
or Belief

10 December 1984
Convention against Torture and Other Cruel, Inhuman or Degrading Treatment or Punishment

28 May 1985
Committee on Economic, Social and Cultural Rights established to monitor implementation of
International Covenant on Economic, Social and Cultural Rights.

4 December 1986
Declaration on the Right to Development

20 November 1989
Convention on the Rights of the Child
– Committee on the Rights of the Child established

15 December 1989
Second Optional Protocol to the International Covenant on Civil and Political Rights — aimed at
the abolition of the death penalty

1990s
14 December 1990
Basic Principles for the Treatment of Principles

18 December 1990
International Convention on the Protection of the Rights of All Migrant Workers and members of
their Families

18 December 1992
Declaration on the Protection of All Persons from Enforced Disappearance
Declaration on the Rights of Persons Belonging to National or Ethnic, Religious or Linguistic
Minorities

14 June 1993
World Conference on Human Rights (Vienna) opens

25 June 1993
Vienna Declaration and Plan of Action

20 December 1993
Declaration on the Elimination of Violence against Women
Third Decade to Combat Racism and Racial Discrimination proclaimed (1995–2004)
Post of United Nations High Commissioner for Human Rights established

21 December 1993
International Decade of the World's Indigenous Peoples proclaimed

23 December 1994
United Nations Decade for Human Rights Education proclaimed (1995–2004)

1995
World Conference on Women's Rights (Beijing)
10 December 1998
Fiftieth Anniversary of the Universal Declaration of Human Rights

2000–
4–8 September 2001
World Conference against Racism, Xenophobia and All Forms of Discrimination (Durban, South Africa)

The history of the UN raises an important point: it is difficult in modern times to separate the development of universal human rights and the development of the UN. Universal human rights and the UN are — for better or worse, effective or otherwise — entwined. The framework of international law and its underpinning of human rights discourse remains integral to the history of the UN itself, even if one of the greatest failings of the UN has been its inability sufficiently to democratize human rights so that knowledge of them extends beyond the legal community. That aside, UN documents in human rights are themselves complex — most commonly divided into 'declarations' (statements of intent by the UN General Assembly that are not legally binding), 'covenants' (a stronger level of guidance by the UN General Assembly but which are non-legally binding pledges and, if agreed by government representatives, are indications that a nation state will adhere to the particular human rights principles) and 'conventions' (the strongest level of UN framework which, when signed by governmental representatives, become legally binding agreements). Conventions require commitments from nation states in order to be ratified or come into force. Conventions also set out in precise terms how the terms of the agreement are to be managed, such as committee structure, composition, procedures for election and terms of reference, and so forth. This is why conventions are always longer documents than basic statements of principle like declarations. These declarations, covenants and conventions are integrally related to the structure and organization of the UN, its history and its *modus operandi*.

The Secretary-General of the UN has made human rights the *central* theme that 'unifies the organization's work in the key areas of peace and security, development, humanitarian assistance and economic and social affairs' and thus '[V]irtually every UN body and specialized agency is involved to some degree in the protection of human rights' (www.un.org, and follow links). The legal framework for international human rights builds on and incorporates the Universal Declaration of Human Rights and is itself incorporated within the International Bill of Human Rights, consisting of five documents:

- Universal Declaration of Human Rights
- International Covenant on Economic, Social and Cultural Rights
- International Covenant on Civil and Political Rights
- Optional Protocol to the International Covenant on Civil and Political Rights
- Second Optional Protocol to the International Covenant on Civil and Political Rights, aiming at the abolition of the death penalty

The major office for *human rights* is the UN High Commission for Human Rights, based in Geneva, Switzerland, with a specially appointed UN High Commissioner for Human Rights — operational details can be found at www.unhchr.ch or through the UN's home page at www.un.org (see also Ghandhi, 2004; Mertus, 2005; Smith, 2005). With the UN's headquarters in New York and its operating centre for human rights in Geneva, these locations in wealthy nations are often cited as reasons why developing nations especially consider the UN to have a western bias (Weiss, Forsythe and Coate, 2004; Ziring, Riggs and Plano, 2005).

The UN, the *Universal Declaration of Human Rights* and Freedom of Expression

When, on that now famous 10 December day in 1948, the General Assembly of the UN adopted and proclaimed the Universal Declaration of Human Rights in thirty articles, it provided a moving testimony to the good intentions of humankind in ridding itself of total-itarianism, genocide and the scourge of world war, as well as being a positive affirmation of human worth and fundamental moral principles. The Declaration provides the neces-sary legal and historical context and a statement of human value. As this document forms the crux of the foundations for human rights, the preamble is worth stating in full:

> Whereas recognition of the inherent dignity and of the equal and inalienable rights of all members of the human family is the foundation of freedom, justice and peace in the world,
> Whereas disregard and contempt for human rights have resulted in barbarous acts which have outraged the conscience of mankind, and the advent of a world in which human beings shall enjoy freedom of speech and belief and freedom from fear and want has been proclaimed as the highest aspiration of the common people,
> Whereas it is essential, if man is not to be compelled to have recourse, as a last resort, to rebellion against tyranny and oppression, that human rights should be protected by the rule of law,
> Whereas it is essential to promote the development of friendly relations between nations,
> Whereas the peoples of the United Nations have in the Charter reaffirmed their faith in fundamental human rights, in the dignity and worth of the human person and in the equal rights of men and women and have determined to promote social progress and better stan-dards of life in larger freedom,

Whereas Member States have pledged themselves to achieve, in co-operation with the United Nations, the promotion of universal respect for and observance of human rights and fundamental freedoms,

Whereas a common understanding of these rights and freedoms is of the greatest importance for the full realization of this pledge,

Now, Therefore THE GENERAL ASSEMBLY proclaims THIS UNIVERSAL DECLARATION OF HUMAN RIGHTS as a common standard of achievement for all peoples and all nations, to the end that every individual and every organ of society, keeping this Declaration constantly in mind, shall strive by teaching and education to promote respect for these rights and freedoms and by progressive measures, national and international, to secure their universal and effective recognition and observance, both among the peoples of Member States themselves and among the peoples of territories under their jurisdiction.

There is little that thirty articles do not themselves cover, at least in basic outline, by way of a statement of moral principle as a foundation for the rights and responsibilities, freedoms and obligations of the individual and the state and international community of nations.

UN Universal Declaration of Human Rights

THE GENERAL ASSEMBLY proclaims THIS UNIVERSAL DECLARATION OF HUMAN RIGHTS as a common standard of achievement for all peoples and all nations, to the end that every individual and every organ of society, keeping this Declaration constantly in mind, shall strive by teaching and education to promote respect for these rights and freedoms.

Article 1
All human beings are born free and equal in dignity and rights.

Article 2
Everyone is entitled to all the rights and freedoms set forth in this Declaration, without distinction of any kind, such as race, colour, sex, language, religion, political or other opinion, national or social origin, property, birth or other status.

Article 3
Everyone has the right to life, liberty and security of person.

Article 4
No one shall be held in slavery or servitude; slavery and the slave trade shall be prohibited in all their forms.

Article 5
No one shall be subjected to torture or to cruel, inhuman or degrading treatment or punishment.

Article 6
Everyone has the right to recognition everywhere as a person before the law.

Article 7
All are equal before the law and are entitled without any discrimination to equal protection of the law.

Article 8
Everyone has the right to an effective remedy by the competent national tribunals for acts violating the fundamental rights.

Article 9
No one shall be subjected to arbitrary arrest, detention or exile.

Article 10
Everyone is entitled in full equality to a fair and public hearing by an independent and impartial tribunal.

Article 11
Everyone charged with a penal offence has the right to be presumed innocent until proved guilty according to law in a public trial.

Article 12
No one shall be subjected to arbitrary interference with privacy, family, home or correspondence.

Article 13
Everyone has the right to freedom of movement and residence within the borders of each state.

Article 14
Everyone has the right to seek and to enjoy in other countries asylum from persecution.

Article 15
Everyone has the right to a nationality.

Article 16
Men and women of full age, without any limitation due to race, nationality or religion, have the right to marry and to found a family.

Article 17
Everyone has the right to own property alone as well as in association with others.

Article 18
Everyone has the right to freedom of thought, conscience and religion.

Article 19
Everyone has the right to freedom of opinion and expression.

Article 20
Everyone has the right to freedom of peaceful assembly and association.

Article 21
Everyone has the right to take part in the government of his country.

Article 22
Everyone, as a member of society, has the right to social security.

Article 23
Everyone has the right to work.

Article 24
Everyone has the right to rest and leisure.

Article 25
Everyone has the right to a standard of living adequate for health and well-being.

Article 26
Everyone has the right to education.

Article 27
Everyone has the right freely to participate in the cultural life of the community.

Article 28
Everyone is entitled to a social and international order in which the rights and freedoms set forth in this Declaration can be fully realized.

Article 29
Everyone has duties to the community in which alone the free and full development of his personality is possible.

Article 30
Nothing in this Declaration may be interpreted as implying for any State, group or person any right to engage in any activity or to perform any act aimed at the destruction of any of the rights and freedoms set forth herein.

See www.un.org and follow link for the Universal Declaration on the UN homepage; see also Amnesty International, www.ai.org

Following this historic Declaration, the General Assembly called upon all Member countries to publicize the text of the Declaration and 'to cause it to be disseminated, displayed, read and expounded ... without distinction based on the political status of countries or territories.' Critical observers (Forsythe, 2000) have pointed out that the thinking is high on ideals but thin on the processes that led to and underlie such wide-ranging anthropological, ethical, philosophical and political thinking. If this identifies a weakness, especially in early UN documents, it also highlights their pragmatic nature. UN declarations and conventions are essentially political documents. Since the UN is at least in essence committed to the principles of democratic process — due representation of views and formal accounting of the acceptability through a voting consensus — such things take time. We have already remarked that the Universal Declaration of Human Rights was drafted by a committee for consideration and approval — but then all modern democratic systems draft laws in this manner rather than by totalitarian decree.

The Universal Declaration of Human Rights set a framework for international governance based on democracy and universal human rights. It was based upon the *de facto* principle that citizens should be able to critique governments and states; and it thereby also attended specifically to freedom of conscience, thought and expression. It did so in much the same way as the *French Declaration of the Rights of Man and of Citizens* did when stating that: 'No man ought to be molested on account of his opinions, not even on account of his religious opinions, provided his avowal of them does not disturb the public order established by the law' (Right X); and 'The unrestrained communication of thoughts and opinions being one of the most precious rights of man, every citizen may speak, write, and publish freely, provided he is responsible for this liberty in cases determined by the law' (Right XI). In the UN's Universal Declaration freedom of expression and freedom of religion are similarly placed side by side: 'Everyone has the right to freedom of thought, conscience and religion' (Article 18) and 'Everyone has the right to freedom of opinion and expression; this right includes freedom to hold opinions without interference and to seek, receive and impart information and ideas through any media and regardless of frontiers (Article 19). It is Articles 18 and 19 that form the basis of all other freedom of expression legislation in international law, including those documents already referred to as the International Bill of Human Rights, International Covenant on Economic, Social and Cultural Rights and the International Covenant on Civil and Political Rights (see Appendix II for a full range of legal sources on freedom of expression).

Summary

Plato was an elitist who did not believe in the masses, except in so far as they might serve the elite. Much of Plato's *Republic* — aside from those chapters not dedicated to eradicating poets — is dedicated to the education of these elite and the formation of what today would be termed a totalitarian state. Unlike many Greek political philosophers, Plato was not fond of democracy: people are to be led and ruled by the wise and powerful, and are to be protected from change. It was not until the European Enlightenment, politically epitomized by Paine's *Rights of Man* and constitutional statements of the period from France and the United States, that we see emergent forms of governance based on universal equality which incorporate terms like human rights as the principles of modern polity. The separation of Church and state in this period heightened the power of the latter over the former in matters of governance. And while, to an extent unknown during the Reformation and Counter-Reformation, the European Enlightenment provided greater freedom of religion, it also provided for freedom *from* religion. One of the unintended consequences of this latter aspect of the Enlightenment was a freedom for militant atheism, the Enlightenment spawning atheistic and totalitarian systems that placed the state above the individual, notably Communism, fascism and Nazism.

Two and a half millennia after Plato, with the defeat of Nazism and the inception of the UN era with its Charter in 1945, two major competing ideologies were liberal democracy — based upon a system of universal human rights protecting the rights of the individual within states — and state communism — which rooted governance in the ideology of class struggle and placed the interest of a controlling state beyond the freedoms of individuals within it. After the Cold War, from 1989 onwards, triumphalist claims were made about the victory of democracy and universal human rights as a basis for state governance globally and implied a supposed end to arguments over universal human rights as a legal set of imposed values consensus (Casanova, 1994; Ayton-Shenker, 1995; Wellman, 2000; Gearon, 2002; Sellars, 2002; Ghandhi, 2004; Smith, 2005). Ironically, it tends to be religious traditions that are again challenging not only freedom of expression but the principle of open governance based on democracy and human rights, with religious fundamentalism arguably the most pervasive contemporary manifestation of totalitarianism.

◆   See Appendix X   ◆

A Typology of Dissent

PAGE 219

◆   The key documents in the UN system covering freedom of expression
and related cultural rights, protections and states' responsibilities are
presented in Appendices II through to IX.   ◆

The adjudication on universal human rights will necessarily be a matter of law, its resolution contingent upon historical and political circumstance. In terms of this universality, however, a wider question and irony might reasonably be raised as to whether an organization like the UN, whose presence is so all-pervasive, does not itself demonstrate certain — albeit benign — totalitarian tendencies similar to those it was created to counteract. The following chapter examines some of the mechanisms that exist at the organizational level of the UN and by which the international community maintains what could be called the state control of freedom.

References

Ayton-Shenker, Diane (1995) 'The Challenge of Human Rights and Cultural Diversity'. Geneva: United Nations Department of Public Information.

Baratta, Joseph Preston (2004) *The Politics of World Federation.* Westport, Connecticut; London: Praeger.

Bennett, Michael N. and Finnemore, Martha (2004) *Rules for the World: International Organizations in Global Politics.* Ithaca, N.Y.: Cornell University Press.

Boulden, Jane and Weiss, Thomas G. (eds.) (2004) *Terrorism and the UN: Before and After September 11.* Bloomington Indiana: Indiana University Press.

Bowles, Newton R. (2004) *The Diplomacy of Hope: The United Nations Since the Cold War.* London: I.B. Tauris.

Casanova (1994) *Religion and Public Governance.* Chicago. Chicago University Press.

Fasulo, Linda M. (2004) *An Insider's Guide to the UN.* New Haven, Connecticut; London: Yale University Press.

Forsythe, David P. (2000) *Human Rights in International Relations.* Cambridge: Cambridge University Press.

Ghandhi, P.R. (eds.) (2004) *Blackstone's Statutes International Human Rights Documents,* 4th edition. Oxford: Oxford University Press.

Krasno, Jean E. (ed.) (2004) *The United Nations: Confronting the Challenges of a Global Society.* Boulder Colorado; London: Lynne Rienner Publishers.

Magee, Bryan (1985) *Karl Popper.* New York: Viking.

Mertus, Julie (2005) *The United Nations and Human Rights.* London: Routledge.

Ryan, Stephen *The United Nations and International Politics.* London: Macmillan, 2000.

Schlesinger, Stephen, C. *Act of Creation: The Founding of the United Nations.* Boulder, Colorado: Westview Press.

Sellars, Kirsten (2002) *The Rise and Rise of Human Rights.* London: Sutton.

Smith, Rhona K.M. (2005) *Textbook on International Human Rights,* 2nd edition. Oxford: Oxford University Press.

United Nations (1993) *World Conference on Human Rights: The Vienna Declaration and Programme of Action.* New York: United Nations.

Weiss, Thomas G., Forsythe, David, P., and Coate, Roger A. (2004) *The United Nations and Changing World Politics.* Boulder, Colorado; Oxford: Westview Press.

Wellman, Carl (2000) *The Proliferation of Rights: Moral Progress or Empty Rhetoric?* Oxford: Westview.

Ziring, Lawrence, Riggs, Robert E. and Plano, Jack C. (2005) *The United Nations: International Organization and World Politics,* 4th edition. Australia; UK: Thomson/Wadsworth.

Selected Electronic Source

> ### *If you only visit one website on The United Nations, go to*
>
> www.un.org
>
> (and follow links to human rights, freedom of expression, and an entire host of issues in international relations, including the full documents referred to this in chapter, including the Universal Declaration of Human Rights (several hundred languages available).
>
> A particularly useful advance database resource for further research is the United Nations Dag Hammarskjöld Library, go to: www.un.org (and follow links).

Freedom of Expression and Human Rights
Contemporary Historical, Literary and Political Contexts

The State Control of Freedom

The UN and Its Inter-Governmental Organizations (IGOs)

Everyone has the right to freedom of thought, conscience and religion.

Article 18, *Universal Declaration of Human Rights*

Everyone has the right to freedom of opinion and expression; this right includes freedom to hold opinions without interference and to seek, receive and impart information and ideas through any media and regardless of frontiers.

Article 19, *Universal Declaration of Human Rights*

If truth is the first casualty of war, freedom of expression remains the first target of the totalitarian. The immediate post-Second World War context was itself centred round re-establishing such civil and political freedoms threatened by totalitarianism, and building an international consensus over shared human values that would later form the basis for human rights norms in international legislation. In the early years of the UN era the prime focus on freedom of expression was in terms of dealing with the specific wartime — and indeed Cold War — issue of propaganda. Such concerns were predominantly, but not exclusively, related to journalism, and to the public and accurate reporting of events which could, if misreported, incite discord between nations. Beyond Articles 18 and 19 in the 1948 Universal Declaration of Human Rights, these preoccupations are made manifest in the 1952 Convention on the International Right of Correction.

When we examine the focus for freedom of expression in the earliest years of the UN, we find pernicious ideology; its propaganda was a major threat to both freedom of expression and international peace and security. We see, particularly, that freedom of expression as a human right is integral to notions of responsibility in reporting and in the wider aspects of media. In the 1952 Convention on the International Right of Correction stress was placed upon the relationship between freedom of expression and the restraints of human rights law. The 1952 Convention was and remains, a defense against propaganda, including ideological bias within the media which is now, of course, more diverse than it was half a century ago. The Convention places freedom of expression integrally within the human rights system: without the maintenance of peace and security that underpin the Convention all human rights are threatened, and the threat is perceived as coming from propaganda, suppression of the press, radio and television, and related infringements of freedoms of expression. Such repressions are invariably indicative that other democratic freedoms and universal human rights are being denied. Freedom of expression is not only a barometer of other potential infringements of human rights but foundational to good and peaceful governance.

The preamble of the Convention on the International Right of Correction begins with the statement that the contracting states desire 'to implement the right of their peoples to be fully and reliably informed' and 'to improve understanding between their peoples through the free flow of information and opinion'. The post-World War Two context is immediately evident with the rejoinder that this will thereby protect humankind 'from the scourge of war, to prevent the recurrence of aggression from any source, and to combat all propaganda which is either designed or likely to provoke or encourage any threat to peace, breach of the peace, or act of aggression'. False reporting and propaganda are as potentially harmful post-conflict as they are in war, the publication of inaccurate reports are a 'danger to the maintenance of friendly relations between peoples and to the preservation of peace'. In a world before mass television, global media and Internet, radio and print journalism were the original principle targets for the Convention, especially in the context of states that did not 'provide for a right of correction of which foreign governments may avail themselves'. The Convention sets out desirability 'to institute such a right on the international level'.

Convention on the International Right of Correction
16 December 1952 (entry into force 24 August 1962)

Article 1 presents definitions of the terms of the Convention:

1. "News dispatch" means news material transmitted in writing or by means of telecommunications, in the form customarily employed by information agencies in transmitting such news material, before publication, to newspapers, news periodicals and broadcasting organizations.

2. "Information agency" means a press, broadcasting, film, television or facsimile organization, public or private, regularly engaged in the collection, and dissemination of news material, created and organized under the laws and regulations of the Contracting State in which the central organization is domiciled and which, in each Contracting State where it operates, functions under the laws and regulations of that State.

3. "Correspondent" means a national of a Contracting State or an individual employed by an information agency of a Contracting State, who in either case is regularly engaged in the collection and the reporting of news material, and who when outside his State is identified as a correspondent by a valid passport or by a similar document internationally acceptable.

Article 2 provides an overview of 'the professional responsibility of correspondents and information agencies' to report facts 'without discrimination and in their proper context and thereby to promote respect for human rights and fundamental freedoms, to further international understanding and co-operation and to contribute to the maintenance of international peace and security'. It also states that 'all correspondents and information agencies should, in the case of news dispatches transmitted or published by them and which have been demonstrated to be false or distorted, follow the customary practice of transmitting through the same channels, or of publishing corrections of such dispatches'. Its concern is with news dispatches 'capable of injuring its relations with other states or its national prestige or dignity transmitted from one country to another by correspondents or information agencies' where such is published abroad and is 'false or distorted'. In such cases, the offended party 'may submit its version of the facts' — defined in the Convention as a 'communiqué' — to the contracting states 'within whose territories such dispatch has been published or disseminated. A copy of the communiqué shall be forwarded at the same time to the correspondent or information agency concerned to enable that correspondent or information agency to correct the news dispatch in question'. Such communiqués 'may be issued only with respect to news dispatches and must be without comment or expression of opinion' and no longer 'than is necessary to correct the alleged inaccuracy or distortion'.

Article 3 states that 'with the least possible delay and in any case not later than five clear days from the date of receiving a communiqué' a State, 'whatever be its opinion concerning the facts in question', shall:

'I (a) Release the communiqué to the correspondents and information agencies operating in its territory through the channels customarily used for the release of news concerning international affairs for publications; and

(b) Transmit the communiqué to the headquarters of the information agency whose correspondent was responsible for originating the dispatch in question, if such headquarters are within its territory.

2. In the event that a Contracting State does not discharge its obligation under this article, with respect to the communiqué of another Contracting State, the latter may accord, on the basis of reciprocity, similar treatment to a communiqué thereafter submitted to it by the defaulting State.'

Article 4 states that if any of the Contracting States to which a communiqué has been transmitted fails to fulfil the set obligations laid down redress may be made to the Secretary-General of the United Nations.

Article 5 states that 'Any dispute between any two or more Contracting States concerning the interpretation or application of the present Convention which is not settled by negotiations shall be referred to the International Court of Justice for decision unless the Contracting States agree to another mode of settlement.'

Articles 6–14 contain reference to administrative detail on the process of signing (**Article 6**) ratification (**Articles 7** and **8**), the extent of the provisions of the Convention (**Article 9**), denunciation (**Article 10**), when the Convention will cease to be in force (**Article 11**), requests for revision (**Article 12**), responsibilities of the Secretary-General in terms of notification (**Article 13**), the translations and deposition of the Convention (**Article 14**).

The 1952 Convention on the International Right of Correction constructs a new, post-Second World War and UN-era discourse of responsibility for fair reporting and the right to amendment of *unfair* reporting and redress against propaganda. The Convention was arguably the first international elaboration upon the right to freedom of expression encapsulated in Article 19 of the Universal Declaration of Human Rights. These post-Second World War and early UN-era years marked the beginning of the Cold War, a protracted period of ideological conflict — freedom of expression was without doubt integrally related to the preservation of world peace and foundational to notions of global governance.

The State Control of Freedom: The UN and Its Intergovernmental Organizations

One of the great achievements of the UN is the creation of a comprehensive body of human rights law, which, according to the Secretary-General 'for the first time in history, provides us with a universal and internationally protected code of human rights, one to which all nations can subscribe and to which all people can aspire.' These include 'economic, social and cultural, as well as political and civil rights' and 'the established mechanisms with which to promote and protect these rights and to assist governments in carrying out their responsibilities' (www.un.org, and follow links). The UN has, therefore, long recognized the necessity of regional or inter-state and inter-governmental organizations to implement its collective policies amongst member nations. This was reiterated by the 1993 World Conference on Human Rights at Vienna:

> Regional arrangements play a fundamental role in promoting and protecting human rights. They should reinforce universal human rights standards, as contained in international human rights instruments, and their protection. The World Conference on Human Rights endorses efforts under way to strengthen these arrangements and to increase their effectiveness, while at the same time stressing the importance of cooperation with the United Nations human rights activities.
>
> The World Conference on Human Rights reiterates the need to consider the possibility of establishing regional and sub-regional arrangements for the promotion and protection of human rights where they do not already exist. (UN, 1993: Para 37)

The existence of a considerable IGO network is indication of the UN's well-established mechanisms for the state and inter-state monitoring and control of human rights. Such an IGO network, at regional and sub-regional levels, can be shown as an indicator of the inter-state and state control of cultural freedoms.

Through a universalizing human rights discourse, the UN has thus developed its global reach not only in legal and political or inter-state organizational terms but in its areas of economic, cultural and social interest. Even if there is often impotence in implementation, there is one rather odd — and perhaps oddly significant — consequence of the notion that universal human rights should govern not only international law but a wide range of cultural freedoms. For if state intrusion into all aspects of social life defines totalitarianism, in its all-encompassing scope of operation, the UN may — albeit in benign form — be less distant from such a polity than we might imagine. Indeed, even the UN's devoted attention to cultural life — acutely evident in concerns over freedom of expression — is an indication of its desire to control and restrict it (Ayton-Shenker, 1995). Immense technological advances have made global governance possible. It may be one of the great ironies of universal human rights and the UN era that, in counteracting totalitarianism with the notion of universal human rights, based on open governance and freedom of expression, the UN created a system for the unremitting and complete control of freedom.

It is amidst this seemingly universal and pervasive context — of human rights, of democratic discourse, of free expression of critique — that an American journalist made himself a worldwide reputation for encapsulating in a phrase the supposed post-Cold War victory of liberal democracy based upon universal human rights above all other political ideologies (Fukuyama, 1992). Thus Francis Fukuyama proudly proclaimed 'the end of history', a refrain with a certain catchy and appealing resonance, but worryingly triumphalist. Given the Marxist emphasis on a deterministic historical determinism, the language of the end of history was no doubt calculated.

We might note, then, that much history has taken place since 1989, and the post-Cold-War era: 9/11, war in Afghanistan, war in Iraq, and the beginning of unpredictable post-7/7 period in England (Baratta, 2004; Barnett and Finnemore, 2004; Bowles, 2004; Boulden and Weiss, 2004; Fasulo, 2004; Krasno, 2004). Indeed, it was in the aftermath of the fall of the

Berlin Wall — defining the end of the Cold War — that another American defined an emergent trend which seemed to suggest that history had not ended but merely entered a new phase after a battle with a newly overcome enemy. It was no accident that 'the end of the civilization' doctrine reappeared (Huntington, 1991), as the 'end of history' thesis had, at the end of the Cold War. Huntington's clash of civilizations notion was that western supremacy had weakened in the face of a decline of its Christian theological beliefs, thus allowing the rise of a powerful, single-minded Islamic world — a battle which Huntington suggests has been a dominating influence upon western history. The one determining difference between the end of the first Gulf War in the early 1990s and the war in Iraq a decade later has been the consolidation of resistance through 'Islamic' militancy. Yet, it is clear that, at present, the consensus over democracy and human rights are of sufficient force to prevail, if simply because of overbearing economic and military might of powerful members of the UN Security Council (Krasno, 2004; Weiss, Forsythe and Coate, 2004; Ziring, Riggs and Plano, 2005). Nevertheless, there remains the longer prospect of a battle over what is a culturally secular and predominantly western notion of democratic governance, universal human rights and freedom of expression. The challenge will be from new forms of totalitarianism, predominantly religiously-motivated and thus transnational, but also emergent from global, inter-state bodies such as the UN.

The apparently easy post-Cold War consensus through democracy and human rights has, therefore, been widely contested, with claims that this consensus has been brought about by strong economic interests, that such consent is *manufactured*, that it is *constructed* and in a sense *enforced*; another, more seemingly benign form of imperialism in a post-colonial era (Said, 1996; Chomsky, 2000; 2002; Herman and Chomsky, 2002). Indeed, the discourse of universal human rights has often been hijacked by economically and politically powerful and media-savvy self interest (Chomsky, 2002; Herman and Chomsky, 2002). Claims by Chomsky et al. relate to the manner in which the language of democracy, liberty and human rights has been used, in particular by the West, as a means of maintaining economic and political control. Political actions in the name of democracy, liberty and human rights can conceal manipulation and the manufacture of consent.

There are a number of related and equally contentious aspects to human rights in the context of this history. Not least here powerful states can make implementation *structurally* inequitable, as one commentator outlines in a succinct summary:

- A study of the discourse of human rights since the Second World War suggests that the rhetoric of human rights has been determined most clearly by the propaganda value it represented.
- The difference in the sort of human rights different states proclaimed was dictated by the political ideology of each state.
- International institutions with power tend to reflect the interests of powerful states.
- International financial institutions have, by their operation, made the protection of economic rights almost impossible for poor states.
- The economic interests of wealthy states have led indirectly but regularly to human rights abuse whether, for instance, through the export of tobacco, the export of pesticides or the export of subsidized food.
- The aftermath of colonialism continues to bedevil colonial peoples in their attempts to promote and secure self-determination.
- Finally, regardless of proclaimed international standards on human rights, there are some states which may regularly, persistently and blatantly ignore world opinion if their strategic or emotional importance is exceptional. (Mansell, 1999: 49)

With the 'defeat' of Soviet Communism, liberal democracy based upon universal human rights may be seen as having prevailed. Mansell's list of the way human rights discourse has been manipulated should make us wary, however, of politically coercive actions that may be justified under the guise of liberty, or human rights, or freedom of expression. Victory for one political force in the name of such liberties may for another be but a more subtle form of control.

Arguably the contentious aspects of human rights are most obvious when intergovernmental or state control of such freedom might seem to be *least* necessary, for example in the sphere of culture. From 1993, for instance, the UN established a Special Rapporteur on the Promotion and Protection of the Right to Freedom of Opinion and Expression. The mandate arose from concerns in Geneva by the High Commission for Human Rights over human rights abused specifically through abuses of freedom of expression:

> concerns at the extensive occurrence of detention, long-term detention and extrajudicial killing, torture, intimidation, persecution and harassment, including through the abuse of legal provisions on defamation and criminal libel as well as on surveillance, search and seizure, and censorship, of threats and acts of violence and of discrimination directed at persons who exercise the right to freedom of opinion and expression, including the right to seek, receive and impart information, and the intrinsically linked rights to freedom of thought, conscience and religion, peaceful assembly and association and the right to take part in the conduct of public affairs, as well as at persons who seek to promote the rights affirmed in the Universal Declaration of Human Rights and the International Covenant on Civil and Political Rights and seek to educate others about them, or who defend those rights and freedoms, including legal professionals and others who represent persons exercising those rights, and calls on states to put an end to these violations and to bring to justice those responsible.

The High Commission for Human Rights requested the Special Rapporteur:

> a)   to gather all relevant information, wherever it might occur, of discrimination against, threats or use of violence and harassment, including persecution and intimidation, directed at persons seeking to exercise or to promote the exercise of the right to freedom of opinion and expression as affirmed in the Universal Declaration of Human Rights and, where applicable, the International Covenant on Civil and Political Rights, taking into account the work being conducted by other mechanisms of the Commission and Sub-Commission which touched on that right, with a view to avoiding duplication of work;
>
> b)   as a matter of high priority, to gather all relevant information, wherever it might occur, of discrimination against, threats or use of violence and harassment, including persecution and intimidation, against professionals in the field of information seeking to exercise or to promote the exercise of the right to freedom of opinion and expression;
>
> c)   to seek and receive credible and reliable information from governments and non-governmental organizations and any other parties who have knowledge of these cases; and to submit annually to the Commission a report covering the activities relating to his or her mandate, containing recommendations to the Commission and providing suggestions on ways and means to better promote and protect the right to freedom of opinion and expression in all its manifestations. (See Appendix 5)

More widely still, the organ of the UN most closely associated with the protection of cultural heritage and cultural freedoms is the United Nations Educational, Scientific and Cultural Organization (UNESCO). UNESCO — based in Paris (www.unesco.org) — was formed in the post-War period to cater for the immediate social and cultural needs of those worst affected by the global conflict. The argument that an organization such as the UN — set up to protect freedoms against totalitarianism — has itself emerged as a force for the very totalitarianism it sought to counteract is undoubtedly contentious, and more contentious when we consider that many of the states belonging to the UN system are not themselves democracies. The argument around cultural control specifically is worthy of further reflection.

UNESCO was founded on 16 November 1945. As with many other organizations formed at that time, its scope and range of activity rapidly expanded (UNESCO, 2002). A key organ for the UN monitoring of cultural human rights machinery (including human rights education), UNESCO has a strong national and regional focus. Today UNESCO defines its 'forms of action' across a wide spectrum (UNESCO, 2002). Education, social and natural science, culture and communication are the means to a far more ambitious goal: 'to build peace in the minds of men'. UNESCO's remit, defined by its title, epitomizes the breadth of freedom of expression — education, science, and culture. Educational, scientific and cultural enterprise is freedom of expression, a freedom of expression that is seen as integral to the preservation of a world heritage:

> Heritage is our legacy from the past, what we live with today, and what we pass on to future generations. Our cultural and natural heritage are both irreplaceable sources of life and inspiration. Places as unique and diverse as the wilds of East Africa's Serengeti, the Pyramids of Egypt, the Great Barrier Reef in Australia and the Baroque cathedrals of Latin America make up our world's heritage. What makes the concept of World Heritage exceptional is its universal application. World Heritage sites belong to all the peoples of the world, irrespective of the territory on which they are located. The United Nations Educational, Scientific and Cultural Organization (UNESCO) seeks to encourage the identification, protection and preservation of cultural and natural heritage around the world considered to be of outstanding value to humanity.

UNESCO's aims are embodied in an international treaty called the Convention concerning the Protection of the World Cultural and Natural Heritage adopted by UNESCO in 1972. They define their World Heritage mission as to:

- encourage countries to sign the World Heritage Convention and to ensure the protection of their natural and cultural heritage;
- encourage States Parties to the Convention to nominate sites within their national territory for inclusion on the World Heritage List;
- encourage States Parties to establish management plans and set up reporting systems on the state of conservation of their World Heritage sites;
- help States Parties safeguard World Heritage properties by providing technical assistance and professional training;
- provide emergency assistance for World Heritage sites in immediate danger;
- support States Parties' public awareness-building activities for World Heritage conservation;
- encourage participation of the local population in the preservation of their cultural and natural heritage;
- encourage international cooperation in the conservation of our world's cultural and natural heritage. (www.unesco.org)

An important aspect of UNESCO's work is to defend against the effects of looting, theft, illegal export and import, and illicit trafficking of cultural property. These are regarded as shared international problems that can only be solved on a global scale and through close collaboration between nation states.

One of the major initiatives here has been the creation of a UNESCO database to make available 'relevant national legislation, in the country of origin as well as abroad, to organizations, institutions, private entities or individuals having a legal question concerning an object that may have been stolen or pillaged, and/or illegally exported, imported or acquired'. With member states being invited to submit relevant national legislation on cultural property, the database will be an aide to UNESCO reinforcement of its campaign to strengthen the ratification and implementation of conventions protecting cultural heritage. The latter legislation includes 1970 UNESCO Convention on the Means of Prohibiting and Preventing the Illicit Import, Export and Transfer of Ownership of Cultural Property and the 1995 UNIDROIT Convention on Stolen or Illegally Exported Cultural Objects. More details can be found at the UNESCO website, www.unesco.org, following links to 'culture'.

◆ See Appendices III and IV ◆

UNESCO

Convention Concerning the Protection of the World
Cultural and Natural Heritage

and

World Heritage Sites List
SEE PAGES 169 AND 179

◆ These Appendices specifically refer to the Work of UNESCO in the field
of cultural freedoms and the protection of cultural heritage. ◆

The scope of UNESCO's work is illustrated also by the links the organization has to many aspects of human rights — from education through to working for democracy and pluralism, and from the range of resolutions over its six decade or so history (UNESCO, 2002). Again, as we have stated, educational, scientific and cultural enterprise is freedom of expression and this freedom of expression is integral to the preservation of a world heritage. A contemporary understanding of freedom of expression implies therefore the widest possible interpretation. It is a right which not only presupposes but demands responsibility to preserve those manifestations of human endeavour which have marked such freedoms in the past and for the future, as well as maintaining the same rights in the present.

If UNESCO's traditional focus on such cultural rights could be seen as somewhat peripheral to the 'hard' politics of international relations and global economics, post-9/11 and post-7/7, such cultural dimensions to global governance can be seen as increasingly at the core of world peace, much the same as the 1952 Convention on the International Right of Correction was in the aftermath of the Second World War. UNESCO's present (2006 and ongoing) commitment to the protection of global civilizations is indicative of this and gives us pause to consider freedom of expression as being as much about preserving the heritage of the past for the future as it is about permitting free expression in the present.

Freedom of expression — of culture in the broadest sense, and ideology or religion — has been shown to be of enduring value within, and indeed inseparable from, the very nature of open societies. If such freedom of expression is irrepressible it is also vulnerable. This is where the positive task of protection of world heritage remains an important legacy of bodies like UNESCO — freedom of expression is not simply about countering repression but also about proactively preserving collective cultural wealth.

Cultural wealth — and the rights around freedom of expression which have allowed it to flourish — is, put simplistically, threatened by three present-day sources. First, religious fundamentalism which opposes aesthetic and alternative theological worldviews is arguably the most pervasive threat to freedom of expression, and as we shall see from the next chapter, a number of sources indicate that religions and religiously dominated states that neglect freedom of religion or belief are likely to neglect not only other aspects of freedom of expression but other human rights (Marshall, 2000). Secondly, ideologically motivated dictatorial and totalitarian states which repress press, media, journalistic and internet freedoms are also likely to be unsympathetic to wider aspects of human rights, including large and populace nations where state communism is the only permitted model of governance. Thirdly, a less obvious threat, the indifference of those avowedly democratic countries that possess freedoms of expression — religious, ideological and aesthetic — and which do not guard against potential threats to its future repression, particularly through a lack of vigilance over the global forces of inter-state governance.

In all, there remains a perennial balance of freedom and legal restriction: in an open democratic society to what extent can freedom be allowed and to what extent should it be restricted. It was a matter which exercised John Stuart Mill. He concluded that only under rare and exceptional circumstances should the freedom to express critique be challenged. The law has always provided a limit to the freedom of citizens and today the maintenance of freedom remains dependent upon statutory and organizational controls, from the UN and IGOs to NGOs — and in effect the state control of freedom. It is impossible to envisage a society that is both ordered and entirely free — each age defines the limits of its freedom. The maintenance of freedom of expression is thus ultimately dependent upon the critical interrogation of any systems of national or international nature — ideological or religious — including those designed for the protection of such freedom.

◆　See Appendix X　◆

A Typology of Dissent

SEE PAGE 219

◆　It is a useful and instructive exercise to contemplate why a Typology of

Dissent is necessary, given the rights and freedoms detailed and

represented in Appendices II through to IX.　◆

Summary

All modern dictators — Hitler, Lenin, Stalin, and Mao — have sought world domination in the name of a unifying ideology with the best interests of the masses supposedly at heart. (The evangelization of the major faiths does not appear dissimilar, for ideology and theology resemble each other in seeking the best for those who know no better. Revolutions are undertaken in the name of the oppressed, inquisitions are fought for the sake of lost souls.) To the extent that it extends to all aspects of public life and to a large degree private life, the UN is — arguably and albeit contentiously stated — a totalitarian organization, preoccupied with extending a uniform legal set of obligations across all nation states and through these to the lives of all human beings, under the rubric of liberty and universal human rights. We could state this very provocatively: Hitler's preoccupation was with world government; his defeat led to the beginnings of one. It is the notion of a single set of moral norms — universal human rights — imposed internationally that remains of critical importance. Stated *less* provocatively there remains an inherent irony in any notion of freedom *controlled* by legal and governmental/inter-governmental means. The cost of cultural and related freedoms may be dependent upon the state control of them.

◆ See Appendices III and IV ◆

UNESCO

Convention Concerning the Protection of the World
Cultural and Natural Heritage

and

World Heritage Sites List

SEE PAGES 169 AND 179

◆ These Appendices specifically refer to the Work of UNESCO in the field of cultural freedoms and the protection of cultural heritage. ◆

Whether this proliferation of rights discourse — the inter-state and state intrusion, for instance, into cultural life — can be regarded as a mark of political progress is open to question (Wellman, 2000), and whether such proliferation is indicative of a benign totalitarianism could be altogether more sinister. Whether cultural heritage and freedom of expression are anything more than peripheral to more important human rights is also worth considering. For example, the cultural aims of UNESCO may lack tangibility or immediacy in comparison with world peace or the eradication of hunger. Yet, aside from those elements of freedom of expression in reporting and democratic critique that are foundational to openness in any society, the programmatic focus of the UN system in recent years has been upon those elements of world heritage (Wehdorn, 2004), including irreplaceable sites, which will mark an enduring historical legacy as to the importance of cultural rights being integral to wider civil and political rights.

◆　See Appendix VIII　◆

Freedom of Expression

Inter-Governmental and Non-Governmental Organizations: Internet Sources

SEE PAGE 205

◆　This Appendix contains a full list of organizations concerned with freedom of expression, including up-to-the-minute case studies. Organizations are listed according to themes relating to freedom of expression: Academic and Education; Artists and Musicians; the Internet; Journalists and the Media; Lawyers and Politicians; Religion; and Writers.　◆

In accepting that freedoms will always be to some extent restricted by historical circumstances, including those presented by law, there remains here — tentatively — a threefold issue of balance between: first, a globalized system of international law based on the principles of universal human rights governed through the UN as an unelected body with appointed representatives; secondly, the interests of sovereign nation states; and, thirdly, individual people, subjects and citizens with religious and related cultural values that often go beyond or even supercede state allegiances. How the freedom of expression of one community is balanced with the protection of another holding another conflicting view of freedom is never clear but part of the pragmatism of law and the contingency of history — and for the future to judge whether the state control of freedom was a measure so intrusive as to harm that which it sought to protect. The more the UN develops its bureaucracy within the lives of individual nations, and especially their cultural life, the closer it will come to govern the meaning systems of individuals, and the more it might be seen to replicate the totalitarian governance it was constructed to combat.

References

Ayton-Shenker, D. (1995) *The Challenge of Human Rights and Cultural Diversity.* Geneva: UN Department of Public Information.

Baratta, Joseph Preston (2004) *The Politics of World Federation.* Westport, Connecticut; London: Praeger.

Barnett, Michael N. and Finnemore, Martha (2004) *Rules for the World: International Organizations in Global Politics.* Ithaca, N.Y.: Cornell University Press.

Boulden, Jane and Weiss, Thomas G. (eds.) (2004) *Terrorism and the UN: Before and After September 11.* Bloomington Indiana: Indiana University Press.

Bowles, Newton R. (2004) *The Diplomacy of Hope: The United Nations Since the Cold War.* London: I.B. Tauris.

Chomsky, Noam (2000) *Rogue States: The Rule of Force in World Affairs*. Cambridge: South End Press.

Chomsky, Noam (2002) *The Umbrella of US Power: The Universal Declaration of Human Rights and the Contradictions of US Policy*. New York: Seven Stories.

Herman, Edward S. and Chomsky, Noam (2002) *Manufacturing Consent: The Political Economy of the Mass Media*. New York: Pantheon.

Fasulo, Linda M. (2004) *An Insider's Guide to the UN*. New Haven, Connecticut; London: Yale University Press.

Fukuyama, Francis (1992) *The End of History and the Last Man*. Washington, DC: American Enterprise Institute.

Ghandhi, P.R. (ed.) (2004) *Blackstone's Statutes International Human Rights Documents*, 4th edition. Oxford: Oxford University Press.

Huntington, Samuel (1992) *The Clash of Civilizations*. London: H. Hamilton.

Krasno, Jean E. (ed.) (2004) *The United Nations: Confronting the Challenges of a Global Society*. Boulder Colorado; London: Lynne Rienner Publishers.

Marshall, Paul (ed.) (2000) *Religious Freedom in the World: A Global Report on Freedom and Persecution.* London: Broadman and Holman.

Mansell, Wade (1999) 'Human Rights' in Christine Bell et al. *Teaching Human Rights*. Coventry: National Centre for Legal Education, University of Warwick.

Mertus, Julie (2005) *The United Nations and Human Rights*. London: Routledge.

Said, Edward (1996) *Culture and Imperialism*. London: Vintage.

Schlesinger, Stephen, C. *Act of Creation: The Founding of the United Nations*. Boulder, Colorado: Westview Press.

Smith, Rhoma K.M. (2005) *Textbook on International Human Rights*, 2nd edition. Oxford: Oxford University Press.

UNESCO (2002) *UNESCO Resolutions, Decisions 1946–2001*. Paris: UNESCO.

United Nations (1993) *World Conference on Human Rights: The Vienna Declaration and Programme of Action.* New York: United Nations.

United Nations (1998) *Report of the UN High Commissioner on Human Rights*. UN: Geneva.

Wehdorn, Manfred (2004) *A Guide to the UNESCO World Heritage Sites*. New York: Springer Wein.

Weiss, Thomas G., Forsythe, David, P., and Coate, Roger A. (2004) *The United Nations and Changing World Politics*. Boulder, Colorado; Oxford: Westview Press.

Wellman, Carl (2000) *The Proliferation of Rights: Moral Progress or Empty Rhetoric?* Oxford: Westview.

Ziring, Lawrence, Riggs, Robert E. and Plano, Jack C. (2005) *The United Nations: International Organization and World Politics*, 4th edition. Australia; UK: Thomson/Wadsworth.

Selected Electronic Sources

If you only visit one website for cultural freedom in the UN,
the following UNESCO links at
www.unesco.org
contain an immense range of up-to-date information on all aspects of
the protection of cultural freedoms.

United Nations Educational, Scientific and Cultural Organization (UNESCO) — Paris, France
www.unesco.org (and follow links)

Division of Human Rights, Democracy, Peace & Tolerance
www.unesco.org (and follow links)

Multiculturalism
www.unesco.org (and follow links)

Linguistic rights
www.unesco.org (and follow links)

Religious rights
www.unesco.org (and follow links)

Cultural heritage
www.unesco.org/culture/heritage (and follow links)

Intercultural dialogue and pluralism
www.unesco.org/culture (and follow links)

World Intellectual Property Organization (WIPO) - Geneva, Switzerland
www.wipo.int (and follow links)

Traditional Knowledge
www.wipo.org/traditionalknowledge (and follow links)

Universal Declaration on Linguistic Rights
www.troc.es/ciemen/mercator (and follow links)

Writing and Human Rights
Towards a Typology for the Interrogation of Dissent

The spirit of revolt can only exist where a theoretic equality conceals great factual inequalities.

Albert Camus' *The Rebel*

Freedom of expression is integrally related — in its possession, in its repression, in its conceptualization — to the manner, context, conditions and time of its articulation. In other words, at some key times within history there have been certain texts which have exercised a powerful influence upon defining the nature and limit of freedom of expression, and indeed wider conceptualizations of liberty and general principles of governance. Whether ancient Greek or early Christian, Reformation or Enlightenment, Nazi totalitarianism or communistic dictatorship of the proletariat, or contemporary democratic and rights-centred libertarian governance in the UN era, each age defines and limits the extent of its liberty; and, in turn, its capacity for freedom of expression according to currently dominant systems of governance.

It was Mill, in the nineteenth century, who articulated the problem of what limits might be placed upon such freedoms in open democratic context — similar in the nineteenth century as they were in the twentieth, as they will be in the twenty-first. What is the nature and natural limit of liberty? Are there circumstances in which freedom of expression needs to be restricted? The answers to these questions — what limits there should there be to liberty and freedom of expression — have their origins in the liberal tradition that Mill did so much to articulate. Achieving the balance between the right of an individual or group to express their ideas freely and the right of others not to be harmed remains a perennial problem for law and government, its resolution the matter for present-day politics and the judgments of history.

In the present volume case study texts have been selected from different historical periods to demonstrate how certain key writings have epitomized issues around the delineation of freedom of expression for their time. Freedom of expression is never statically defined, however, and once written many key historical texts continue to exercise a profound influence upon subsequent centuries, long after they were originally written. In the context of our discussions we might frequently place books as victims — objects and cultural artefacts to be burnt or otherwise repressed as a symbol of cultural and wider intolerance. Yet books themselves and indeed their authors — as well as subsequent interpreters and exegetes — are often the instigators of oppression against dissent. It is barely possible to think of a systematic oppression that was not founded upon a text from which the inspiration to burn or otherwise destroy originated — whether the purgative fires of the Inquisition or the furnaces of the death camps — such violence will have its origins in some written form or another, ideas originating inevitably in the edicts or the interpretations of a book, whether through the misuse of a religious text such as the Bible or in following the hatred of a book like *Mein Kampf* to its natural, murderous conclusion. We might regard the twenty-five centuries of our study — overviews through key texts — as representing writings that have exercised influence to greater or lesser degrees. Sometimes the influence of texts like those of Plato or Augustine have been both benign and malignant and spread over many centuries, other texts like *Mein Kampf* have exercised a sharp and rapid, almost instantaneously murderous effect.

Writing and Human Rights: Towards a Typology for the Interrogation of Dissent

Writing has always been the essential means of promulgating a notion of rights: conventions, declarations, bills of rights, books all manifestly present written statements defining the roles and responsibilities of citizens within a state. Though the significance of other forms of cultural expression such as music and information media cannot be downplayed (Jones, 2001; Commonwealth Secretariat, 2003; Blecha, 2004; Randall, 2005), the relationship between writing and human rights is interdependent; language and writing are integrally related to the development of all enduring philosophies and theologies — tolerant and totalitarian. The burning of books is thus historically always the epitome of *in*tolerance. Open debate about freedom of expression — whether literary, political or religious — is, as we see today, central to issues of peace and security. Throughout history, freedom of expression remains fundamental rather than peripheral to politics, justice and the social order, and in contemporary language we conceptualize this through human rights discourse. The denial of freedom of expression is all too likely to anticipate, under the correctly fraught political contexts, macabre infringements of human rights.

In this regard, it is possible to discern two trends that are equally applicable to post-Cold War, post-9/11 and post-7/7 contexts: the *decline* of Communist state ideology as a source of repressive measures against freedom of expression and the *rise* of theologically inspired repression. Written in a pre-9/11 and pre-7/7 world, Ayton Shenker's brief but important UN Report — *The Challenge of Human Rights Diversity* — summarizes the post-Cold War phenomenon, especially the emergent tensions between cultural and especially religious traditions and universal human rights:

> The end of super-power rivalry, and the growing North-South disparity in wealth and access to resources, coincide with an alarming increase in violence, poverty and unemployment, homelessness, displaced persons and the erosion of environmental stability . . . At the same time previously isolated peoples are being brought together by the increasing integration of markets, the emergence of new regional political alliance, and remarkable advances in telecommunications, biotechnology and transportation that have prompted demographic shift. The resulting confluence of peoples and cultures is, in an increasingly global, multi-

cultural world, brimming with tension, confusion and conflict in the process of pluralism. There is an understandable urge to return to old traditional cultures, fundamental values, and the familiar, seemingly — of one's identity. Without a secure sense of identity amidst the turmoil people may resort to isolationism, ethnocentrism and intolerance. (Ayton-Shenker 1995: 1)

Ayton-Shenker argues that cultural relativism (the word fundamentalism is not used) is a potential threat to universal human rights and that neither state nor religious tradition can override rights established by international law. This is a defence against charges of moral imperialism often brought against the UN itself. She argues that this hard-won consensus is a legal safeguard, not the province of any particular region or set of cultural traditions:

> More directly, human rights facilitate respect for and protection of cultural diversity through the establishment of cultural rights embodied in instruments of human rights law. These include: the International Bill of Human Rights; the Convention on the Rights of the Child; the International Convention on the Elimination of Racial Discrimination; the Declaration on Race and Racial Prejudice; the Elimination of all Forms of Intolerance and of Discrimination based Religion or Belief; the Declaration on the Principles of International Cultural Co-Operation; the Declaration on the Rights of Persons Belonging to National or Ethnic, Linguistic Minorities; the Declaration on the Right to Development; the Convention on the Protection of the Rights of All Migrant Workers and Their Families; and the ILO Convention No. 169 on the Rights of Tribal Peoples. (Ayton-Shenker 1995: 2)

The suppression of freedom of public religion in Cold War states coincided with the resurgence of religion in global governance in a post-Cold War world. Trends in post-Cold War and post-9/11 and 7/7 are thus closely interrelated, but in ways which are still being outplayed.

The Index of Censorship (Petrie 2002) provides evidence of such new patterns of post-Cold War repression — after the fall of Soviet Communism, the twin influences of the rise of nationalism and trans-national religious fundamentalism. In some cases the nationalism is supported by and founded upon a religious intolerance, as for example in Georgia, Stalin's birthplace, the Caucus region south of Russia. Here, after many years of Communist repression, the resurgence of Orthodox Christianity, particularly by the country's most famous son, has led to a re-discovery of Georgia's distinctive roots in Christian tradition, including the founding of Georgia as a nation. This nationalism however has not instilled a toleration of religious minorities in a country inexperienced in either democracy or its new freedoms. The resurgence of trans-national religious fundamentalism has been apparent since the end of the Cold War — facilitated by the removal of the communistic repressions of religious, cultural and national differences (de Baets, 2001; Jones, 2001; Gearon 2002). In recognition of the plight of persecuted writers, Human Rights Watch provides Hellman–Hammett Grants — small awards of financial assistance — to writers (literary and journalistic) who have suffered persecution. The Hellman–Hammett Grants are named after Lillian Hellman and Dashiell Hammett who were interrogated in the 1950s by the Un-American Activities Committee headed by Wisconsin Senator Joseph R. McCarthy. Details of the award and its origins, as well as biographies of persecuted writers, those who have received awards, can be found at www.hrw.org, and by following links. As gauged by these Hellman-Hammett awards, pre- and post-9/11 infringements of freedoms of expression show notable increases in two forms of repression: nationalistically-based repression within, and religiously-based repressions within and beyond the borders of states.

◆ See Appendix VIII ◆

Freedom of Expression

Inter-Governmental and Non-Governmental Organizations: Internet Sources

PAGE 205

◆ Read this Appendix for details of NGOs working on issues of freedom of expression — and for up-to-the-minute sources on present-day, geo-political contexts. ◆

Many Non-Governmental Organizations are committed to the area of religious freedom and present evidence on the ground of such developments, within former communist countries and beyond. The International Association for Freedom of Religion, for instance, presents the following case studies from March 2001 until March 2003 under five headings, all concerned with the repression of religious freedoms in the light of religion's post-Cold War resurgence:

1. Restrictive legislation

- Passage of a restrictive religion law, widely criticized for its overly broad interpretations of what is considered appropriate religious practice. (France)
- Strict registration requirements and general monopoly of the Orthodox Church in some regions, resulting in discrimination of other churches and religions. (Russia)
- A law was drafted, which gave only certain churches and communities the status of a legal entity. Others would have had to fulfil various conditions in order to be registered. (Serbia)
- Passage of a restrictive religion law, which prohibits religions that have existed in the country for less than 20 years from publishing literature or setting up missions. (Belarus)

2. Violence against specific religious or belief groups

- Escalating group violence against worshippers of non-Orthodox faiths, especially Evangelical Christians and Jehovah's Witnesses. The government has failed to prosecute those responsible. (Georgia)
- Assaults on Jews and vandalizing of their homes, businesses, and places of worship. (Belgium, Germany, and the UK)
- Physical assaults on Muslims, firebombing of mosques, and hate speeches directed towards the Muslim community. (USA and Australia)
- Bloody religious clashes between Muslims and Christians (N. Nigeria) and between Muslims and Hindus. (India)

3. Human rights discriminations against religious or belief groups

- Prohibitions on the wearing of headscarves for Muslim women. (Turkey)
- Muslims are denied rights of citizenship and cannot receive national identity cards. Among other things, this effects their ability to get jobs. (Burma)
- Members of the Bahá'í Faith are denied pensions and opportunities for students to go on to tertiary education are also denied. (Iran)

- Town councils have refused to register the residencies of certain belief groups. (Japan)

4. Incidents involving religious property

- Destruction of two Buddhist statues, which were renowned as both religious and archaeological treasures. (Afghanistan)
- Destruction of mosques by security forces as well as series of attacks on Orthodox churches by unknown arsonists. (Macedonia)
- Lack of restitution of property to mosques and churches, which continue to be state owned. (Bulgaria and Romania)
- Public worship by non-Muslims is banned and places of worship other than mosques are not permitted. (Saudi Arabia)

5. Arrests and detentions

- Both Buddhist and Christian leaders continue to face arbitrary detention and arrest. (Vietnam)
- Only the Russian Orthodox Church and the state-approved Spiritual Directorate of Muslims are officially registered. Prayer meetings of other religious groups are frequently raided and worshippers detained. (Turkmenistan)
- Several thousand Muslims are in jail for religious reasons. (Uzbekistan)
- Members of the banned Falun Gong spiritual movement have been detained, arrested, or sent to labour camps. (China)
- Jehovah's Witnesses are jailed for their beliefs related to conscientious objection to military service. (Armenia)

For reasons such as those listed above, freedom of religion is increasingly becoming integrated with issues of freedom of expression — we are witnessing a close association of Article 18 (on freedom of religion) and Article 19 (on freedom of expression).

Such trends represent a somewhat remarkable reversal of the seemingly unstoppable post-Enlightenment secularization. Haynes's work (1998) builds on Casanova's (1994) foundational challenge to the secularization thesis — that in modern society religion becomes less and less relevant to public governance. This principle has been central to the historical separation of religion and the state in many modern democracies. And since the formation of the UN, human rights issues related to religion or belief have been the focus of several international instruments:

- The Universal Declaration of Human Rights (1948)
- The Arcot Krishnaswami Study (1959)
- The International Covenant on Civil and Political Rights (1966)
- The International Covenant on Social, Economic and Cultural Rights (1966)
- The Declaration on the Elimination of All Forms of Intolerance and Discrimination Based on Religion or Belief (1981)
- Declaration on the Rights of Persons Belonging to National or Ethnic, Religious and Linguistic Minorities (18 December 1992)
- Oslo Declaration on Freedom of Religion and Belief (1998)
- World Conference against Racism, Xenophobia and Related Forms of Discrimination (September, 2002)

  For full texts, follow links at www.unhchr.org

As Lerner comments, Article 18 greatly influenced the texts incorporated in the 1966 Covenants, and was influential in regional treaties and the 1981 Declaration, and subsequent pronouncements (Lerner 2000; cf. Baratta, 2004; Barnett, 2004).

There are three general points to note from such developments. First, after a long neglect (or low level treatment) of religion explicitly, the UN, from the late 1970s particularly, began to recognize the international significance of religion for a stable world order. The preamble to the UN Declaration on the Elimination of All Forms of Intolerance and Discrimination Based on Religion or Belief (1981) restates the wider context of Charter of the UN. Notably this reiterates the 'dignity and equality inherent in all human beings', international commitment on the promotion of universal human rights and fundamental freedoms for all, 'without distinction as to race, sex, language or religion' and 'the principles of non-discrimination and equality before the law and the right to freedom of thought, conscience, religion and belief'. During the 1990s, religion emerges explicitly in numerous international statements, gaining a new and unprecedented prominence. First, there was the Cairo Declaration on Human Rights in Islam (1990), the Fundamental Agreement between the Holy See and the State of Israel (1993). The Vienna Declaration and Plan of Action (1993) and the follow-up to the World Conference on Human Rights (1998) also gave some prominence to religion, important in their respective post-Yugoslavia and post-Rwanda contexts, a prominence given to religion that culminated in the Oslo Declaration on Freedom of Religion and Belief (1998). Secondly, and indicated by both the 1981 Declaration and the 1998 Oslo Declaration, the notion of freedom of religion was itself extended to freedom of religion and belief to allow for a wider interpretation of worldviews. Thirdly, this in turn has had the effect of linking in a fairly direct way rights of 'freedom of thought, conscience and religion' to 'later generation rights' of human solidarity (Wellman, 2000), most notable in the linking of religious intolerance to the ending of racism, xenophobia and discrimination more broadly. For example, we might note that the 1981 Declaration on the Elimination of All Forms of Intolerance and of Discrimination Based on Religion or Belief was followed just over a decade later by the UN Declaration on the Rights of Persons Belonging to National or Ethnic, Religious, and Linguistic Minorities (1992). While a post-9/11 and post 7/7 context has *further* highlighted the issue of potential violent conflict in worldview, the issue of this fissure between universal rights and particular cultural, especially religious traditions has, clearly, been a critical issue for many years before these dates; the cruel historical irony here should not be lost: the World Conference Against Racism, Xenophobia and Other Forms of Discrimination in Durban, South Africa (September 2001) concluded its business on an 'optimistic note', according to one major human rights organization, on 10 September 2001 (HRW, 2001).

The broad trend — linking freedom of religion or belief and freedom of expression — is more widely confirmed by two important contexts, both US-based, where religion and rights are seen as a barometer of wider democratic freedoms: the United States legislature and an American based NGO called Freedom House. First, the 1998 International Religious Freedom Act made it a requirement for the US Secretary of State to publish an Annual Report on religious freedom worldwide. Published each September, the Annual Report on International Religious Freedom is submitted to the Committee on International Relations at the US House of Representatives and the Committee on Foreign Relations of the US Senate by the Department of State. The report is extensive and provides country-by-country accounts of religious freedoms, the infringements of and improvements in relation to such rights to belief. It is available at www.house.gov/international_relations and www.state.gov, following links for the required year. The Report contains an extremely useful executive summary. Fundamentally, the US Department of State clearly links a country's record on freedom of religion to the issue of whether preserving this will respect other fundamental rights:

> A commitment to the inviolable and universal dignity of the human person is at the core of U.S. human rights policy abroad, including the policy of advocating religious freedom. Governments that protect religious freedom for all their citizens are more likely to protect the other fundamental human rights. Encouraging stable, healthy democracies is a vital national interest in the United States. The spread of democracy makes for good neighbours, economic prosperity, increased trade, and a decrease in conflict. (US Department of State, 2001)

The Report reiterates how, in the international domain, 'freedom of religion and conscience is one of the foundational rights in the post War system of human rights instruments.' It again makes explicit how in 'recent years, the international commitment to religious freedom has increased'. A major criticism is that the US softens criticism of countries with which it has strong alliances — for example, many of the countries heavily criticized in the 2001 Report (published pre-9/11) were less critiqued when, a year later, they were allied with the US in the 'war on terror'. For a broad and systematic critique of this US law on religious freedom, made by John Shattuck in a 2002 keynote paper to a Harvard Conference on Religion, Democracy and Human Rights entitled 'Religion, Rights and Terrorism' (go to www.harvard.edu and follow links).

Secondly, Freedom House's major achievement has been the publication of a highly accessible global survey of religious freedom (Marshall, 2000). The Freedom House global survey reviewed the state of religious freedom in the majority of the world's countries, providing useful snapshot insights into the political context of religious life in each. The survey criteria were developed from the UN Declaration on the Elimination of All Forms of Intolerance and of Discrimination Based on Religion or Belief, and related UN instruments. Even so, its assessment of the level of religious freedom may seem a little crude (there is a 1–7 scale, with 7 being the least intolerant and the US gaining an unambiguous 1). Marshall relates freedom of religion and freedom of expression, but suggests a survey of religious freedom is 'different from surveying particular human rights, such as press freedom, which focus only on particular organizations or practices. With freedom of the press, one can look at the intensity of controls on particular media and the weight of penalties applied with those controls. But, unlike press freedom, religious freedom cannot be focused on the freedoms of certain organizations and individuals. Religious freedom cuts across a wide range of human rights.'

There are too a number of NGOs specifically concerned with freedom of expression, where religious factors are increasingly coming to the fore. International P.E.N. is one such organization. International P.E.N. (Poets, Essayists, Novelists) has three guiding principles:

- To promote intellectual cooperation and understanding among writers.
- To create a world community of writers that emphasizes the central role of literature in the development of world culture.
- To defend literature against the many threats to its survival that the modern world poses.

Presidents of PEN have included Alberto Moravia, Heinrich Böll, Arthur Miller, Pierre Emmanuel, Mario Vargas Llosa and György Konrád. PEN's history is an illustrious one, existing 'to promote friendship and intellectual co-operation among writers everywhere, regardless of their political or other views' and 'to fight for freedom of expression and to defend vigorously writers suffering from oppressive regimes'. It was founded in London in 1921 by Mrs. C. A. Dawson Scott, its first president was John Galsworthy. Early members included Joseph Conrad, George Bernard Shaw and H. G. Wells. The P.E.N. Charter is based on resolutions passed at its International Congresses. P.E.N. affirms that:

1. Literature, national though it be in origin, knows no frontiers, and should remain common currency between nations in spite of political or international upheavals.
2. In all circumstances, and particularly in time of war, works of art, the patrimony of humanity at large, should be left untouched by national or political passion.
3. Members of P.E.N. should at all times use what influence they have in favour of good understanding and mutual respect between nations; they pledge themselves to do their utmost to dispel race, class and national hatreds, and to champion the ideal of one humanity living in peace in one world.
4. P.E.N. stands for the principle of unhampered transmission of thought within each nation and between all nations, and members pledge themselves to oppose any form of suppression of freedom of expression in the country and community to which they belong, as well as throughout the world wherever this is possible. P.E.N. declares for a free press and opposes arbitrary censorship in time of peace. It believes that the necessary advance of the world towards a more highly organized political and economic order renders a free criticism of governments, administrations and institutions imperative. And since freedom implies voluntary restraint, members pledge themselves to oppose such evils of a free press as mendacious publication, deliberate falsehood and distortion of facts for political and personal ends.

• Membership of P.E.N. is open to all qualified writers, editors and translators who subscribe to these aims, without regard to nationality, language, race, colour or religion.

Issues of freedom of expression colliding with freedom of religion are widely evident. For instance, the English PEN campaign *against* incitement *against* religious hate laws is based on the argument that these will inculcate unacceptable restrictions upon freedom of expression (www.pen.org.uk).

Freedom of expression — whether religious, theological or ideological — remains an increasingly key and acute barometer of wider issues of liberty, democracy and human rights in an open society. The following typology represents a means of gradating such a barometer in terms of freedom of expression — a means by which to assess whether in particular contexts the aspect of freedom of expression is under challenge and from what ideological or theological source. This five-point scale can be termed a 'typology for interrogation of dissent'.

A Typology for the Interrogation of Dissent

1. What are the areas of greatest tension between freedom of religion or belief (political/ ideological/ theological) and freedom of expression (aesthetic — artistic, literary, musical — other) and in what media (electronic, film, print, reportage, other)?
2. Is there a shift towards ideological repression? (Is this nation-state based or trans-national?)
3. Is there a shift towards increased religious repression? (Is *this* nation-state based or trans-national?)
4. Where does the pressure for *repression* of freedom of expression arise? (Is it governmental agency, inter-governmental or non-governmental organizations? Is it religiously led groups who institute pressure on governments — yet very often governments wish to separate

religion from state — or governments who are instituting pressure on religiously led groups? Are there shifts in this trend motivated by particular events?)

5. Where does the pressure for *liberalization* of freedom of expression arise — from secular or religious sources or a combination of both? (Is it governmental agency, inter-governmental or non-governmental organizations? Is it religiously led groups who institute pressure on governments — yet very often governments wish to separate religion from state — or governments who are instituting pressure on religiously led groups? Are there shifts in this trend motivated by particular events?)

The interdisciplinary implications — historical and legal, literary and philosophical, religious and theological, socio-cultural and political — are required to open further debate about freedom of expression and its centrality to issues of peace and security, encouraging conversation within and between the academy, and governmental, inter-governmental and non-governmental organizations. A typology of dissent can be tested in a range of such contexts. A typology of dissent is here presented as a means of disaggregating and interrogating the terms of and tensions between freedom of expression and its repression. In such an interrogation, writing and dissent are integrally related — we have seen that the text can just as often be the source of oppression as liberty from it.

◆   See Appendix X   ◆

A Typology of Dissent

PAGE 219

◆   The key documents in the UN system covering freedom of expression and related cultural rights, protections and states' responsibilities are presented in Appendices II through to IX. Again, Appendix VIII provides a list of inter-governmental and non-governmental organizations working with freedom of expression, often in the context of wider human rights work.   ◆

Summary

In *The Origins of Totalitarianism* Arendt (1951) asserts a three-fold phase in the historical development of all-pervasive state control. She presents an historical survey that traces the emergence of totalitarianism: from Christian anti-Semitism, through imperialism and the economic and cultural colonial expansions of the modern period when total state control first became truly possible. Indeed, this last point is central to Arendt's argument — she sees totalitarianism as being possible only in the modern world, even therefore, frighteningly epitomizing it. Only in the modern world — scientific, technologically efficient, and industrial — can the dictatorial impulse be made so efficient as to aspire to total control, and if necessary total annihilation of dissent. The Nazi concentration camps were a first instance of industrialized mass death, and one of the prime demonstrations that totalitarian control by the state is only possible when the means of control can achieve such totality. If the modern era has produced the most effective, if short-lived, totalitarian regimes, it is likely that the possibility of a state exercising, with modern technologies, total control, remains a risk for the modern world — we have seen how even a benign organization like the UN can demonstrate aspects of a totalitarian state the more it intrudes into the cultural.

Freedom of expression nevertheless remains, in all contexts, fundamental — rather than peripheral — to human rights discourse, and open debate about freedom of expression is as central to modern governance as it is to issues of peace and security. Freedom of expression — as we note from the 1952 Convention on the International Right of Correction — is always amongst the first victim of wars, just as the twin weapons of censorship and propaganda are the allies of any dictatorial peace, regardless of ideology. At times of tyranny and oppression, the writer, the artist, the film-maker and the musician can all provide a powerful focus for resistance. Oppressive regimes ensure that such forms of artistic expression, along with all aspects of the media, are controlled. The Index on Censorship defined the Cold War struggle against such repression, the 'embarrassment of tyrannies' (Webb and Bell, 1997). Today (as Appendix 8 shows), far from being a political luxury, freedom of expression is foundational to democracies, and anathema to dictatorships.

The relationship between the repression of freedom of expression and totalitarianism is always therefore a close one — as historical, literary and political texts from Plato through Hitler to Mao reveal. Modern political history, that of totalitarianism in particular, reveals mass slaughter that began with and was later consolidated by ideological repression — in Stalin's Russia, in Hitler's Germany, in Pol Pot's Cambodia, in Saddam Hussein's Iraq (Power, 2001). One of the great lessons taught by the history of totalitarianism is its impulse to end the discourse or cultural conversation of the other. The dictatorial impulse is to repress not only the voice of dissent but the life of the dissenter. The contemporary — that is the UN era — discourse of universal human rights arises from the historical circumstances of such totalitarianism. There is thus a direct causal and integral link between the repressions of totalitarianism and universal human rights, between writing and human rights.

If each age defines and limits the extent of freedom of expression within its system of governance and polity, then writers have always been necessary to articulate such determinations, and to give voice to dissent. This wider relationship between writing and freedom of expression has been evident throughout the literary texts of religious and political history — from Plato and Augustine through Luther and Paine to Marx and Mill, Hitler and Mao. Again, in the UN era there is an integral connection between the form of words that materialized in the UN Charter of 1945, the 1948 Universal Declaration of Human Rights, and the totalitarianism that provoked these declarations. Totalitarianism, and the genocide which this has so often engendered, is the ultimate attempt at silencing dissent: it was from the violence of totalitarianism that the words of the UN's Universal Declaration of Human Rights arose. The contemporary need to protect freedom of expression remains as urgent as ever; historical, literary and political contexts over more than two and a half millennia demonstrate why.

References

Arendt, Hannah [1951] (1966) *The Origins of Totalitarianism*. New York: Harcourt, Brace and World.

Ayton-Shenker, Diana (1995) 'The Challenge of Human Rights and Cultural Diversity'. Geneva: United Nations Department of Public Information.

Baratta, Joseph Preston (2004) *The Politics of World Federation*. Westport, Connecticut; London: Praeger.

Barnett, Michael N. and Finnemore, Martha (2004) *Rules for the World: International Organizations in Global Politics*. Ithaca, N.Y.: Cornell University Press.

Blecha, Peter (2004) *Taboo Tunes: A History of Banned Bands and Censored Songs*. San Francisco: Backbeat Books

Bloom, Irene, Martin, J. Paul and Proudfoot, Wayne L. (eds.) (2000) *Religious Diversity and Human Rights*. New York: Columbia University Press.

Casanova, Jose (1994) *Public Religions in the Modern World*. Chicago: Chicago University Press

Cloonan, Martin and Garofalo (eds.) (2003) *Policing Pop*. Philadelphia: Temple University Press.

Commonwealth Secretariat (2003) *Freedom of Expression, Association and Assembly: Best Practice*. London: Commonwealth Secretariat.

de Baets, Antoon (2001) *Censorship of Historical Thought: A World Guide, 1945–2000*. Westport, Conn: Greenwood Press.

Forsythe, David P. (2000) *Human Rights in International Relations*, third edition. Cambridge: Cambridge University Press.

Gearon, Liam (2002) (ed.) *Religion and Human Rights: A Reader*. Brighton and Portland: Sussex Academic Press.

Gupta, Suman (2003) *Reading Harry Potter*. Basingstoke: Palgrave.

Haynes, Jeffrey (1998) *Religion in Global Politics*. Harlow: Longman.

HRW (2001) 'Racism Conference Ends on Optimistic Note', Human Rights Watch News Report, 10 September 2001. New York: Human Rights Watch.

International Association for Religious Freedom (2001) *Centennial Reflections International Association for Religious Freedom, 1900–2000*. Assen, The Netherlands: Van Gorcum.

Jones, Derek (ed.) (2001) *Censorship: A World Encyclopedia*, four volumes. London: Fitzroy Dearborn.

Lerner, Nathan (2000) *Religion, Beliefs, and Human Rights*. Maryknoll, New York: Orbis.

Magee, Bryan (1985) *Karl Popper*. New York: Viking.

Marshall, Paul (ed.) (2000) *Religious Freedom in the World: A Global Report on Freedom and Persecution*. London: Broadman and Holman.

Mostyn, Trevor (2002) *Censorship in Islamic Societies*. London: Saqi.

Nurser, John (2005) *For All the Peoples and All Nations: Christian Churches and Human Rights*. Geneva: WCC Publications.

Petrie, Ruth (2002) *The Fall of Communism and the Rise of Nationalism: The Index Reader*. London: Index on Censorship.

Pipes, Daniel (2003) *The Rushdie Affair: The Novel, the Ayatollah, and the West*, 2nd edition. New Brunswick, N.J.; London: Transaction.

Power, Samantha (2001) *A Problem from Hell: America and the Age of Genocide*. New York: Basic Books.

Randall, Annie J. (ed.) (2005) *Music, Power and Politics*. New York; London: Routledge.

Selected Electronic Sources

If you only visit one website on Writing and Human Rights, go to
The International Freedom of Expression Exchange,
an immense hub of links for freedom of expression internationally.
www.ifex.org

Appendices

PART
III

Appendices

Appendix I

CHARTER OF THE UNITED NATIONS
Signed San Francisco, June 1945
Overview

Charter of the United Nations

Preamble

We the Peoples of the United Nations Determined

➤ to save succeeding generations from the scourge of war, which twice in our lifetime has brought untold sorrow to mankind, and

➤ to reaffirm faith in fundamental human rights, in the dignity and worth of the human person, in the equal rights of men and women and of nations large and small, and

➤ to establish conditions under which justice and respect for the obligations arising from treaties and other sources of international law can be maintained, and

➤ to promote social progress and better standards of life in larger freedom,

And for these Ends

➤ to practice tolerance and live together in peace with one another as good neighbors, and

➤ to unite our strength to maintain international peace and security, and

➤ to ensure by the acceptance of principles and the institution of methods, that armed force shall not be used, save in the common interest, and

➤ to employ international machinery for the promotion of the economic and social advancement of all peoples,

Have Resolved to Combine our Efforts to Accomplish these Aims

Accordingly, our respective Governments, through representatives assembled in the city of San Francisco, who have exhibited their full powers found to be in good and due form, have agreed to the present Charter of the United Nations and do hereby establish an international organization to be known as the United Nations.

Chapter I   Purposes and Principles

Article 1

The Purposes of the United Nations are:

1. To maintain international peace and security, and to that end: to take effective collective measures for the prevention and removal of threats to the peace, and for the suppression of acts of aggression or other breaches of the peace, and to bring about by peaceful means, and in conformity with the principles of justice and international law, adjustment or settlement of international disputes or situations which might lead to a breach of the peace;

2. To develop friendly relations among nations based on respect for the principle of equal rights and self-determination of peoples, and to take other appropriate measures to strengthen universal peace;

3. To achieve international cooperation in solving international problems of an economic, social, cultural, or humanitarian character, and in promoting and encouraging respect for human rights and for fundamental freedoms for all without distinction as to race, sex, language, or religion; and

4. To be a center for harmonizing the actions of nations in the attainment of these common ends.

Article 2

The Organization and its Members, in pursuit of the Purposes stated in Article 1, shall act in accordance with the following Principles.

1. The Organization is based on the principle of the sovereign equality of all its Members.

2. All Members, in order to ensure to all of them the rights and benefits resulting from

membership, shall fulfill in good faith the obligations assumed by them in accordance with the present Charter.

3. All Members shall settle their international disputes by peaceful means in such a manner that international peace and security, and justice, are not endangered.

4. All Members shall refrain in their international relations from the threat or use of force against the territorial integrity or political independence of any state, or in any other manner inconsistent with the Purposes of the United Nations.

5. All Members shall give the United Nations every assistance in any action it takes in accordance with the present Charter, and shall refrain from giving assistance to any state against which the United Nations is taking preventive or enforcement action.

6. The Organization shall ensure that states which are not Members of the United Nations act in accordance with these Principles so far as may be necessary for the maintenance of international peace and security.

7. Nothing contained in the present Charter shall authorize the United Nations to intervene in matters which are essentially within the domestic jurisdiction of any state or shall require the Members to submit such matters to settlement under the present Charter . . .

Chapter II   Membership

Article 3

The original Members of the United Nations shall be the states which, having participated in the United Nations Conference on International Organization at San Francisco, or having previously signed the Declaration by United Nations of January 1, 1942, sign the present Charter and ratify it in accordance with Article 110.

Article 4

1. Membership in the United Nations is open to all other peace-loving states which accept the obligations contained in the present Charter and, in the judgment of the Organization, are able and willing to carry out these obligations.

2. The admission of any such state to membership in the United Nations will be effected by a decision of the General Assembly upon the recommendation of the Security Council.

Article 5

A member of the United Nations against which preventive or enforcement action has been taken by the Security Council may be suspended from the exercise of the rights and privileges of membership by the General Assembly upon the recommendation of the Security Council. The exercise of these rights and privileges may be restored by the Security Council.

Article 6

A Member of the United Nations which has persistently violated the Principles contained in the present Charter may be expelled from the Organization by the General Assembly upon the recommendation of the Security Council.

Chapter III   Organs

Article 7

1. There are established as the principal organs of the United Nations: a General Assembly, a Security Council, an Economic and Social Council, a Trusteeship Council, an International Court of Justice, and a Secretariat.

2. Such subsidiary organs as may be found necessary may be established in accordance with the present Charter.

Article 8
The United Nations shall place no restrictions on the eligibility of men and women to partic-ipate in any capacity and under conditions of equality in its principal and subsidiary organs.

Chapter IV   The General Assembly

Composition

Article 9
1. The General Assembly shall consist of all the Members of the United Nations.
2. Each member shall have not more than five representatives in the General Assembly.

Functions and Powers

Article 10
The General Assembly may discuss any questions or any matters within the scope of the present Charter or relating to the powers and functions of any organs provided for in the present Charter, and, except as provided in Article 12, may make recommendations to the Members of the United Nations or to the Security Council or to both on any such questions or matters.

Article 11
1. The General Assembly may consider the general principles of cooperation in the mainte-nance of international peace and security, including the principles governing disarmament and the regulation of armaments, and may make recommendations with regard to such principles to the Members or to the Security Council or to both.
2. The General Assembly may discuss any questions relating to the maintenance of interna-tional peace and security brought before it by any Member of the United Nations, or by the Security Council, or by a state which is not a Member of the United Nations in accordance with Article 35, paragraph 2, and, except as provided in Article 12, may make recommendations with regard to any such questions to the state or states concerned or to the Security Council or to both. Any such question on which action is necessary shall be referred to the Security Council by the General Assembly either before or after discussion.
3. The General Assembly may call the attention of the Security Council to situations which are likely to endanger international peace and security.
4. The powers of the General Assembly set forth in this Article shall not limit the general scope of Article 10.

Article 12
1. While the Security Council is exercising in respect of any dispute or situation the func-tions assigned to it in the present Charter, the General Assembly shall not make any recommendation with regard to that dispute or situation unless the Security Council so requests.
2. The Secretary-General, with the consent of the Security Council, shall notify the General Assembly at each session of any matters relative to the maintenance of international peace and security which are being dealt with by the Security Council and shall similarly notify the General Assembly, or the Members of the United Nations if the General Assembly is not in session, immediately the Security Council ceases to deal with such matters.

Article 13
1. The General Assembly shall initiate studies and make recommendations for the purpose of:
(a) promoting international cooperation in the political field and encouraging the progres-sive development of international law and its codification;

(b) promoting international cooperation in the economic, social, cultural, educational, and health fields, and assisting in the realization of human rights and fundamental freedoms for all without distinction as to race, sex, language, or religion.

2. The further responsibilities, functions and powers of the General Assembly with respect to matters mentioned in paragraph 1(b) above are set forth in Chapters IX and X.

Article 14

Subject to the provisions of Article 12, the General Assembly may recommend measures for the peaceful adjustment of any situation, regardless of origin, which it deems likely to impair the general welfare or friendly relations among nations, including situations resulting from a violation of the provisions of the present Charter setting forth the Purposes and Principles of the United Nations.

Article 15

1. The General Assembly shall receive and consider annual and special reports from the Security Council; these reports shall include an account of the measures that the Security Council has decided upon or taken to maintain international peace and security.

2. The General Assembly shall receive and consider reports from the other organs of the United Nations.

Chapter V   The Security Council

Article 23

The Security Council shall consist of fifteen Members of the United Nations. The Republic of China, France, the Union of Soviet Socialist Republics, the United Kingdom of Great Britain and Northern Ireland, and the United States of America shall be permanent members of the Security Council. The General Assembly shall elect ten other Members of the United Nations to be non-permanent members of the Security Council, due regard being specially paid, in the first instance to the contribution of Members of the United Nations to the maintenance of international peace and security and to the other purposes of the Organization, and also to equitable geographical distribution.

The non-permanent members of the Security Council shall be elected for a term of two years. In the first election of the non-permanent members after the increase of the membership of the Security Council from eleven to fifteen, two of the four additional members shall be chosen for a term of one year. A retiring member shall not be eligible for immediate re-election.

Each member of the Security Council shall have one representative.

Functions and Powers

Article 24

1. In order to ensure prompt and effective action by the United Nations, its Members confer on the Security Council primary responsibility for the maintenance of international peace and security, and agree that in carrying out its duties under this responsibility the Security Council acts on their behalf.

2. In discharging these duties the Security Council shall act in accordance with the Purposes and Principles of the United Nations. The specific powers granted to the Security Council for the discharge of these duties are laid down in Chapters VI, VII, VIII, and XII.

3. The Security Council shall submit annual and, when necessary, special reports to the General Assembly for its consideration.

Article 25

The Members of the United Nations agree to accept and carry out the decisions of the Security Council in accordance with the present Charter.

Article 26

In order to promote the establishment and maintenance of international peace and security with the least diversion for armaments of the world's human and economic resources, the Security Council shall be responsible for formulating, with the assistance of the Military Staff Committee referred to in Article 47, plans to be submitted to the Members of the United Nations for the establishment of a system for the regulation of armaments.

Appendix II

FREEDOM OF EXPRESSION IN INTERNATIONAL LAW: THE UNITED NATIONS AND RELATED REGIONAL INTER-GOVERNMENTAL INSTRUMENTS

UNIVERSAL DECLARATION OF HUMAN RIGHTS

Adopted and proclaimed by the UN General Assembly, 10 December 1948.

Article 19

Everyone has the right to freedom of opinion and expression; this right includes freedom to hold opinions without interference and to seek, receive and impart information and ideas through any media and regardless of frontiers.

Article 20

1. Everyone has the right to freedom of peaceful assembly and association.
2. No one may be compelled to belong to an association.

Article 29

1. Everyone has duties to the community in which alone the free and full development of his personality is possible.
2. In the exercise of his rights and freedoms, everyone shall be subject only to such limitations as are determined by law solely for the purpose of securing due recognition and respect for the rights and freedoms of others and of meeting the just requirements of morality, public order and the general welfare in a democratic society.

INTERNATIONAL COVENANT ON CIVIL AND POLITICAL RIGHTS

Adopted and opened for signature, ratification and accession by UN General Assembly, 16 December 1966. Entered into force 23 March 1976.

Article 2

2. Where not already provided for by existing legislative or other measures, each State Party to the present Covenant undertakes to take the necessary steps, in accordance with its constitutional processes and with the provisions of the present Covenant, to adopt such legislative or other measures as may be necessary to give effect to the rights recognized in the present Covenant.
3. Each State Party to the present Covenant undertakes:
(a) To ensure that any person whose rights or freedoms as herein recognized are violated

shall have an effective remedy, notwithstanding that the violation has been committed by persons acting in an official capacity;

(b) To ensure that any person claiming such a remedy shall have his right thereto determined by competent judicial, administrative or legislative authorities, or by any other competent authority provided for by the legal system of the State, and to develop the possibilities of judicial remedy;

(c) To ensure that the competent authorities shall enforce such remedies when granted.

Article 5

1. Nothing in the present Covenant may be interpreted as implying for any State, group or person any right to engage in any activity or perform any act aimed at the destruction of any of the rights and freedoms recognized herein or at their limitation to a greater extent than is provided for in the present Covenant.

Article 14

1. All persons shall be equal before the courts and tribunals. In the determination of any criminal charge against him, or of his rights and obligations in a suit at law, everyone shall be entitled to a fair and public hearing by a competent, independent and impartial tribunal established by law. The Press and the public may be excluded from all or part of a trial for reasons of morals, public order (*ordre public*) or national security in a democratic society, or when the interest of the private lives of the Parties so requires, or to the extent strictly necessary in the opinion of the court in special circumstances where publicity would prejudice the interests of justice; but any judgment rendered in a criminal case or in a suit at law shall be made public except where the interest of juvenile persons otherwise requires or the proceedings concern matrimonial disputes or the guardianship of children.

Article 17

1. No one shall be subjected to arbitrary or unlawful interference with his privacy, family, home or correspondence, nor to unlawful attacks on his honour and reputation.

2. Everyone has the right to the protection of the law against such interference or attacks.

Article 19

1. Everyone shall have the right to hold opinions without interference.

2. Everyone shall have the right to freedom of expression; this right shall include freedom to seek, receive and impart information and ideas of all kinds, regardless of frontiers, either orally, in writing or in print, in the form of art, or through any other media of his choice.

3. The exercise of the rights provided for in paragraph 2 of this article carries with it special duties and responsibilities. It may therefore be subject to certain restrictions, but these shall only be such as are provided by law and are necessary:

(a) For respect of the rights or reputations of others;

(b) For the protection of national security or of public order (*ordre public*), or of public health or morals.

Article 20

1. Any propaganda for war shall be prohibited by law.

2. Any advocacy of national, racial or religious hatred that constitutes incitement to discrimination, hostility or violence shall be prohibited by law.

Article 21

The right of peaceful assembly shall be recognized. No restrictions may be placed on the exercise of this right other than those imposed in conformity with the law and which are necessary in a democratic society in the interests of national security or public safety, public order (*ordre public*), the protection of public health or morals or the protection of the rights and freedoms of others.

Article 22

1. Everyone shall have the right to freedom of association with others, including the right to form and join trade unions for the protection of his interests.

2. No restrictions may be placed on the exercise of this right other than those which are prescribed by law and which are necessary in a democratic society in the interests of national security or public safety, public order, the protection of public health or morals or the protection of the rights and freedoms of others. This article shall not prevent the imposition of lawful restrictions on members of the armed forces and of the police in their exercise of this right.

INTERNATIONAL CONVENTION ON THE ELIMINATION OF ALL FORMS OF RACIAL DISCRIMINATION

Adopted and opened for signature, ratification and accession by the UN General Assembly, 21 December 1965. Entered into force 4 January 1969.

Article 4

States Parties condemn all propaganda and all organizations which are based on ideas or theories of superiority of one race or group of persons of one colour or ethnic origin, or which attempt to justify or promote racial hatred and discrimination in any form, and undertake to adopt immediate and positive measures designed to eradicate all incitement to, or acts of, such discrimination and, to this end, with due regard to the principles embodied in the Universal Declaration of Human Rights and the rights expressly set forth in article 5 of this Convention, *inter alia*:

(a) Shall declare an offence publishable by law all dissemination of ideas based on racial superiority or hatred, incitement to racial discrimination, as well as all acts of violence or incitement to such acts against any race or group of persons of another colour or ethnic origin, and also the provision of any assistance to racist activities, including the financing thereof;

(b) Shall declare illegal and prohibit organizations, and also organized and all other propaganda activities, which promote and incite racial discrimination, and shall recognize participation in such organizations or activities as an offence punishable by law;

(c) Shall not permit public authorities or public institutions, national or local, to promote or incite racial discrimination.

REGIONAL AND INTER-GOVERNMENTAL STATEMENTS
ORGANIZATION OF AFRICAN UNITY (OAU)
AFRICAN CHARTER ON HUMAN AND PEOPLES' RIGHTS

Adopted by the OAU on 27 June 1981. Entered into force in October 1986.

Article 1

The Member States of the Organization of African Unity parties to the present Charter shall recognize the rights, duties and freedoms enshrined in this Charter and shall undertake to adopt legislative or other measures to give effect to them.

Article 2

Every individual shall be entitled to the enjoyment of the rights and freedoms recognized and guaranteed in the present Charter without distinction of any kind such as race, ethnic group, colour, sex, language, religion, political or any other opinion, national and social origin, fortune, birth or other status.

Article 9

1. Every individual shall have the right to receive information.

2. Every individual shall have the right to express and disseminate his opinions within the law.

Article 10

1. Every individual shall have the right to free association provided that he abides by the law.

2. Subject to the obligation of solidarity provided for in Article 29 no one may be compelled to join an association.

Article 11

Every individual shall have the right to assemble freely with others. The exercise of this right shall be subject only to necessary restrictions provided for by law in particular those enacted in the interest of national security, the safety, health, ethics and rights and freedoms of others.

Article 25

States parties to the present Charter shall have the duty to promote and ensure through teaching, education and publication, the respect of the rights and freedoms contained in the present Charter and to see to it that these freedoms and rights as well as corresponding obligations and duties are understood.

Article 27

1. Every individual shall have duties towards his family and society, the State and other legally recognized communities and the international community.

2. The rights and freedoms of each individual shall be exercised with due regard to the rights of others, collective security, morality and common interest.

Article 28

Every individual shall have the duty to respect and consider his fellow beings without discrimination, and to maintain relations aimed at promoting, safeguarding and reinforcing mutual respect and tolerance.

ORGANIZATION OF AMERICAN STATES
AMERICAN CONVENTION ON HUMAN RIGHTS

Adopted by the OAS on 22 November 1969. Entered into force 18 July 1978.

Article 1: Obligation to Respect Rights

1. The States Parties to this Convention undertake to respect the rights and freedoms recognized herein and to ensure to all persons subject to their jurisdiction the free and full exercise of those rights and freedoms, without any discrimination for reasons of race, color, sex, language, religion, political or other opinion, national or social origin, economic status, birth, or any other social condition.

Article 2: Domestic Legal Effects

Where the exercise of any of the rights or freedoms referred to in Article 1 is not already ensured by legislative or other provisions, the States Parties undertake to adopt, in accordance with their constitutional processes and the provisions of this Convention, such legislative or other measures as may be necessary to give effect to those rights or freedoms.

Article 8: Right to a Fair Trial

1. Every person has the right to a hearing, with due guarantees and within a reasonable time, by a competent, independent and impartial tribunal, previously established by law, in the substantiation of any accusation of a criminal nature made against him or for the determination of his rights and obligations of a civil, labor, fiscal, or any other nature.

5. Criminal proceedings shall be public, except insofar as may be necessary to protect the interests of justice.

Article 11: Right to Privacy

1. Everyone has the right to have his honor respected and his dignity recognized.

2. No one may be the object of arbitrary or abusive interference with his private life, his family, his home, or his correspondence, or of unlawful attacks on his honor or reputation.

3. Everyone has the right to the protection of the law against such interference or attacks.

Article 13: Freedom of Thought and Expression

1. Everyone has the right to freedom of thought and expression. This right includes freedom to seek, receive, and impart information and ideas of all kinds, regardless of frontiers, either orally, in writing, in print, in the form of art, or through any other medium of one's choice.

2. The exercise of the right provided for in the foregoing paragraph shall not be subject to prior censorship but shall be subject to subsequent imposition of liability, which shall be expressly established by law to the extent necessary to ensure:

(a) respect for the rights or reputations of others; or

(b) the protection of national security, public order, or public health or morals.

3. The right of expression may not be restricted by indirect methods or means, such as the abuse of government or private controls over newsprint, radio broadcasting frequencies, or equipment used in the dissemination of information, or by any other means tending to impede the communication and circulation of ideas and opinions.

4. Notwithstanding the provisions of paragraph 2 above, public entertainments may be subject by law to prior censorship for the sole purpose of regulating access to them for the moral protection of childhood and adolescence.

5. Any propaganda for war and any advocacy of national, racial, or religious hatred that constitute incitements to lawless violence or to any other similar illegal action against any person or group of persons on any grounds including those of race, color, religion, language, or national origin shall be considered as offenses punishable by law.

Article 14: Right of Reply

1. Anyone injured by inaccurate or offensive statements or ideas disseminated to the public in general by a legally regulated medium of communication has the right to reply or to make a correction using the same communications outlet, under such conditions as the law may establish.

2. The correction or reply shall not in any case remit other legal liabilities that may have been incurred.

3. For the effective protection of honor and reputation, every publisher, and every newspaper, motion picture, radio, and television company, shall have a person responsible who is not protected by immunities or special privileges.

Article 15: Right of Assembly
The right of peaceful assembly, without arms, is recognized. No restrictions may be placed on the exercise of this right other than those imposed in conformity with the law and necessary in a democratic society in the interest of national security, public safety or public order, or to protect public health or morals or the rights or freedoms of others.

Article 16: Freedom of Association
1. Everyone has the right to associate freely for ideological, religious, political, economic, labor, social, cultural, sports, or other purposes.

2. The exercise of this right shall be subject only to such restrictions established by law as may be necessary in a democratic society, in the interest of national security, public safety or public order, or to protect public health or morals or the rights and freedoms of others.

Article 29: Restrictions Regarding Interpretation
No provision of this Convention shall be interpreted as:

(a) permitting any State Party, group, or person to suppress the enjoyment or exercise of the rights and freedoms recognized in this Convention or to restrict them to a greater extent than is provided for herein;

(b) restricting the enjoyment or exercise of any right or freedom recognized by virtue of the laws of any State Party or by virtue of another convention to which one of the said states is a party;

(c) precluding other rights or guarantees that are inherent in the human personality or derived from representative democracy as a form of government; or

(d) excluding or limiting the effect that the American Declaration of the Rights and Duties of Man and other international acts of the same nature may have.

AMERICAN DECLARATION OF THE RIGHTS AND DUTIES OF MAN

Approved by the Ninth International Conference of American States on 2 May 1948.

Article 4
Every person has the right to freedom of investigation, of opinion, and of the expression and dissemination of ideas, by any medium whatsoever.

Article 5
Every person has the right to the protection of the law against abusive attacks upon his honor, his reputation, and his private and family life.

Article 21
Every person has the right to assemble peaceably with others in a formal public meeting or an informal gathering, in connection with matters of common interest of any nature.

Article 22
Every person has the right to associate with others to promote, exercise and protect his legitimate interests of a political, economic, religious, social, cultural, professional, labor union or other nature.

For further legal and related sources see www.ifex.org, particularly links to Article 19.

COUNCIL OF EUROPE
EUROPEAN CONVENTION ON HUMAN RIGHTS
(Convention for the Protection of Human Rights and Fundamental Freedoms)

Signed by Contracting States of the Council of Europe on 4 November 1950. Entered into force 3 September 1953.

Article 6
1. In the determination of his civil rights and obligations or of any criminal charge against him, everyone is entitled to a fair and public hearing within a reasonable time by an independent and impartial tribunal established by law. Judgment shall be pronounced publicly but the press and public may be excluded from all or part of the trial in the interests of morals, public order or national security in a democratic society, where the interests of juveniles or the protection of the private life of the parties so require, or to the extent strictly necessary in the opinion of the court in special circumstances where publicity would prejudice the interests of justice.

Article 8
1. Everyone has the right to respect for his private and family life, his home and his correspondence.
2. There shall be no interference by a public authority with the exercise of this right except such as is in accordance with the law and is necessary in a democratic society in the interests of national security, public safety or the economic well-being of the country, for the prevention of disorder or crime, for the protection of health or morals, or for the protection of the rights and freedoms of others.

Article 10
1. Everyone has the right to freedom of expression. This right shall include freedom to hold opinions and to receive and impart information and ideas without interference by public authority and regardless of frontiers. This Article shall not prevent States from requiring the licensing of broadcasting, television or cinema enterprises.
2. The exercise of these freedoms, since it carries with it duties and responsibilities, may be subject to such formalities, conditions, restrictions or penalties as are prescribed by law and are necessary in a democratic society, in the interests of national security, territorial integrity of public safety, for the prevention of disorder or crime, for the protection of health or morals, for the protection of the reputation or rights of others, for preventing the disclosure of information received in confidence, or for maintaining the authority and impartiality of the judiciary.

Article 11
1. Everyone has the right to freedom of peaceful assembly and to freedom of association with others, including the right to form and to join trade unions for the protection of his interests.
2. No restrictions shall be placed on the exercise of these rights other than such as are prescribed by law and are necessary in a democratic society in the interests of national security or public safety, for the prevention of disorder or crime, for the protection of health or morals or for the protection of the rights and freedoms of others. This Article shall not prevent the imposition of lawful restrictions on the exercise of these rights by members of the armed forces, of the police or of the administration of the State.

Article 14
The enjoyment of the rights and freedoms set forth in this Convention shall be secured without discrimination on any ground such as sex, race, colour, language, religion, political or

other opinion, national or social origin, association with a national minority, property, birth or other status.

Article 16
Nothing in Articles 10, 11 and 14 shall be regarded as preventing the High Contracting Parties from imposing restrictions on the political activity of aliens.

Article 17
Nothing in this Convention may be interpreted as implying for any State, group or person any right to engage in any activity or perform any act aimed at the destruction of any of the rights and freedoms set forth herein or at their limitation to a greater extent than is provided for in the Convention.

For related sources of information on international legal sources, see www.ifex.org

Appendix III

UNESCO

CONVENTION CONCERNING THE PROTECTION OF THE WORLD CULTURAL AND NATURAL HERITAGE

THE GENERAL CONFERENCE of the United Nations Educational, Scientific and Cultural Organization meeting in Paris from 17 October to 21 November 1972, at its seventeenth session,

Noting that the cultural heritage and the natural heritage are increasingly threatened with destruction not only by the traditional causes of decay, but also by changing social and economic conditions which aggravate the situation with even more formidable phenomena of damage or destruction,

Considering that deterioration or disappearance of any item of the cultural or natural heritage constitutes a harmful impoverishment of the heritage of all the nations of the world,

Considering that protection of this heritage at the national level often remains incomplete because of the scale of the resources which it requires and of the insufficient economic, scientific, and technological resources of the country where the property to be protected is situated,

Recalling that the Constitution of the Organization provides that it will maintain, increase, and diffuse knowledge, by assuring the conservation and protection of the world's heritage, and recommending to the nations concerned the necessary international conventions,

Considering that the existing international conventions, recommendations and resolutions concerning cultural and natural property demonstrate the importance, for all the peoples of the world, of safeguarding this unique and irreplaceable property, to whatever people it may belong,

Considering that parts of the cultural or natural heritage are of outstanding interest and therefore need to be preserved as part of the world heritage of mankind as a whole,

Considering that, in view of the magnitude and gravity of the new dangers threatening them, it is incumbent on the international community as a whole to participate in the protection of the cultural and natural heritage of outstanding universal value, by the granting of collective assistance which, although not taking the place of action by the State concerned, will serve as an efficient complement thereto,

Considering that it is essential for this purpose to adopt new provisions in the form of a convention establishing an effective system of collective protection of the cultural and natural heritage of outstanding universal value, organized on a permanent basis and in accordance with modern scientific methods,

Having decided, at its sixteenth session, that this question should be made the subject of an international convention,

Adopts this sixteenth day of November 1972 this Convention.

I. DEFINITION OF THE CULTURAL AND NATURAL HERITAGE
Article 1

For the purposes of this Convention, the following shall be considered as "cultural heritage": monuments: architectural works, works of monumental sculpture and painting, elements or structures of an archaeological nature, inscriptions, cave dwellings and combinations of features, which are of outstanding universal value from the point of view of history, art or science; groups of buildings: groups of separate or connected buildings which, because of their architecture, their homogeneity or their place in the landscape, are of outstanding universal value from the point of view of history, art or science; sites: works of man or the combined works of nature and man, and areas including archaeological sites which are of outstanding universal value from the historical, aesthetic, ethnological or anthropological point of view.

Article 2

For the purposes of this Convention, the following shall be considered as 'natural heritage: natural features consisting of physical and biological formations or groups of such formations, which are of outstanding universal value from the aesthetic or scientific point of view; geological and physiographical formations and precisely delineated areas which constitute the habitat of threatened species of animals and plants of outstanding universal value from the point of view of science or conservation; natural sites or precisely delineated natural areas of outstanding universal value from the point of view of science, conservation or natural beauty.

Article 3

It is for each State Party to this Convention to identify and delineate the different properties situated on its territory mentioned in Articles 1 and 2 above.

II. NATIONAL PROTECTION AND INTERNATIONAL PROTECTION OF THE CULTURAL AND NATURAL HERITAGE

Article 4

Each State Party to this Convention recognizes that the duty of ensuring the identification, protection, conservation, presentation and transmission to future generations of the cultural and natural heritage referred to in Articles 1 and 2 and situated on its territory, belongs primarily to that State. It will do all it can to this end, to the utmost of its own resources and, where appropriate, with any international assistance and co-operation, in particular, financial, artistic, scientific and technical, which it may be able to obtain.

Article 5

To ensure that effective and active measures are taken for the protection, conservation and presentation of the cultural and natural heritage situated on its territory, each State Party to this Convention shall endeavor, in so far as possible, and as appropriate for each country:

to adopt a general policy which aims to give the cultural and natural heritage a function in the life of the community and to integrate the protection of that heritage into comprehensive planning programmes;

to set up within its territories, where such services do not exist, one or more services for the protection, conservation and presentation of the cultural and natural heritage with an appropriate staff and possessing the means to discharge their functions;

to develop scientific and technical studies and research and to work out such operating methods as will make the State capable of counteracting the dangers that threaten its cultural or natural heritage;

to take the appropriate legal, scientific, technical, administrative and financial measures necessary for the identification, protection, conservation, presentation and rehabilitation of this heritage; and

to foster the establishment or development of national or regional centres for training in the protection, conservation and presentation of the cultural and natural heritage and to encourage scientific research in this field.

Article 6

Whilst fully respecting the sovereignty of the States on whose territory the cultural and natural heritage mentioned in Articles 1 and 2 is situated, and without prejudice to property right provided by national legislation, the States Parties to this Convention recognize that such heritage constitutes a world heritage for whose protection it is the duty of the international community as a whole to co-operate.

The States Parties undertake, in accordance with the provisions of this Convention, to give their help in the identification, protection, conservation and presentation of the cultural and natural heritage referred to in paragraphs 2 and 4 of Article 11 if the States on whose territory it is situated so request.

Each State Party to this Convention undertakes not to take any deliberate measures which might damage directly or indirectly the cultural and natural heritage referred to in Articles 1 and 2 situated on the territory of other States Parties to this Convention.

Article 7

For the purpose of this Convention, international protection of the world cultural and natural heritage shall be understood to mean the establishment of a system of international co-operation and assistance designed to support States Parties to the Convention in their efforts to conserve and identify that heritage.

III. INTERGOVERNMENTAL COMMITTEE FOR THE PROTECTION OF THE WORLD CULTURAL AND NATURAL HERITAGE

Article 8

An Intergovernmental Committee for the Protection of the Cultural and Natural Heritage of Outstanding Universal Value, called the World Heritage Committee, is hereby established within the United Nations Educational, Scientific and Cultural Organization. It shall be composed of 15 States Parties to the Convention, elected by States Parties to the Convention meeting in general assembly during the ordinary session of the General Conference of the United Nations Educational, Scientific and Cultural Organization. The number of States members of the Committee shall be increased to 21 as from the date of the ordinary session of the General Conference following the entry into force of this Convention for at least 40 States.

Election of members of the Committee shall ensure an equitable representation of the different regions and cultures of the world.

A representative of the International Centre for the Study of the Preservation and Restoration of Cultural Property (Rome Centre), a representative of the International Council of Monuments and Sites (ICOMOS) and a representative of the International Union for Conservation of Nature and Natural Resources (IUCN), to whom may be added, at the request of States Parties to the Convention meeting in general assembly during the ordinary sessions of the General Conference of the United Nations Educational, Scientific and Cultural Organization, representatives of other intergovernmental or non-governmental organizations, with similar objectives, may attend the meetings of the Committee in an advisory capacity.

Article 9

The term of office of States members of the World Heritage Committee shall extend from the end of the ordinary session of the General Conference during which they are elected until the end of its third subsequent ordinary session.

The term of office of one-third of the members designated at the time of the first election shall, however, cease at the end of the first ordinary session of the General Conference following that at which they were elected; and the term of office of a further third of the members designated at the same time shall cease at the end of the second ordinary session of the General Conference following that at which they were elected. The names of these members shall be chosen by lot by the President of the General Conference of the United Nations Educational, Scientific and Cultural Organization after the first election.

States members of the Committee shall choose as their representatives persons qualified in the field of the cultural or natural heritage.

Article 10

The World Heritage Committee shall adopt its Rules of Procedure.

The Committee may at any time invite public or private organizations or individuals to participate in its meetings for consultation on particular problems.

The Committee may create such consultative bodies as it deems necessary for the performance of its functions.

Article 11

Every State Party to this Convention shall, in so far as possible, submit to the World Heritage Committee an inventory of property forming part of the cultural and natural heritage, situated in its territory and suitable for inclusion in the list provided for in paragraph 2 of this Article. This inventory, which shall not be considered exhaustive, shall include documentation about the location of the property in question and its significance.

On the basis of the inventories submitted by States in accordance with paragraph 1, the Committee shall establish, keep up to date and publish, under the title of World Heritage List a list of properties forming part of the cultural heritage and natural heritage, as defined in Articles 1 and 2 of this Convention, which it considers as having outstanding universal value in terms of such criteria as it shall have established. An updated list shall be distributed at least every two years.

The inclusion of a property in the World Heritage List requires the consent of the State concerned. The inclusion of a property situated in a territory, sovereignty or jurisdiction over which is claimed by more than one State shall in no way prejudice the rights of the parties to the dispute.

The Committee shall establish, keep up to date and publish, whenever circumstances shall so require, under the title of List of World Heritage in Danger, a list of the property appearing in the World Heritage List for the conservation of which major operations are necessary and for which assistance has been requested under this Convention. This list shall contain an estimate of the cost of such operations. The list may include only such property forming part of the cultural and natural heritage as is threatened by serious and specific dangers, such as the threat of disappearance caused by accelerated deterioration, large-scale public or private projects or rapid urban or tourist development projects; destruction caused by changes in the use or ownership of the land; major alterations due to unknown causes; abandonment for any reason whatsoever; the outbreak or the threat of an armed conflict; calamities and cataclysms; serious fires, earthquakes, landslides; volcanic eruptions; changes in water level, floods and tidal waves. The Committee may at any time, in case of urgent need, make a new entry in the List of World Heritage in Danger and publicize such entry immediately.

The Committee shall define the criteria on the basis of which a property belonging to the cultural or natural heritage may be included in either of the lists mentioned in paragraphs 2 and 4 of this article.

Before refusing a request for inclusion in one of the two lists mentioned in paragraphs 2 and 4 of this article, the Committee shall consult the State Party in whose territory the cultural or natural property in question is situated.

The Committee shall, with the agreement of the States concerned, co-ordinate and encourage the studies and research needed for the drawing up of the lists referred to in paragraphs 2 and 4 of this article.

Article 12

The fact that a property belonging to the cultural or natural heritage has not been included in either of the two lists mentioned in paragraphs 2 and 4 of Article 11 shall in no way be construed to mean that it does not have an outstanding universal value for purposes other than those resulting from inclusion in these lists.

Article 13

The World Heritage Committee shall receive and study requests for international assistance formulated by States Parties to this Convention with respect to property forming part of the cultural or natural heritage, situated in their territories, and included or potentially suitable for inclusion in the lists mentioned referred to in paragraphs 2 and 4 of Article 11. The purpose of such requests may be to secure the protection, conservation, presentation or rehabilitation of such property.

Requests for international assistance under paragraph 1 of this article may also be concerned with identification of cultural or natural property defined in Articles 1 and 2, when preliminary investigations have shown that further inquiries would be justified.

The Committee shall decide on the action to be taken with regard to these requests, determine where appropriate, the nature and extent of its assistance, and authorize the conclusion, on its behalf, of the necessary arrangements with the government concerned.

The Committee shall determine an order of priorities for its operations. It shall in so doing bear in mind the respective importance for the world cultural and natural heritage of the property requiring protection, the need to give international assistance to the property most representative of a natural environment or of the genius and the history of the peoples of the world, the urgency of the work to be done, the resources available to the States on whose territory the threatened property is situated and in particular the extent to which they are able to safeguard such property by their own means.

The Committee shall draw up, keep up to date and publicize a list of property for which international assistance has been granted.

The Committee shall decide on the use of the resources of the Fund established under Article 15 of this Convention. It shall seek ways of increasing these resources and shall take all useful steps to this end.

The Committee shall co-operate with international and national governmental and non-governmental organizations having objectives similar to those of this Convention. For the implementation of its programmes and projects, the Committee may call on such organizations, particularly the International Centre for the Study of the Preservation and Restoration of cultural Property (the Rome Centre), the International Council of Monuments and Sites (ICOMOS) and the International Union for Conservation of Nature and Natural Resources (IUCN), as well as on public and private bodies and individuals.

Decisions of the Committee shall be taken by a majority of two-thirds of its members present and voting. A majority of the members of the Committee shall constitute a quorum.

Article 14

The World Heritage Committee shall be assisted by a Secretariat appointed by the Director-General of the United Nations Educational, Scientific and Cultural Organization.

The Director-General of the United Nations Educational, Scientific and Cultural Organization, utilizing to the fullest extent possible the services of the International Centre for the Study of the Preservation and the Restoration of Cultural Property (the Rome Centre), the International Council of Monuments and Sites (ICOMOS) and the International Union for Conservation of Nature and Natural Resources (IUCN) in their respective areas of competence and capability, shall prepare the Committee's documentation and the agenda of its meetings and shall have the responsibility for the implementation of its decisions.

IV. FUND FOR THE PROTECTION OF THE WORLD CULTURAL AND NATURAL HERITAGE

Article 15

A Fund for the Protection of the World Cultural and Natural Heritage of Outstanding Universal Value, called "the World Heritage Fund", is hereby established.

The Fund shall constitute a trust fund, in conformity with the provisions of the Financial Regulations of the United Nations Educational, Scientific and Cultural Organization.

The resources of the Fund shall consist of:

compulsory and voluntary contributions made by States Parties to this Convention,

Contributions, gifts or bequests which may be made by:

other States;

the United Nations Educational, Scientific and Cultural Organization, other organizations of the United Nations system, particularly the United Nations Development Programme or other intergovernmental organizations;

public or private bodies or individuals;

any interest due on the resources of the Fund;

funds raised by collections and receipts from events organized for the benefit of the fund; and

all other resources authorized by the Fund's regulations, as drawn up by the World Heritage Committee.

Contributions to the Fund and other forms of assistance made available to the Committee may be used only for such purposes as the Committee shall define. The Committee may accept contributions to be used only for a certain programme or project, provided that the Committee shall have decided on the implementation of such programme or project. No political conditions may be attached to contributions made to the Fund.

Article 16

Without prejudice to any supplementary voluntary contribution, the States Parties to this Convention undertake to pay regularly, every two years, to the World Heritage Fund, contributions, the amount of which, in the form of a uniform percentage applicable to all States, shall be determined by the General Assembly of States Parties to the Convention, meeting during the sessions of the General Conference of the United Nations Educational, Scientific and Cultural Organization. This decision of the General Assembly requires the majority of the States Parties present and voting, which have not made the declaration referred to in paragraph 2 of this Article. In no case shall the compulsory contribution of States Parties to the Convention exceed 1% of the contribution to the regular budget of the United Nations Educational, Scientific and Cultural Organization.

However, each State referred to in Article 31 or in Article 32 of this Convention may declare, at the time of the deposit of its instrument of ratification, acceptance or accession, that it shall not be bound by the provisions of paragraph 1 of this Article.

A State Party to the Convention which has made the declaration referred to in paragraph 2 of this Article may at any time withdraw the said declaration by notifying the Director-General of the United Nations Educational, Scientific and Cultural Organization. However, the withdrawal of the declaration shall not take effect in regard to the compulsory contribution due by the State until the date of the subsequent General Assembly of States parties to the Convention.

In order that the Committee may be able to plan its operations effectively, the contributions of States Parties to this Convention which have made the declaration referred to in paragraph 2 of this Article, shall be paid on a regular basis, at least every two years, and should not be less than the contributions which they should have paid if they had been bound by the provisions of paragraph 1 of this Article.

Any State Party to the Convention which is in arrears with the payment of its compulsory or voluntary contribution for the current year and the calendar year immediately preceding it shall not be eligible as a Member of the World Heritage Committee, although this provision shall not apply to the first election.

The terms of office of any such State which is already a member of the Committee shall terminate at the time of the elections provided for in Article 8, paragraph 1 of this Convention.

Article 17

The States Parties to this Convention shall consider or encourage the establishment of national public and private foundations or associations whose purpose is to invite donations for the protection of the cultural and natural heritage as defined in Articles 1 and 2 of this Convention.

Article 18

The States Parties to this Convention shall give their assistance to international fund-raising campaigns organized for the World Heritage Fund under the auspices of the United Nations Educational, Scientific and Cultural Organization. They shall facilitate collections made by the bodies mentioned in paragraph 3 of Article 15 for this purpose.

V. CONDITIONS AND ARRANGEMENTS FOR INTERNATIONAL ASSISTANCE

Article 19

Any State Party to this Convention may request international assistance for property forming part of the cultural or natural heritage of outstanding universal value situated within its territory. It shall submit with its request such information and documentation provided for in Article 21 as it has in its possession and as will enable the Committee to come to a decision.

Article 20

Subject to the provisions of paragraph 2 of Article 13, sub-paragraph (c) of Article 22 and Article 23, international assistance provided for by this Convention may be granted only to property forming part of the cultural and natural heritage which the World Heritage Committee has decided, or may decide, to enter in one of the lists mentioned in paragraphs 2 and 4 of Article 11.

Article 21

The World Heritage Committee shall define the procedure by which requests to it for international assistance shall be considered and shall specify the content of the request, which should define the operation contemplated, the work that is necessary, the expected cost thereof, the degree of urgency and the reasons why the resources of the State requesting assistance do not allow it to meet all the expenses. Such requests must be supported by experts' reports whenever possible.

Requests based upon disasters or natural calamities should, by reasons of the urgent work which they may involve, be given immediate, priority consideration by the Committee, which should have a reserve fund at its disposal against such contingencies.

Before coming to a decision, the Committee shall carry out such studies and consultations as it deems necessary.

Article 22

Assistance granted by the World Heritage Committee may take the following forms:

studies concerning the artistic, scientific and technical problems raised by the protection, conservation, presentation and rehabilitation of the cultural and natural heritage, as defined in paragraphs 2 and 4 of Article 11 of this Convention;

provisions of experts, technicians and skilled labour to ensure that the approved work is correctly carried out;

training of staff and specialists at all levels in the field of identification, protection, conservation, presentation and rehabilitation of the cultural and natural heritage;

supply of equipment which the State concerned does not possess or is not in a position to acquire;

low-interest or interest-free loans which might be repayable on a long-term basis;

the granting, in exceptional cases and for special reasons, of non-repayable subsidies.

Article 23

The World Heritage Committee may also provide international assistance to national or regional centres for the training of staff and specialists at all levels in the field of identification, protection, conservation, presentation and rehabilitation of the cultural and natural heritage.

Article 24

International assistance on a large scale shall be preceded by detailed scientific, economic and technical studies. These studies shall draw upon the most advanced techniques for the protection, conservation, presentation and rehabilitation of the natural and cultural heritage and shall be consistent with the objectives of this Convention. The studies shall also seek means of making rational use of the resources available in the State concerned.

Article 25

As a general rule, only part of the cost of work necessary shall be borne by the international community. The contribution of the State benefiting from international assistance shall constitute a substantial share of the resources devoted to each programme or project, unless its resources do not permit this.

Article 26

The World Heritage Committee and the recipient State shall define in the agreement they conclude the conditions in which a programme or project for which international assistance under the terms of this Convention is provided, shall be carried out. It shall be the responsibility of the State receiving such international assistance to continue to protect, conserve and present the property so safeguarded, in observance of the conditions laid down by the agreement.

VI. EDUCATIONAL PROGRAMMES

Article 27

The States Parties to this Convention shall endeavor by all appropriate means, and in particular by educational and information programmes, to strengthen appreciation and respect by their peoples of the cultural and natural heritage defined in Articles 1 and 2 of the Convention.

They shall undertake to keep the public broadly informed of the dangers threatening this heritage and of the activities carried on in pursuance of this Convention.

Article 28

States Parties to this Convention which receive international assistance under the Convention shall take appropriate measures to make known the importance of the property for which assistance has been received and the role played by such assistance.

VII. REPORTS

Article 29

The States Parties to this Convention shall, in the reports which they submit to the General Conference of the United Nations Educational, Scientific and Cultural Organization on dates and in a manner to be determined by it, give information on the legislative and administrative provisions which they have adopted and other action which they have taken for the application of this Convention, together with details of the experience acquired in this field.

These reports shall be brought to the attention of the World Heritage Committee.

The Committee shall submit a report on its activities at each of the ordinary sessions of the General Conference of the United Nations Educational, Scientific and Cultural Organization.

VIII. FINAL CLAUSES

Article 30

This Convention is drawn up in Arabic, English, French, Russian and Spanish, the five texts being equally authoritative.

Article 31

This Convention shall be subject to ratification or acceptance by States members of the United Nations Educational, Scientific and Cultural Organization in accordance with their respective constitutional procedures.

The instruments of ratification or acceptance shall be deposited with the Director-General of the United Nations Educational, Scientific and Cultural Organization.

Article 32

This Convention shall be open to accession by all States not members of the United Nations Educational, Scientific and Cultural Organization which are invited by the General Conference of the Organization to accede to it.

Accession shall be effected by the deposit of an instrument of accession with the Director-General of the United Nations Educational, Scientific and Cultural Organization.

Article 33

This Convention shall enter into force three months after the date of the deposit of the twentieth instrument of ratification, acceptance or accession, but only with respect to those States which have deposited their respective instruments of ratification, acceptance or accession on or before that date. It shall enter into force with respect to any other State three months after the deposit of its instrument of ratification, acceptance or accession.

Article 34

The following provisions shall apply to those States Parties to this Convention which have a federal or non-unitary constitutional system:

with regard to the provisions of this Convention, the implementation of which comes under the legal jurisdiction of the federal or central legislative power, the obligations of the federal or central government shall be the same as for those States parties which are not federal States;

with regard to the provisions of this Convention, the implementation of which comes under the legal jurisdiction of individual constituent States, countries, provinces or cantons that are not obliged by the constitutional system of the federation to take legislative measures, the federal government shall inform the competent authorities of such States, countries, provinces or cantons of the said provisions, with its recommendation for their adoption.

Article 35

Each State Party to this Convention may denounce the Convention.

The denunciation shall be notified by an instrument in writing, deposited with the Director-General of the United Nations Educational, Scientific and Cultural Organization

The denunciation shall take effect twelve months after the receipt of the instrument of denunciation. It shall not affect the financial obligations of the denouncing State until the date on which the withdrawal takes effect.

Article 36

The Director-General of the United Nations Educational, Scientific and Cultural Organization shall inform the States members of the Organization, the States not members of the Organization which are referred to in Article 32, as well as the United Nations, of the deposit of all the instruments of ratification, acceptance, or accession provided for in Articles 31 and 32, and of the denunciations provided for in Article 35.

Article 37

This Convention may be revised by the General Conference of the United Nations Educational, Scientific and Cultural Organization. Any such revision shall, however, bind only the States which shall become Parties to the revising convention.

If the General Conference should adopt a new convention revising this Convention in whole or in part, then, unless the new convention otherwise provides, this Convention shall cease to be open to ratification, acceptance or accession, as from the date on which the new revising convention enters into force.

Article 38

In conformity with Article 102 of the Charter of the United Nations, this Convention shall be registered with the Secretariat of the United Nations at the request of the Director-General of the United Nations Educational, Scientific and Cultural Organization.

Done in Paris, this twenty-third day of November 1972, in two authentic copies bearing the signature of the President of the seventeenth session of the General Conference and of the Director-General of the United Nations Educational, Scientific and Cultural Organization, which shall be deposited in the archives of the United Nations Educational, Scientific and Cultural Organization, and certified true copies of which shall be delivered to all the States referred to in Articles 31 and 32 as well as to the United Nations.

Appendix IV

UNESCO

WORLD HERITAGE SITES LIST
(Results by Country)

Afghanistan
- Minaret and Archaeological Remains of Jam (2002)
- Cultural Landscape and Archaeological Remains of the Bamiyan Valley (2003)

Albania
- Butrint (1992, 1999)
- Museum-City of Gjirokastra (2005)

Algeria
- Al Qal'a of Beni Hammad (1980)
- Djémila (1982)
- M'Zab Valley (1982)
- Tassili n'Ajjer (1982)
- Timgad (1982)
- Tipasa (1982)
- Kasbah of Algiers (1992)

Andorra
- Madriu-Perafita-Claror Valley (2004)

Argentina
- Los Glaciares (1981)
- Iguazu National Park (1984)
- Cueva de las Manos, Río Pinturas (1999)
- Península Valdés (1999)
- Ischigualasto / Talampaya Natural Parks (2000)
- Jesuit Block and Estancias of Córdoba (2000)
- Quebrada de Humahuaca (2003)

Armenia
- Monasteries of Haghpat and Sanahin (1996, 2000)
- Cathedral and Churches of Echmiatsin and the Archaeological Site of Zvartnots (2000)
- Monastery of Geghard and the Upper Azat Valley (2000)

Australia
- Great Barrier Reef (1981)
- Kakadu National Park (1981, 1987, 1992)
- Willandra Lakes Region (1981)
- Lord Howe Island Group (1982)
- Tasmanian Wilderness (1982, 1989)
- Central Eastern Rainforest Reserves (Australia) (1986, 1994)
- Uluru-Kata Tjuta National Park (1987, 1994)
- Wet Tropics of Queensland (1988)

- Shark Bay, Western Australia (1991)
- Fraser Island (1992)
- Australian Fossil Mammal Sites (Riversleigh/ Naracote) (1994)
- Heard and McDonald Islands (1997)
- Macquarie Island (1997)
- Greater Blue Mountains Area (2000)
- Purnululu National Park (2003)
- Royal Exhibition Building and Carlton Gardens (2004)

Austria
- Historic Centre of the City of Salzburg (1996)
- Palace and Gardens of Schönbrunn (1996)
- Hallstatt-Dachstein Salzkammergut Cultural Landscape (1997)
- Semmering Railway (1998)
- City of Graz — Historic Centre (1999)
- Wachau Cultural Landscape (2000)
- Historic Centre of Vienna (2001)

Azerbaijan
- Walled City of Baku with the Shirvanshah's Palace and Maiden Tower (2000)

Bahrain
- Qal'at al-Bahrain Archaeological Site (2005)

Bangladesh
- Historic Mosque City of Bagerhat (1985)
- Ruins of the Buddhist Vihara at Paharpur (1985)
- The Sundarbans (1997)

Belarus
- Mir Castle Complex (2000)
- Architectural, Residential and Cultural Complex of the Radziwill Family at Nesviz(2005)
-

Belgium
- Flemish Béguinages (1998)
- Grand-Place, Brussels (1998)
- The Four Lifts on the Canal du Centre and their Environs, La Louvière and Le Roeulx (Hainault) (1998)
- Historic Centre of Brugge (2000)
- Major Town Houses of the Architect Victor Horta (Brussels) (2000)
- Neolithic Flint Mines at Spiennes (Mons) (2000)
- Notre-Dame Cathedral in Tournai (2000)
- Plantin-Moretus House-Workshops-Museum Complex (2005)

Belize
- Belize Barrier-Reef Reserve System (1996)

Benin
- Royal Palaces of Abomey (1985)

Bolivia
- City of Potosi (1987)
- Jesuit Missions of the Chiquitos (1990)
- Historic City of Sucre (1991)
- Fuerte de Samaipata (1998)
- Noel Kempff Mercado National Park (2000)
- Tiwanaku: Spiritual and Political Centre of the Tiwanaku Culture (2000)

Bosnia and Herzegovina
- Old Bridge Area of the Old City of Mostar (2005)

Botswana
- Tsodilo (2001)

Brazil
- Historic Town of Ouro Preto (1980)
- Historic Centre of the Town of Olinda (1982)
- Jesuit Missions of the Guaranis: San Ignacio Mini, Santa Ana, Nuestra Señora de Loreto and Santa Maria Mayor (Argentina), Ruins of Sao Miguel das Missoes (Brazil) (1983, 1984)
- Historic Centre of Salvador de Bahia (1985)
- Sanctuary of Bom Jesus do Congonhas (1985)
- Iguaçu National Park (1986)
- Brasilia (1987)
- Serra da Capivara National Park (1991)
- Historic Centre of São Luis (1997)
- Atlantic Forest Southeast Reserves (1999)
- Discovery Coast Atlantic Forest Reserves (1999)
- Historic Centre of the Town of Diamantina (1999)
- Central Amazon Conservation Complex (2000, 2003)
- Pantanal Conservation Area (2000)
- Brazilian Atlantic Islands: Fernando de Noronha and Atol das Rocas Reserves (2001)
- Cerrado Protected Areas: Chapada dos Veadeiros and Emas National Parks (2001)
- Historic Centre of the Town of Goiás (2001)

Bulgaria
- Boyana Church (1979)
- Madara Rider (1979)
- Rock-hewn Churches of Ivanovo (1979)
- Thracian Tomb of Kazanlak (1979)
- Ancient City of Nessebar (1983)
- Pirin National Park (1983)
- Rila Monastery (1983)
- Srebarna Nature Reserve (1983)
- Thracian Tomb of Sveshtari (1985)

Cambodia
- Angkor (1992)

Cameron
- Dja Faunal Reserve (1987)

Canada
- L'Anse aux Meadows National Historic Site (1978)
- Nahanni National Park (1978)
- Dinosaur Provincial Park (1979)
- Head-Smashed-In Buffalo Jump (1981)
- SGaang Gwaii (Anthony Island) (1981)
- Wood Buffalo National Park (1983)
- Canadian Rocky Mountain Parks (1984, 1990)
- Historic District of Québec (1985)
- Gros Morne National Park (1987)
- Old Town Lunenburg (1995)
- Miguasha National Park (1999)

Central African Republic

- Manovo-Gounda St Floris National Park (1988)

Chile
- Rapa Nui National Park (1995)
- Churches of Chiloé (2000)
- Historic Quarter of the Seaport City of Valparaíso (2003)
- Humberstone and Santa Laura Saltpeter Works (2005)

China
- Imperial Palaces of the Ming and Qing Dynasties in Beijing and Shenyang (1987, 2004)
- Mausoleum of the First Qin Emperor (1987)
- Mogao Caves (1987)
- Mount Taishan (1987)
- Peking Man Site at Zhoukoudian (1987)
- The Great Wall (1987)
- Mount Huangshan (1990)
- Huanglong Scenic and Historic Interest Area (1992)
- Jiuzhaigou Valley Scenic and Historic Interest Area (1992)
- Wulingyuan Scenic and Historic Interest Area (1992)
- Ancient Building Complex in the Wudang Mountains (1994)
- Historic Ensemble of the Potala Palace, Lhasa (1994, 2000, 2001)
- Mountain Resort and its Outlying Temples, Chengde (1994)
- Temple and Cemetery of Confucius and the Kong Family Mansion in Qufu (1994)
- Lushan National Park (1996)
- Mount Emei Scenic Area, including Leshan Giant Buddha Scenic Area (1996)
- Ancient City of Ping Yao (1997)
- Classical Gardens of Suzhou (1997, 2000)
- Old Town of Lijiang (1997)
- Summer Palace, an Imperial Garden in Beijing (1998)
- Temple of Heaven: an Imperial Sacrificial Altar in Beijing (1998)
- Dazu Rock Carvings (1999)
- Mount Wuyi (1999)
- Ancient Villages in Southern Anhui — Xidi and Hongcun (2000)
- Imperial Tombs of the Ming and Qing Dynasties (2000, 2003, 2004)
- Longmen Grottoes (2000)
- Mount Qingcheng and the Dujiangyan Irrigation System (2000)

- Yungang Grottoes (2001)
- Three Parallel Rivers of Yunnan Protected Areas (2003)
- Capital Cities and Tombs of the Ancient Koguryo Kingdom (2004)
- Historic Centre of Macao (2005)

Colombia
- Port, Fortresses and Group of Monuments, Cartagena (1984)
- Los Katios National Park (1994)
- Historic Centre of Santa Cruz de Mompox (1995)
- National Archeological Park of Tierradentro (1995)
- San Agustín Archeological Park (1995)

Costa Rica
- Cocos Island National Park (1997, 2002)
- Area de Conservación Guanacaste (1999, 2004)

Cote d'Ivoire
- Taï National Park (1982)
- Comoé National Park (1983)

Croatia
- Historical Complex of Split with the Palace of Diocletian (1979)
- Old City of Dubrovnik (1979, 1994)
- Plitvice Lakes National Park (1979, 2000)
- Episcopal Complex of the Euphrasian Basilica in the Historic Centre of Poreè (1997)
- Historic City of Trogir (1997)
- The Cathedral of St James in Šibenik (2000)

Cuba
- Old Havana and its Fortifications (1982)
- Trinidad and the Valley de los Ingenios (1988)
- San Pedro de la Roca Castle, Santiago de Cuba (1997)
- Desembarco del Granma National Park (1999)
- Viñales Valley (1999)
- Archaeological Landscape of the First Coffee Plantations in the Southeast of Cuba (2000)
- Alejandro de Humboldt National Park (2001)
- Urban Historic Centre of Cienfuegos (2005)

Cyprus
- Paphos (1980)
- Painted Churches in the Troodos Region (1985, 2001)
- Choirokoitia (1998)

Czech Republic
- Historic Centre of Èeský Krumlov (1992)
- Historic Centre of Prague (1992)
- Historic Centre of Telè (1992)
- Pilgrimage Church of St John of Nepomuk at Zelená Hora (1994)
- Kutná Hora: Historical Town Centre with the Church of St Barbara and the Cathedral of Our Lady at Sedlec (1995)
- Lednice-Valtice Cultural Landscape (1996)

- Gardens and Castle at Kromìøí (1998)
- Holašovice Historical Village Reservation (1998)
- Litomyšl Castle (1999)
- Holy Trinity Column in Olomouc (2000)
- Tugendhat Villa in Brno (2001)
- Jewish Quarter and St Procopius' Basilica in Trebíc (2003)

Democratic People's Republic of Korea
- Complex of Koguryo Tombs (2004)

Democratic Republic of the Congo
- Virunga National Park (1979)
- Garamba National Park (1980)
- Kahuzi-Biega National Park (1980)
- Salonga National Park (1984)
- Okapi Wildlife Reserve (1996)

Denmark
- Jelling Mounds, Runic Stones and Church (1994)
- Roskilde Cathedral (1995)
- Kronborg Castle (2000)
- Ilulissat Icefjord (2004)

Dominica
- Morne Trois Pitons National Park (1997)
- Dominican Republic
- Colonial City of Santo Domingo (1990)

Ecuador
- City of Quito (1978)
- Galapagos Islands (1978, 2001)
- Sangay National Park (1983)
- Historic Centre of Santa Ana de los Ríos de Cuenca (1999)

Egypt
- Abu Mena (1979)
- Ancient Thebes with its Necropolis (1979)
- Islamic Cairo (1979)
- Memphis and its Necropolis — the Pyramid Fields from Giza to Dahshur (1979)
- Nubian Monuments from Abu Simbel to Philae (1979)
- Saint Catherine Area (2002)
- Wadi Al-Hitan (Whale Valley) (2005)

El Salvador
- Joya de Ceren Archaeoloical Site (1993)

Estonia
- Historic Centre (Old Town) of Tallinn (1997)

Ethiopia
- Rock-hewn Churches, Lalibela (1978)
- Simien National Park (1978)
- Fasil Ghebbi, Gondar Region (1979)
- Aksum (1980)
- Lower Valley of the Awash (1980)
- Lower Valley of the Omo (1980)
- Tiya (1980)

Finland
- Fortress of Suomenlinna (1991)
- Old Rauma (1991)
- Petäjävesi Old Church (1994)
- Verla Groundwood and Board Mill (1996)
- Bronze Age Burial Site of Sammallahdenmäki (1999)
- Struve Geodetic Arc (2005)

France
- Chartres Cathedral (1979)
- Decorated Grottoes of the Vézère Valley (1979)
- Mont-Saint-Michel and its Bay (1979)
- Palace and Park of Versailles (1979)
- Vézelay, Church and Hill (1979)
- Amiens Cathedral (1981)
- Cistercian Abbey of Fontenay (1981)
- Palace and Park of Fontainebleau (1981)
- Roman and Romanesque Monuments of Arles (1981)
- Roman Theatre and its Surroundings and the "Triumphal Arch" of Orange (1981)
- Royal Saltworks of Arc-et-Senans (1982)
- Cape Girolata, Cape Porto, Scandola Nature Reserve and the Piana Calanches in Corsica (1983)
- Church of Saint-Savin sur Gartempe (1983)
- Place Stanislas, Place de la Carrière and Place d'Alliance in Nancy (1983)
- Pont du Gard (Roman Aqueduct) (1985)
- Strasbourg — Grande île (1988)
- Cathedral of Notre-Dame, Former Abbey of Saint-Remi and Palace of Tau, Reims (1991)
- Paris, Banks of the Seine (1991)
- Bourges Cathedral (1992)
- Historic Centre of Avignon (1995)
- Canal du Midi (1996)
- Historic Fortified City of Carcassonne (1997)
- Historic Site of Lyons (1998)
- Routes of Santiago de Compostela in France (1998)
- Belfries of Belgium and France (1999, 2005)
- Jurisdiction of Saint-Emilion (1999)
- The Loire Valley between Sully-sur-Loire and Chalonnes (2000)
- Provins, Town of Medieval Fairs (2001)
- Le Havre, the city rebuilt by Auguste Perret (2005)

Gambia
- James Island and Related Sites (2003)

Georgia
- Bagrati Cathedral and Gelati Monastery (1994)
- Historical Monuments of Mtskheta (1994)
- Upper Svaneti (1996)

Germany
- Aachen Cathedral (1978)
- Speyer Cathedral (1981)
- Würzburg Residence with the Court Gardens and Residence Square (1981)
- Pilgrimage Church of Wies (1983)
- Castles of Augustusburg and Falkenlust at Brühl (1984)
- St Mary's Cathedral and St Michael's Church at Hildesheim (1985)
- Roman Monuments, Cathedral of St Peter and Church of Our Lady in Trier (1986)
- Hanseatic City of Lübeck (1987)
- Palaces and Parks of Potsdam and Berlin (1990, 1992, 1999)
- Abbey and Altenmünster of Lorsch (1991)
- Mines of Rammelsberg and Historic Town of Goslar (1992)
- Maulbronn Monastery Complex (1993)
- Town of Bamberg (1993)
- Collegiate Church, Castle, and Old Town of Quedlinburg (1994)
- Völklingen Ironworks (1994)
- Messel Pit Fossil Site (1995)
- Bauhaus and its Sites in Weimar and Dessau (1996)
- Cologne Cathedral (1996)
- Luther Memorials in Eisleben and Wittenberg (1996)
- Classical Weimar (1998)
- Museumsinsel (Museum Island), Berlin (1999)
- Wartburg Castle (1999)
- Garden Kingdom of Dessau-Wörlitz (2000)
- Monastic Island of Reichenau (2000)
- Zollverein Coal Mine Industrial Complex in Essen (2001)
- Historic Centres of Stralsund and Wismar (2002)
- Upper Middle Rhine Valley (2002)
- Dresden Elbe Valley (2004)
- Muskauer Park / Park Muzakowski (2004)
- Town Hall and Roland on the Marketplace of Bremen (2004)

Ghana
- Forts and Castles, Volta Greater Accra, Central and Western Regions (1979)
- Asante Traditional Buildings (1980)

Greece
- Temple of Apollo Epicurius at Bassae (1986)
- Acropolis, Athens (1987)
- Archaeological Site of Delphi (1987)
- Archaeological Site of Epidaurus (1988)
- Medieval City of Rhodes (1988)
- Meteora (1988)

- Mount Athos (1988)
- Paleochristian and Byzantine Monuments of Thessalonika (1988)
- Archaeological Site of Olympia (1989)
- Mystras (1989)
- Delos (1990)
- Monasteries of Daphni, Hossios Luckas and Nea Moni of Chios (1990)
- Pythagoreion and Heraion of Samos (1992)
- Archaeological Site of Vergina (1996)
- Archaeological Sites of Mycenae and Tiryns (1999)
- Historic Centre (Chorá) with the Monastery of Saint John "the Theologian" and the Cave of the Apocalypse on the Island of Pátmos (1999)

Guatemala
- Antigua Guatemala (1979)
- Tikal National Park (1979)
- Archaeological Park and Ruins of Quirigua (1981)

Guinea
- Mount Nimba Strict Nature Reserve (1981, 1982)

Haiti
- National History Park — Citadel, Sans Souci, Ramiers (1982)

Holy See
- Vatican City (1984)

Honduras
- Maya Site of Copan (1980)
- Río Plátano Biosphere Reserve (1982)

Hungary
- Budapest, including the Banks of the Danube, the Buda Castle Quarter and Andrássy Avenue (1987, 2002)
- Old Village of Hollókö and its Surroundings (1987)
- Millenary Benedictine Abbey of Pannonhalma and its Natural Environment (1996)
- Hortobágy National Park — the Puszta (1999)
- Early Christian Necropolis of Pécs (Sopianae) (2000)
- Fertö/Neusiedlersee Cultural Landscape (2001)
- Tokaj Wine Region Historic Cultural Landscape (2002)

Iceland
- Þingvellir National Park (2004)

India
- Agra Fort (1983)
- Ajanta Caves (1983)
- Ellora Caves (1983)
- Taj Mahal (1983)
- Group of Monuments at Mahabalipuram (1984)
- Sun Temple, Konarak (1984)
- Kaziranga National Park (1985)

- Keoladeo National Park (1985)
- Manas Wildlife Sanctuary (1985)
- Churches and Convents of Goa (1986)
- Fatehpur Sikri (1986)
- Group of Monuments at Hampi (1986)
- Khajuraho Group of Monuments (1986)
- Elephanta Caves (1987)
- Great Living Chola Temples (1987, 2004)
- Group of Monuments at Pattadakal (1987)
- Sundarbans National Park (1987)
- Nanda Devi and Valley of Flowers National Parks (1988, 2005)
- Buddhist Monuments at Sanchi (1989)
- Humayun's Tomb, Delhi (1993)
- Qutb Minar and its Monuments, Delhi (1993)
- Mountain Railways of India (1999, 2005)
- Mahabodhi Temple Complex at Bodh Gaya (2002)
- Rock Shelters of Bhimbetka (2003)
- Champaner-Pavagadh Archaeological Park (2004)
- Chhatrapati Shivaji Terminus (formerly Victoria Terminus) (2004)

Indonesia
- Borobudur Temple Compounds (1991)
- Komodo National Park (1991)
- Prambanan Temple Compounds (1991)
- Ujung Kulon National Park (1991)
- Sangiran Early Man Site (1996)
- Lorentz National Park (1999)
- Tropical Rainforest Heritage of Sumatra (2004)

Iran (Islamic Republic of)
- Meidan Emam, Esfahan (1979)
- Persepolis (1979)
- Tchogha Zanbil (1979)
- Takht-e Soleyman (2003)
- Bam and its Cultural Landscape (2004)
- Pasargadae (2004)
- Soltaniyeh (2005)

Iraq
- Hatra (1985)
- Ashur (Qal'at Sherqat) (2003)

Ireland
- Archaeological Ensemble of the Bend of the Boyne (1993)
- Skellig Michael (1996)

Israel
- Masada (2001)
- Old City of Acre (2001)
- White City of Tel-Aviv — the Modern Movement (2003)
- Biblical Tels — Megiddo, Hazor, Beer Sheba (2005)

- Incense Route — Desert Cities in the Negev (2005)

Italy
- Rock Drawings in Valcamonica (1979)
- Church and Dominican Convent of Santa Maria delle Grazie with "The Last Supper" by Leonardo da Vinci (1980)
- Historic Centre of Rome, the Properties of the Holy See in that City Enjoying Extraterritorial Rights and San Paolo Fuori le Mura (1980, 1990)
- Historic Centre of Florence (1982)
- Piazza del Duomo, Pisa (1987)
- Venice and its Lagoon (1987)
- Historic Centre of San Gimignano (1990)
- I Sassi di Matera (1993)
- City of Vicenza and the Palladian Villas of the Veneto (1994, 1996)
- Crespi d'Adda (1995)
- Ferrara, City of the Renaissance, and its Po Delta (1995, 1999)
- Historic Centre of Naples (1995)
- Historic Centre of Siena (1995)
- Castel del Monte (1996)
- Early Christian Monuments of Ravenna (1996)
- Historic Centre of the City of Pienza (1996)
- The Trulli of Alberobello (1996)
- 18th-Century Royal Palace at Caserta, with the Park, the Aqueduct of Vanvitelli, and the San Leucio Complex (1997)
- Archaeological Area of Agrigento (1997)
- Archaeological Areas of Pompei, Herculaneum and Torre Annunziata (1997)
- Botanical Garden (Orto Botanico), Padua (1997)
- Cathedral, Torre Civica and Piazza Grande, Modena (1997)
- Costiera Amalfitana (1997)
- Portovenere, Cinque Terre, and the Islands (Palmaria, Tino and Tinetto) (1997)
- Residences of the Royal House of Savoy (1997)
- Su Nuraxi di Barumini (1997)
- Villa Romana del Casale (1997)
- Archaeological Area and the Patriarchal Basilica of Aquileia (1998)
- Cilento and Vallo di Diano National Park with the Archeological sites of Paestum and Velia, and the Certosa di Padula (1998)
- Historic Centre of Urbino (1998)
- Villa Adriana (Tivoli) (1999)
- Assisi, the Basilica of San Francesco and Other Franciscan Sites (2000)
- City of Verona (2000)
- Isole Eolie (Aeolian Islands) (2000)
- Villa d'Este, Tivoli (2001)
- Late Baroque Towns of the Val di Noto (South-eastern Sicily) (2002)
- Sacri Monti of Piedmont and Lombardy (2003)
- Etruscan Necropolises of Cerveteri and Tarquinia (2004)
- Val d'Orcia (2004)
- Syracuse and the Rocky Necropolis of Pantalica (2005)

Japan
- Buddhist Monuments in the Horyu-ji Area (1993)
- Himeji-jo (1993)

- Shirakami-Sanchi (1993)
- Yakushima (1993)
- Historic Monuments of Ancient Kyoto (Kyoto, Uji and Otsu Cities) (1994)
- Historic Villages of Shirakawa-go and Gokayama (1995)
- Hiroshima Peace Memorial (Genbaku Dome) (1996)
- Itsukushima Shinto Shrine (1996)
- Historic Monuments of Ancient Nara (1998)
- Shrines and Temples of Nikko (1999)
- Gusuku Sites and Related Properties of the Kingdom of Ryukyu (2000)
- Sacred Sites and Pilgrimage Routes in the Kii Mountain Range (2004)
- Shiretoko (2005)

Jerusalem (Site proposed by Jordan)
- Old City of Jerusalem and its Walls (1981)

Jordan
- Petra (1985)
- Quseir Amra (1985)
- Um er-Rasas (Kastrom Mefa'a) (2004)

Kazakhstan
- Mausoleum of Khoja Ahmed Yasawi (2003)
- Petroglyphs within the Archaeological Landscape of Tamgaly (2004)

Kenya
- Lake Turkana National Parks (1997, 2001)
- Mount Kenya National Park / Natural Forest (1997)
- Lamu Old Town (2001)

Lao People's Democratic Republic
- Town of Luang Prabang (1995)
- Vat Phou and Associated Ancient Settlements within the Champasak Cultural Landscape (2001)

Latvia
- Historic Centre of Riga (1997)

Lebanon
- Anjar (1984)
- Baalbek (1984)
- Byblos (1984)
- Tyre (1984)
- Ouadi Qadisha (the Holy Valley) and the Forest of the Cedars of God (Horsh Arz el-Rab) (1998)

Libyan Arab Jamahiriya
- Archaeological Site of Cyrene (1982)
- Archaeological Site of Leptis Magna (1982)
- Archaeological Site of Sabratha (1982)
- Rock-Art Sites of Tadrart Acacus (1985)
- Old Town of Ghadames (1986)

Lithuania
- Vilnius Historic Centre (1994)
- Curonian Spit (2000)
- Kernave Archaeological Site (Cultural Reserve of Kernave) (2004)

Luxembourg
- City of Luxembourg: its Old Quarters and Fortifications (1994)

Madagascar
- Tsingy de Bemaraha Strict Nature Reserve (1990)
- Royal Hill of Ambohimanga (2001)

Malawi
- Lake Malawi National Park (1984)

Malaysia
- Gunung Mulu National Park (2000)
- Kinabalu Park (2000)

Mali
- Old Towns of Djenné (1988)
- Timbuktu (1988)
- Cliff of Bandiagara (Land of the Dogons) (1989)
- Tomb of Askia (2004)

Malta
- City of Valletta (1980)
- Hal Saflieni Hypogeum (1980)
- Megalithic Temples of Malta (1980, 1992)

Mauritania
- Banc d'Arguin National Park (1989)
- Ancient Ksour of Ouadane, Chinguetti, Tichitt and Oualata (1996)

Mexico
- Historic Centre of Mexico City and Xochimilco (1987)
- Historic Centre of Oaxaca and Archaeological Site of Monte Albán (1987)
- Historic Centre of Puebla (1987)
- Pre-Hispanic City and National Park of Palenque (1987)
- Pre-Hispanic City of Teotihuacan (1987)
- Sian Ka'an (1987)
- Historic Town of Guanajuato and Adjacent Mines (1988)
- Pre-Hispanic City of Chichen-Itza (1988)
- Historic Centre of Morelia (1991)
- El Tajin, Pre-Hispanic City (1992)
- Historic Centre of Zacatecas (1993)
- Rock Paintings of the Sierra de San Francisco (1993)
- Whale Sanctuary of El Vizcaino (1993)
- Earliest 16th-Century Monasteries on the Slopes of Popocatepetl (1994)
- Historic Monuments Zone of Querétaro (1996)
- Pre-Hispanic Town of Uxmal (1996)

- Hospicio Cabañas, Guadalajara (1997)
- Archeological Zone of Paquimé, Casas Grandes (1998)
- Historic Monuments Zone of Tlacotalpan (1998)
- Archaeological Monuments Zone of Xochicalco (1999)
- Historic Fortified Town of Campeche (1999)
- Ancient Maya City of Calakmul, Campeche (2002)
- Franciscan Missions in the Sierra Gorda of Querétaro (2003)
- Luis Barragán House and Studio (2004)
- Islands and Protected Areas of the Gulf of California (2005)

Mongolia
- Uvs Nuur Basin (2003)
- Orkhon Valley Cultural Landscape (2004)

Morocco
- Medina of Fez (1981)
- Medina of Marrakesh (1985)
- Ksar of Ait-Ben-Haddou (1987)
- Historic City of Meknes (1996)
- Archaeological Site of Volubilis (1997)
- Medina of Tétouan (formerly known as Titawin) (1997)
- Medina of Essaouira (formerly Mogador) (2001)
- Portuguese City of Mazagan (El Jadida) (2004)

Mozambique
- Island of Mozambique (1991)

Nepal
- Kathmandu Valley (1979)
- Sagarmatha National Park (1979)
- Royal Chitwan National Park (1984)
- Lumbini, the Birthplace of the Lord Buddha (1997)

Netherlands
- Schokland and Surroundings (1995)
- Defence Line of Amsterdam (1996)
- Historic Area of Willemstad, Inner City and Harbour, Netherlands Antilles (1997)
- Mill Network at Kinderdijk-Elshout (1997)
- Ir.D.F. Woudagemaal (D.F. Wouda Steam Pumping Station) (1998)
- Droogmakerij de Beemster (Beemster Polder) (1999)
- Rietveld Schröderhuis (Rietveld Schröder House) (2000)

New Zealand
- Te Wahipounamu — South West New Zealand (1990)
- Tongariro National Park (1990, 1993)
- New Zealand Sub-Antarctic Islands (1998)

Nicaragua
- Ruins of León Viejo (2000)

Niger
- Air and Ténéré Natural Reserves (1991)
- W National Park of Niger (1996)

Nigeria
- Sukur Cultural Landscape (1999)
- Osun-Osogbo Sacred Grove (2005)

Norway
- Bryggen (1979)
- Urnes Stave Church (1979)
- Røros (1980)
- Rock Drawings of Alta (1985)
- Vegaøyan — The Vega Archipelago (2004)
- West Norwegian Fjords — Geirangerfjord and Nærøyfjord (2005)

Oman
- Bahla Fort (1987)
- Archaeological Sites of Bat, Al-Khutm and Al-Ayn (1988)
- Arabian Oryx Sanctuary (1994)
- The Land of Frankincense (2000)

Pakistan
- Archaeological Ruins at Moenjodaro (1980)
- Buddhist Ruins of Takht-i-Bahi and Neighbouring City Remains at Sahr-i-Bahlol (1980)
- Taxila (1980)
- Fort and Shalamar Gardens in Lahore (1981)
- Historical Monuments of Thatta (1981)
- Rohtas Fort (1997)

Panama
- Fortifications on the Caribbean Side of Panama: Portobelo-San Lorenzo (1980)
- Darien National Park (1981)
- Talamanca Range-La Amistad Reserves / La Amistad National Park (1983, 1990)
- Archaeological Site of Panamá Viejo and Historic District of Panamá (1997, 2003)
- Coiba National Park and its Special Zone of Marine Protection (2005)

Paraguay
- Jesuit Missions of La Santisima Trinidad de Parana and Jesus de Tavarangue (1993)

Peru
- City of Cuzco (1983)
- Historic Sanctuary of Machu Picchu (1983)
- Chavin (Archaeological Site) (1985)
- Huascaran National Park (1985
- Chan Chan Archaelogical Zone (1986)
- Manu National Park (1987)
- Historic Centre of Lima (1988, 1991)
- Rio Abiseo National Park (1990, 1992)
- Lines and Geoglyphs of Nasca and Pampas de Jumana (1994)
- Historical Centre of the City of Arequipa (2000)

Philippines
- Baroque Churches of the Philippines (1993)
- Tubbataha Reef Marine Park (1993)
- Rice Terraces of the Philippine Cordilleras (1995)
- Historic Town of Vigan (1999)
- Puerto-Princesa Subterranean River National Park (1999)

Poland
- Cracow's Historic Centre (1978)
- Wieliczka Salt Mine (1978)
- Auschwitz Concentration Camp (1979)
- Belovezhskaya Pushcha / Bialowieża Forest (1979, 1992)
- Historic Centre of Warsaw (1980)
- Old City of Zamoœæ (1992)
- Castle of the Teutonic Order in Malbork (1997)
- Medieval Town of Toruñ (1997)
- Kalwaria Zebrzydowska: the Mannerist Architectural and Park Landscape Complex and Pilgrimage Park (1999)
- Churches of Peace in Jawor and Swidnica (2001)
- Wooden Churches of Southern Little Poland (2003)

Portugal
- Central Zone of the Town of Angra do Heroismo in the Azores (1983)
- Convent of Christ in Tomar (1983)
- Monastery of Batalha (1983)
- Monastery of the Hieronymites and Tower of Belem in Lisbon (1983)
- Historic Centre of Evora (1986)
- Monastery of Alcobaça (1989)
- Cultural Landscape of Sintra (1995)
- Historic Centre of Oporto (1996)
- Prehistoric Rock-Art Sites in the Côa Valley (1998)
- Laurisilva of Madeira (1999)
- Alto Douro Wine Region (2001)
- Historic Centre of Guimarães (2001)
- Landscape of the Pico Island Vineyard Culture (2004)

Republic of Korea
- Haeinsa Temple Janggyeong Panjeon, the Depositories for the Tripitaka Koreana Woodblocks (1995)
- Jongmyo Shrine (1995)
- Seokguram Grotto and Bulguksa Temple (1995)
- Changdeokgung Palace Complex (1997)
- Hwaseong Fortress (1997)
- Gochang, Hwasun, and Ganghwa Dolmen Sites (2000)
- Gyeongju Historic Areas (2000)

Romania
- Danube Delta (1991)
- Churches of Moldavia (1993)
- Monastery of Horezu (1993)
- Villages with Fortified Churches in Transylvania (1993, 1999)

- Dacian Fortresses of the Orastie Mountains (1999)
- Historic Centre of Sighiþoara (1999)
- Wooden Churches of Maramureþ (1999)

Russian Federation
- Historic Centre of Saint Petersburg and Related Groups of Monuments (1990)
- Kizhi Pogost (1990)
- Kremlin and Red Square, Moscow (1990)
- Cultural and Historic Ensemble of the Solovetsky Islands (1992)
- Historic Monuments of Novgorod and Surroundings (1992)
- White Monuments of Vladimir and Suzdal (1992)
- Architectural Ensemble of the Trinity Sergius Lavra in Sergiev Posad (1993)
- Church of the Ascension, Kolomenskoye (1994)
- Virgin Komi Forests (1995)
- Lake Baikal (1996)
- Volcanoes of Kamchatka (1996, 2001)
- Golden Mountains of Altai (1998)
- Western Caucasus (1999)
- Historic and Architectural Complex of the Kazan Kremlin (2000)
- The Ensemble of Ferrapontov Monastery (2000)
- Central Sikhote-Alin (2001)
- Citadel, Ancient City and Fortress Buildings of Derbent (2003)
- Ensemble of the Novodevichy Convent (2004)
- Natural System of Wrangel Island Reserve (2004)
- Historical Centre of the City of Yaroslavl (2005)

Saint Kitts and Nevis
- Brimstone Hill Fortress National Park (1999)

Saint Lucia
- Pitons Management Area (2004)

Senegal
- Island of Gorée (1978)
- Djoudj National Bird Sanctuary (1981)
- Niokolo-Koba National Park (1981)
- Island of Saint-Louis (2000)

Serbia and Montenegro
- Natural and Culturo-Historical Region of Kotor (1979)
- Stari Ras and Sopoèani (1979)
- Durmitor National Park (1980)
- Studenica Monastery (1986)
- Deèani Monastery (2004)

Seychelles
- Aldabra Atoll (1982)
- Vallée de Mai Nature Reserve (1983)

Slovakia
- Banská Štiavnica (1993)

- Spišský Hrad and its Associated Cultural Monuments (1993)
- Vlkolínec (1993)
- Caves of Aggtelek Karst and Slovak Karst (1995, 2000)
- Bardejov Town Conservation Reserve (2000)

Slovenia
- Škocjan Caves (1986)

Solomon Islands
- East Rennell (1998)

South Africa
- Fossil Hominid Sites of Sterkfontein, Swartkrans, Kromdraai, and Environs (1999, 2005)
- Greater St Lucia Wetland Park (1999)
- Robben Island (1999)
- UKhahlamba / Drakensberg Park (2000)
- Mapungubwe Cultural Landscape (2003)
- Cape Floral Region Protected Areas (2004)
- Vredefort Dome (2005)

Spain
- Alhambra, Generalife and Albayzín, Granada (1984, 1994)
- Burgos Cathedral (1984)
- Historic Centre of Cordoba (1984, 1994)
- Monastery and Site of the Escurial, Madrid (1984)
- Works of Antoni Gaudí (1984, 2005)
- Altamira Cave (1985)
- Monuments of Oviedo and the Kingdom of the Asturias (1985, 1998)
- Old Town of Avila with its Extra-Muros Churches (1985)
- Old Town of Segovia and its Aqueduct (1985)
- Santiago de Compostela (Old Town) (1985)
- Garajonay National Park (1986)
- Historic City of Toledo (1986)
- Mudejar Architecture of Aragon (1986, 2001)
- Old Town of Cáceres (1986)
- Cathedral, Alcazar and Archivo de Indias in Seville (1987)
- Old City of Salamanca (1988)
- Poblet Monastery (1991)
- Archaeological Ensemble of Mérida (1993)
- Route of Santiago de Compostela (1993)
- Royal Monastery of Santa Maria de Guadalupe (1993)
- Doñana National Park (1994)
- Historic Walled Town of Cuenca (1996)
- La Lonja de la Seda de Valencia (1996)
- Las Médulas (1997)
- Pyrénées — Mont Perdu (1997, 1999)
- San Millán Yuso and Suso Monasteries (1997)
- The Palau de la Música Catalana and the Hospital de Sant Pau, Barcelona (1997)
- Rock-Art of the Mediterranean Basin on the Iberian Peninsula (1998)
- University and Historic Precinct of Alcalá de Henares (1998)
- Ibiza, biodiversity and culture (1999)

- San Cristóbal de La Laguna (1999)
- Archaeological Ensemble of Tárraco (2000)
- Archaeological Site of Atapuerca (2000)
- Catalan Romanesque Churches of the Vall de Boí (2000)
- Palmeral of Elche (2000)
- Roman Walls of Lugo (2000)
- Aranjuez Cultural Landscape (2001)
- Renaissance Monumental Ensembles of Úbeda and Baeza (2003)

Sri Lanka
- Ancient City of Polonnaruwa (1982)
- Ancient City of Sigiriya (1982)
- Sacred City of Anuradhapura (1982)
- Old Town of Galle and its Fortifications (1988)
- Sacred City of Kandy (1988)
- Sinharaja Forest Reserve (1988)
- Golden Temple of Dambulla (1991)

Sudan
- Gebel Barkal and the Sites of the Napatan Region (2003)

Suriname
- Central Suriname Nature Reserve (2000)
- Historic Inner City of Paramaribo (2002)

Sweden
- Royal Domain of Drottningholm (1991)
- Birka and Hovgården (1993)
- Engelsberg Ironworks (1993)
- Rock Carvings in Tanum (1994)
- Skogskyrkogården (1994)
- Hanseatic Town of Visby (1995)
- Church Village of Gammelstad, Luleå (1996)
- Laponian Area (1996)
- Naval Port of Karlskrona (1998)
- Agricultural Landscape of Southern Öland (2000)
- High Coast (2000)
- Mining Area of the Great Copper Mountain in Falun (2001)
- Varberg Radio Station (2004)

Switzerland
- Benedictine Convent of St John at Müstair (1983)
- Convent of St Gall (1983)
- Old City of Berne (1983)
- Three Castles, Defensive Wall and Ramparts of the Market-town of Bellinzone (2000)
- Jungfrau-Aletsch-Bietschhorn (2001)
- Monte San Giorgio (2003)

Syrian Arab Republic
- Ancient City of Damascus (1979)
- Ancient City of Bosra (1980)

- Site of Palmyra (1980)
- Ancient City of Aleppo (1986)

Thailand
- Historic City of Ayutthaya and Associated Historic Towns (1991)
- Historic Town of Sukhotai and Associated Historic Towns (1991)
- Thungyai — Huai Kha Khaeng Wildlife Sanctuaries (1991)
- Ban Chiang Archaeological Site (1992)
- Dong Phayayen — Khao Yai Forest Complex (2005)

The Former Yugoslav Republic of Macedonia
- Ohrid Region with its Cultural and Historical Aspect and its Natural Environment (1979, 1980)

Togo
- Koutammakou, the Land of the Batammariba (2004)

Tunisia
- Amphitheatre of El Jem (1979)
- Medina of Tunis (1979)
- Site of Carthage (1979)
- Ichkeul National Park (1980)
- Punic Town of Kerkuane and its Necropolis (1985, 1986)
- Kairouan (1988)
- Medina of Sousse (1988)
- Dougga/Thugga (1997)

Turkey
- Göreme National Park and the Rock Sites of Cappadocia (1985)
- Great Mosque and Hospital of Divriði (1985)
- Historic Areas of Istanbul (1985)
- Hattusha (1986)
- Nemrut Dað (1987)
- Hierapolis-Pamukkale (1988)
- Xanthos-Letoon (1988)
- City of Safranbolu (1994)
- Archaeological Site of Troy (1998)

Turkmenistan
- State Historical and Cultural Park (1999)
- Kunya-Urgench (2005)

Uganda
- Bwindi Impenetrable National Park (1994)
- Rwenzori Mountains National Park (1994)
- Tombs of Buganda Kings at Kasubi (2001)

Ukraine
- Kiev: Saint-Sophia Cathedral and Related Monastic Buildings, Kiev-Pechersk Lavra (1990)
- L'viv — the Ensemble of the Historic Centre (1998)

United Kingdom of Great Britain and Northern Ireland

- Castles and Town Walls of King Edward in Gwynedd (1986)
- Durham Castle and Cathedral (1986)
- Giant's Causeway and Causeway Coast (1986)
- Ironbridge Gorge (1986)
- St Kilda (1986, 2004, 2005)
- Stonehenge, Avebury and Associated Sites (1986)
- Studley Royal Park including the Ruins of Fountains Abbey (1986)
- Blenheim Palace (1987)
- City of Bath (1987)
- Frontiers of the Roman Empire (1987, 2005)
- Westminster Palace, Westminster Abbey and Saint Margaret's Church (1987)
- Canterbury Cathedral, St Augustine's Abbey, and St Martin's Church (1988)
- Henderson Island (1988)
- Tower of London (1988)
- Gough and Inaccessible Islands (1995, 2004)
- Old and New Towns of Edinburgh (1995)
- Maritime Greenwich (1997)
- Heart of Neolithic Orkney (1999)
- Blaenavon Industrial Landscape (2000)
- Historic Town of St George and Related Fortifications, Bermuda (2000)
- Derwent Valley Mills (2001)
- Dorset and East Devon Coast (2001)
- New Lanark (2001)
- Saltaire (2001)
- Royal Botanic Gardens, Kew (2003)
- Liverpool — Maritime Mercantile City (2004)

United Republic of Tanzania

- Ngorongoro Conservation Area (1979)
- Ruins of Kilwa Kisiwani and Ruins of Songo Mnara (1981)
- Serengeti National Park (1981)
- Selous Game Reserve (1982)
- Kilimanjaro National Park (1987)
- Stone Town of Zanzibar (2000)

United States of America

- Mesa Verde (1978)
- Yellowstone (1978)
- Everglades National Park (1979)
- Grand Canyon National Park (1979)
- Independence Hall (1979)
- Kluane/Wrangell-St Elias/Glacier Bay/Tatshenshini-Alsek (1979, 1992, 1994)
- Redwood National Park (1980)
- Mammoth Cave National Park (1981)
- Olympic National Park (1981)
- Cahokia Mounds State Historic Site (1982)
- Great Smoky Mountains National Park (1983)
- La Fortaleza and San Juan Historic Site in Puerto Rico (1983)
- Statue of Liberty (1984)
- Yosemite National Park (1984)

- Chaco Culture National Historical Park (1987)
- Hawaii Volcanoes National Park (1987)
- Monticello and the University of Virginia in Charlottesville (1987)
- Pueblo de Taos (1992)
- Carlsbad Caverns National Park (1995)
- Waterton Glacier International Peace Park (1995)

Uruguay
- Historic Quarter of the City of Colonia del Sacramento (1995)

Uzbekistan
- Itchan Kala (1990)
- Historic Centre of Bukhara (1993)
- Historic Centre of Shakhrisyabz (2000)
- Samarkand — Crossroads of Cultures (2001)

Venezuela
- Coro and its Port (1993)
- Canaima National Park (1994)
- Ciudad Universitaria de Caracas (2000)

Vietnam
- Complex of Hué Monuments (1993)
- Ha Long Bay (1994, 2000)
- Hoi An Ancient Town (1999)
- My Son Sanctuary (1999)
- Phong Nha-Ke Bang National Park (2003)

Yemen
- Old Walled City of Shibam (1982)
- Old City of Sana'a (1986)
- Historic Town of Zabid (1993)

Zimbabwe
- Mana Pools National Park, Sapi and Chewore Safari Areas (1984)
- Great Zimbabwe National Monument (1986)
- Khami Ruins National Monument (1986)
- Mosi-oa-Tunya / Victoria Falls (1989)
- Matobo Hills (2003)

Appendix V

UNITED NATIONS

Special Rapporteur on the Promotion and Protection of the Right to Freedom of Opinion and Expression

— The Mandate —

The United Nations Commission on Human Rights, in resolution 1993/45 of 5 March 1993, decided to appoint a Special Rapporteur on the promotion and protection of the right to freedom of opinion and expression.

The Commission on Human Rights:

expressing concerns at the extensive occurrence of detention, long-term detention and extra-judicial killing, torture, intimidation, persecution and harassment, including through the abuse of legal provisions on defamation and criminal libel as well as on surveillance, search and seizure, and censorship, of threats and acts of violence and of discrimination directed at persons who exercise the right to freedom of opinion and expression, including the right to seek, receive and impart information, and the intrinsically linked rights to freedom of thought, conscience and religion, peaceful assembly and association and the right to take part in the conduct of public affairs, as well as at persons who seek to promote the rights affirmed in the Universal Declaration of Human Rights and the International Covenant on Civil and Political Rights and seek to educate others about them, or who defend those rights and freedoms, including legal profes-sionals and others who represent persons exercising those rights, and calls on States to put an end to these violations and to bring to justice those responsible;

requested the Special Rapporteur:

(a) to gather all relevant information, wherever it might occur, of discrimination against, threats or use of violence and harassment, including persecution and intimidation, directed at persons seeking to exercise or to promote the exercise of the right to freedom of opinion and expression as affirmed in the Universal Declaration of Human Rights and, where applicable, the International Covenant on Civil and Political Rights, taking into account the work being conducted by other mechanisms of the Commission and Sub-Commission which touched on that right, with a view to avoiding duplication of work;

(b) as a matter of high priority, to gather all relevant information, wherever it might occur, of discrimination against, threats or use of violence and harassment, including persecution and intimidation, against professionals in the field of information seeking to exercise or to promote the exercise of the right to freedom of opinion and expression;

(c) to seek and receive credible and reliable information from governments and non-govern-mental organizations and any other parties who have knowledge of these cases; and to submit annually to the Commission a report covering the activities relating to his or her mandate, containing recommendations to the Commission and providing suggestions on ways and means to better promote and protect the right to freedom of opinion and expression in all its manifes-tations.

The mandate of the Special Rapporteur was extended by the Commission on Human Rights in Resolution 2002/48, at its 58th session. The Commission on Human Rights invited the Special Rapporteur to continue to carry out his activities in Resolution 2003/42 and Resolution 2004/42.

In the discharge of his mandate the Special Rapporteur:

(a) Transmits urgent appeals and communications to States with regard to individuals or professionals in the field of information who have been reported to be discriminated against, threatened with the use of violence, persecuted, intimidated or harassed for seeking to exercise or to promote the exercise of the right to freedom of opinion and expression.

(b) Undertakes fact-finding country visits.

(c) Submits annual reports on activities, identification of trends and methods of work, and addressing specific thematic issues to the Commission.

Special Rapporteurs:
Mr. Ambeyi Ligabo (Kenya), since August 2002
Mr. Abid Hussain (India), from 1993 to July 2002

Appendix VI

UNITED NATIONS

Special Rapporteur of the Commission on Human Rights on Freedom of Religion or Belief

— The Mandate —

The United Nations Commission on Human Rights decided, in resolution 1986/20 subsequently renewed, to appoint a special rapporteur on religious intolerance. The Commission requested the Special Rapporteur:

– to examine incidents and governmental actions in all parts of the world which were inconsistent with the provisions of the Declaration on the Elimination of All Forms of Intolerance and of Discrimination Based on Religion or Belief, and to recommend remedial measures for such situations.

– to apply a gender perspective in the reporting process, including in information collection and in recommendations;

– within the terms of his mandate and in the context of recommending remedial measures, to take into account the experience of various States as to which measures are most effective in promoting freedom of religion and belief and countering all forms of;

– to continue to bear in mind the need to be able to respond effectively to credible and reliable information that comes before him, to seek the views and comments of the Government concerned on any information which he intends to include in his report, and to continue to carry out his work with discretion and independence.

In the discharge of his mandate the Special Rapporteur:

(a) transmits urgent appeals and communications to States with regard to cases that represent infringements of or impediments to the exercise of the right to freedom of religion and belief.

(b) undertakes fact-finding country visits.

(c) submits annual reports to the Commission on human rights, and General Assembly, on the activities, trends and methods of work.

Special Rapporteurs:
Ms. Asma Jahangir (Pakistan), 2004
Mr. Abdelfattah Amor (Tunisia), since 1993–2004
Mr. Angelo d'Almeida Ribeiro (Portugal), 1986–1993

Appendix VII

UNITED NATIONS

Declaration on the Elimination of All Forms of Intolerance and of Discrimination Based on Religion or Belief (1981)

The General Assembly,

Considering that one of the basic principles of the Charter of the United Nations is that of the dignity and equality inherent in all human beings, and that all Member States have pledged themselves to take joint and separate action in co-operation with the Organization to promote and encourage universal respect for and observance of human rights and fundamental freedoms for all, without distinction as to race, sex, language or religion,

Considering that the Universal Declaration of Human Rights and the International Covenants on Human Rights proclaim the principles of nondiscrimination and equality before the law and the right to freedom of thought, conscience, religion and belief,

Considering that the disregard and infringement of human rights and fundamental freedoms, in particular of the right to freedom of thought, conscience, religion or whatever belief, have brought, directly or indirectly, wars and great suffering to mankind, especially where they serve as a means of foreign interference in the internal affairs of other States and amount to kindling hatred between peoples and nations,

Considering that religion or belief, for anyone who professes either, is one of the fundamental elements in his conception of life and that freedom of religion or belief should be fully respected and guaranteed,

Considering that it is essential to promote understanding, tolerance and respect in matters relating to freedom of religion and belief and to ensure that the use of religion or belief for ends inconsistent with the Charter of the United Nations, other relevant instruments of the United Nations and the purposes and principles of the present Declaration is inadmissible,

Convinced that freedom of religion and belief should also contribute to the attainment of the goals of world peace, social justice and friendship among peoples and to the elimination of ideologies or practices of colonialism and racial discrimination,

Noting with satisfaction the adoption of several, and the coming into force of some, conventions, under the aegis of the United Nations and of the specialized agencies, for the elimination of various forms of discrimination,

Concerned by manifestations of intolerance and by the existence of discrimination in matters of religion or belief still in evidence in some areas of the world,

Resolved to adopt all necessary measures for the speedy elimination of such intolerance in all its forms and manifestations and to prevent and combat discrimination on the ground of religion or belief,

Proclaims this Declaration on the Elimination of All Forms of Intolerance and of Discrimination Based on Religion or Belief:

Article 1

1. Everyone shall have the right to freedom of thought, conscience and religion. This right shall include freedom to have a religion or whatever belief of his choice, and freedom, either individually or in community with others and in public or private, to manifest his religion or belief in worship, observance, practice and teaching.

2. No one shall be subject to coercion which would impair his freedom to have a religion or belief of his choice.

3. Freedom to manifest one's religion or belief may be subject only to such limitations as are prescribed by law and are necessary to protect public safety, order, health or morals or the fundamental rights and freedoms of others.

Article 2

1. No one shall be subject to discrimination by any State, institution, group of persons, or person on the grounds of religion or other belief.

2. For the purposes of the present Declaration, the expression "intolerance and discrimination based on religion or belief" means any distinction, exclusion, restriction or preference based on religion or belief and having as its purpose or as its effect nullification or impairment of the recognition, enjoyment or exercise of human rights and fundamental freedoms on an equal basis.

Article 3

Discrimination between human being on the grounds of religion or belief constitutes an affront to human dignity and a disavowal of the principles of the Charter of the United Nations, and shall be condemned as a violation of the human rights and fundamental freedoms proclaimed in the Universal Declaration of Human Rights and enunciated in detail in the International Covenants on Human Rights, and as an obstacle to friendly and peaceful relations between nations.

Article 4

1. All States shall take effective measures to prevent and eliminate discrimination on the grounds of religion or belief in the recognition, exercise and enjoyment of human rights and fundamental freedoms in all fields of civil, economic, political, social and cultural life.

2. All States shall make all efforts to enact or rescind legislation where necessary to prohibit any such discrimination, and to take all appropriate measures to combat intolerance on the grounds of religion or other beliefs in this matter.

Article 5

1. The parents or, as the case may be, the legal guardians of the child have the right to organize the life within the family in accordance with their religion or belief and bearing in mind the moral education in which they believe the child should be brought up.

2. Every child shall enjoy the right to have access to education in the matter of religion or belief in accordance with the wishes of his parents or, as the case may be, legal guardians, and shall not be compelled to receive teaching on religion or belief against the wishes of his parents or legal guardians, the best interests of the child being the guiding principle.

3. The child shall be protected from any form of discrimination on the ground of religion or belief. He shall be brought up in a spirit of understanding, tolerance, friendship among peoples, peace and universal brotherhood, respect for freedom of religion or belief of others, and in full consciousness that his energy and talents should be devoted to the service of his fellow men.

4. In the case of a child who is not under the care either of his parents or of legal guardians, due account shall be taken of their expressed wishes or of any other proof of their wishes in the matter of religion or belief, the best interests of the child being the guiding principle.

5. Practices of a religion or belief in which a child is brought up must not be injurious to his physical or mental health or to his full development, taking into account article 1, paragraph 3, of the present Declaration.

Article 6

In accordance with article I of the present Declaration, and subject to the provisions of article 1, paragraph 3, the right to freedom of thought, conscience, religion or belief shall include, inter alia, the following freedoms:

(a) To worship or assemble in connection with a religion or belief, and to establish and maintain places for these purposes;

(b) To establish and maintain appropriate charitable or humanitarian institutions;

(c) To make, acquire and use to an adequate extent the necessary articles and materials related to the rites or customs of a religion or belief;

(d) To write, issue and disseminate relevant publications in these areas;

(e) To teach a religion or belief in places suitable for these purposes;

(f) To solicit and receive voluntary financial and other contributions from individuals and institutions;

(g) To train, appoint, elect or designate by succession appropriate leaders called for by the requirements and standards of any religion or belief;

(h) To observe days of rest and to celebrate holidays and ceremonies in accordance with the precepts of one's religion or belief;

(i) To establish and maintain communications with individuals and communities in matters of religion and belief at the national and international levels.

Article 7
The rights and freedoms set forth in the present Declaration shall be accorded in national legislation in such a manner that everyone shall be able to avail himself of such rights and freedoms in practice.

Article 8
Nothing in the present Declaration shall be construed as restricting or derogating from any right defined in the Universal Declaration of Human Rights and the International Covenants on Human Rights.

Appendix VIII

FREEDOM OF EXPRESSION

INTER-GOVERNMENTAL AND NON-GOVERNMENTAL ORGANISATIONS: INTERNET SOURCES

FREEDOM OF EXPRESSION ORGANISATIONS

1. Academic and Educational Freedom of Expression
2. Artists, Musicians and Freedom of Expression
3. Internet and Freedom of Expression
4. Journalists, the Media and Freedom of Expression
5. Lawyers, Politicians and Freedom of Expression
6. Religion and Freedom of Expression
7. Writers and Freedom of Expression

FREEDOM OF EXPRESSION ORGANISATIONS
(INCORPORATING THE MANY GENERIC HUMAN RIGHTS ORGANISATIONS LISTED ABOVE)

1. Academic and Educational Freedom of Expression
American Association for the Advancement of Science — Human Rights Program
http://www.shr.aaas.org

American Library Association — Office for Intellectual Freedom (United States)
http://www.ala.org

Amnesty International
http://www.ai.org

Bonfire of Liberties — Censorship of the Humanities
http://www.humanities-interactive.org (and follow links)

Committee of Concerned Scientists
http://www.libertynet.org

Human Rights Watch
http://www.hrw.org

International Human Rights Network of Academies and Scholarly Societies
http://www.nationalacademies.org

National Academy of Sciences — Committee on Human Rights
http://www.nationalacademies.org

Network for Education and Academic Rights (NEAR)
http://www.nearinternational.org

Network of Concerned Historians
http://www.odur.let.rug.nl

New York Academy of Sciences — Committee on Human Rights
http://www.nyas.org

OneWorld.net
(Portal link for in excess of 1000 NGOs worldwide)
http://www.oneworld.net

Scholars at Risk Network — University of Chicago
http://www.scholarsatrisk.uchicago.edu (and follow links — shifts university centre periodically)

Scholars at Risk Program — Massey College, University of Toronto
http://www.pencanada.ca (and follow links)

Statewatch
(United Kingdom)
http://www.statewatch.org

United Nations Educational, Scientific and Cultural Organization (France)
http://www.unesco.org

United Nations Office of the High Commissioner for Human Rights (Switzerland)
http://www.unhchr.ch

2.   Artists, Musicians and Freedom of Expression

American Arts Alliance (United States)
http://www.artswire.org

American Communication Association (United States)
http://www.uark.edu

American Library Association — Office for Intellectual Freedom (United States)
http://www.ala.org (and follow links)

Amnesty International
http://www.ai.org

Artists Without Frontiers (United Kingdom)
http://www.artistswithoutfrontiers.com

Association for Progressive Communications (United States)
http://www.apc.org

Association Internationale de Defense des Artistes (AIDA) (Netherlands)
http://www.aidainternational.nl

Human Rights Watch
http://www.hrw.org

International Publishers Association Switzerland
http://www.ipa-uie.org

live8
http://www.live8.org

Music Industry Human Rights Association
http://www.mihra.org

OneWorld.net
(Portal link for in excess of 1000 NGOs worldwide)
http://www.oneworld.net

Orbicom — The International Network of UNESCO Chairs and Associates in Communications (Canada)
http://www.orbicomuqam.ca

Statewatch (United Kingdom)
http://www.statewatch.org

The Nations Online Project (countries of the world online)
http://www.nationsonline

United Nations Educational, Scientific and Cultural Organization (France)
http://www.unesco.org (and follow links)

3. Internet and Freedom of Expression
Amnesty International
http://www.ai.org (and follow links)

Center for Democracy and Technology (United States)
http://www.cdt.org

Citizens Internet Empowerment Coalition (United States)
http://www.ciec.org

Cyberspace Law Web Guide (United States)
http://www.findlaw.com (and follow links)

Electronic Frontier Canada (Canada)
http://www.efc.org.ca

Electronic Frontiers Australia (Australia)
http://www.efc.org.au

Global Internet Liberty Campaign (International)
http://www.gilc.org

Human Rights Watch
hrw.org (and follow links)

Information Policy Blog (international media links)
http://www.i-policy.typepad.com

Internet Free Expression Alliance (United States)
http://www.ifea.net

MoveOn.org (United States)
http://www.moveon.org

OneWorld.net
(Portal link for in excess of 1000 NGOs worldwide)
http://www.oneworld.net

Open Net Initiative
http://www.opennetinitiative.net

Oxford Internet Institute
http://www.oii.ox.uk

Statewatch (United Kingdom)
http://www.statewatch.org

United Nations Educational, Scientific and Cultural Organization (France)
http://www.unesco.org

United Nations Office of the High Commissioner for Human Rights (Switzerland)
http://www.unhchr.ch

4.   Journalists, the Media and Freedom of Expression

African Women's Media Center (Senegal)
http://www.awmc.com/

Alliance of Independent Journalists (Aliansi Jurnalis Independen, AJI) (IFEX
Member/Indonesia)
http//www.aijnews.org.id/

American Society of Journalists and Authors (United States)
http://www.asja.org

Amnesty International
http://www.ai.org

Asia Pacific Media Network (United States)
http://www.asiamedia.ucla.edu

Association of American Publishers — International Freedom to Publish Committee
(United States)
http://www.publishers.org (and follow links)

Association of European Journalists (Belgium)
http://www.aej.org

Australian Press Council (Australia)
http://www.presscouncil.org.au

Baltic Media Centre — International Media Development (Denmark)
http://www.bmc.dk (and follow link)

BBC World Service Trust (United Kingdom)
http://www.bbc.co.worldservice (and follow link)

BIA, the Independent Communications Network (Turkey)
http://www.bianet.org

Burma Media Association (Thailand)
http://www.bmaonline.net

Canadian Association of Journalists (Canada)
http://www.eagle.ca/caj

Caribbean Media Network (Jamaica)
http://www.caribbean-media.net/ (and follow links)

Center for Journalism in Extreme Situations (Russia/IFEX Member)
http://www.cjes.ru/english (and follow links)

Center for Media and Public Affairs (United States)
http://www.cmpa.com

Center for War, Peace and the News Media (United States)
http://www.nyu.edu (and follow links)

Centro de Reportes Informativos sobre Guatemala (CERIGUA) (Guatemala/IFEX Member)
http://www.cerigua.org/ (and follow links)

Common Ground Productions (A division of Search for Common Ground, United States)
http://www.cfcg.org (and follow links)

Commonwealth Press Union (United Kingdom)
http://www.cpu.org.uk/

Dart Centre for Journalism and Trauma A global resource for journalists who cover violence
http://www.dartcenter.org (and follow links)

DevMedia (Media for Development and Democracy) (Canada)
http://www.devmedia.org

Ethiopian Free Press Journalists' Association (Ethiopia)
http://www.ifex.org (and follow links)

European Institute for the Media (Germany)
http://www.eimorg (and follow links)

European Journalism Centre (Netherlands)
http://www.ejc.nl

European Newspaper Publishers' Association (Belgium)
http://www.enpa.be

International Freedom of Expression Exchange
http://www.ifex.org

FAIR — Fairness and Accuracy in Reporting (United States)
http://www.fair.org

Fédération professionelle des journalistes du Québec (IFEX Member/Canada)
http://www.fpjq.org

Freie Presse Deutschland (Germany)
http://www.freiepress.org

Guatemalan Association of Journalists, Press Freedom Committee (Comisión de Libertad de Prensa de la Asociación de Periodistas de Guatemala) (IFEX Member/Guatemala)
http://www.ifex.org/ (and follow links)

Hong Kong Journalists Association (China — Hong Kong)
http://www.hkja.org.hk

Human Rights Watch
http://www.hrw.org

Independent Association of Georgian Journalists (Georgia)
http://www.iagj.ge

Independent Journalism Center (IFEX Member/Moldova)
http://www.ijc.aitp.md (and follow links)

Independent Journalism Centre (IFEX Member/Nigeria)
http://www.ijc-nigeria.org (and follow links)

Institute for Global Communications (United States)
http://www.igc.org

Institute for Media, Policy and Civil Society (IMPACS) (Canada)
http://www.impacs.bc.ca

Institute for War and Peace Reporting (United Kingdom)
http://www.iwpr.net

Inter American Press Association (IFEX Member, United States)
http://www.sipiapa.com

International Center for Journalists (United States)
http://www.icfj.org

International Federation of Journalists (IFEX Member/Belgium)
http://www.ifj.org (and follow links)

International Press Institute (Austria)
http://www.freemedia.at

International Research & Exchanges Board (IREX) (US and International)
http://www.irex.org

International Women's Media Foundation (United States)
http://www.iwmf.org

Internews (United States)
http://www.internews.org

Journalists' Trade Union (IFEX Member/Azerbaijan)
http://www.juhiaz.org

Media Action International (Switzerland)
http://www.mediaaction.org

Media Alliance (United States)
http://www.media-alliance.org

Media Coalition (United States)
http://www.mediacoalition.org

Media Diversity Institute (United Kingdom)
http://www.media-diversity.org

Media Institute (IFEX Member/Kenya)
http://www.kenyanew.com

National Press Club of Canada (Canada)
http://www.pressclub.on.ca

One World Radio (United Kingdom)
http://www.oneworld.net (and follow links)

OneWorld.net
(Portal link for in excess of 1000 NGOs worldwide)
http://www.oneworld.net

Pacific Islands News Association (IFEX Member/Fiji)
http://www.ifex.net (and follow links)

Pakistan Press Foundation (IFEX Member/Pakistan)
http://www.oneworld.org/ppf

Panos (International)
http://www.panos.org.uk/

Paraguay Union of Journalists (Sindicato de Periodistas del Paraguay) (IFEX Member, Paraguay)
http://www.ifex.org (and follow links)

Philippine Center for Investigative Journalism (Philippines)
http://www.pcij.org

Press Now (Netherlands)
http://www.xs4all.nl (and follow links)
RAP 21 — African Press Network for the 21st Century (An electronic network of African media from 40 countries)
http://www.rap21.org (and follow links)

Society of Professional Journalists (IFEX Member, United States)
http://www.spj.org (and follow links)

South African National Editors Forum (South Africa)
http://www.sanef.org.za

South East Europe Media Organisation (SEEMO) (Austria)
http://www.seema.at

Statewatch (United Kingdom)
http://www.statewatch.org

Thai Journalists Association (IFEX Member, Thailand)
http://www.tja.or.th

The Hoot (India)
http://www.thehoot.org

The Media Institute (United States)
http://www.mediainst.org

United Nations Educational, Scientific and Cultural Organization (France)
http://www.unesco.org

United Nations Office of the High Commissioner for Human Rights (Switzerland)
http://www.unhchr.ch

West African Journalists Association (Union des Journalistes de l'Afrique de l'Ouest) (IFEX
Member, Senegal)
http://www.ujao.org

World Association for Christian Communication (United Kingdom)
http://www.wacc.org.uk

World Association of Community Radio Broadcasters (AMARC) (IFEX Member, Canada)
http://www.amarc.org

World Association of Newspapers (France)
http://www.wan-press.info

World Free Press Institute (United States)
http://www.pressfreedom.org

World Press Institute (United States)
http://www.worldpressinstitute.org

Zambia Independent Media Association (Zambia)
http://www.zima.co.zm

5.   Lawyers, Politicians and Freedom of Expression
Amnesty International
http://www.ai.org

Benton Foundation(United States)
http://www.benton.org

Canadian Centre for International Studies and Cooperation (Canada)
http://www.ceci.org

Center for Democratic Communications of the National Lawyers Guild (United States)
http://www.nlgcdc.org

Centre for Democratic Institutions (Australia)
http://www.cdi.anu.edu.au

Communications Assistance Foundation (CAF/SCO) (Netherlands)
http://www.villa.intermax.nl (and follow links)

Hivos International (Netherlands)
http://www.hivos.nl

Human Rights Watch
http://www.hrw.org

International Crisis Group (Global organisation that works to prevent and resolve conflict)
http://www.crisisweb.org

International Institute for Democracy (France)
http://www.iidemocracy.coe.int

International Institute for Democracy and Electoral Assistance (IDEA) (Sweden)
http://www.idea.int

International Peace Research Institute
(Norway)
http://www.prio.org

United Nations Educational, Scientific and Cultural Organization (France)
http://www.unesco.org

United Nations Office of the High Commissioner for Human Rights (Switzerland)
http://www.unhchr.ch

International Publishers Association Switzerland
http://www.ipa-uie.org

McCormick Tribune Foundation — Journalism Program (United States)
http://www.rrmtf.org/journalism

Mertz Gilmore Foundation (United States)
http://www.metzgilmore.org

Netaid — Join the Fight Against Poverty (United States)
http://www.netaid.org

Netherlands Institute for Southern Africa Media and Freedom of Expression Programme
http://www.niza.nl

Northern Ireland Human Rights Commission
http://www.nihrc.org

North–South Institute (Canada)
http://www.nsi-ins.ca

OneWorld.net
(Portal link for in excess of 1000 NGOs worldwide)
http://www.oneworld.net

Open Society Institute and Soros Foundations Network (United States)
http://www.soros.org

Orbicom — The International Network of UNESCO Chairs and Associates in communications (Canada)
http://www.orbicom.uqam.ca

Oxfam (International)
http://www.oxfam.org

Panos (International)
http://www.panos.org.uk

Partners for Media in Africa (France)
http://www.gret.org

People for the American Way (United States)
http://www.pfaw.org

Prisoners of Conscience Appeal Fund
http://www.prisonersofconscience.org

Probidad (El Salvador)
http://www.probidad.org

Relief Web (UN information gateway for humanitarian crises)
http://www.reliefweb.int

Statewatch (United Kingdom)
http://statewatch.org

The Nations Online Project (A portal to the countries of the world)
http://www.nationsonline.org

United Nations Educational, Scientific and Cultural Organization (France)
http://www.unesco.org

United Nations Office of the High Commissioner for Human Rights (Switzerland)
http://www.unhchr.ch

World Movement for Democracy (United States)
http://www.wmd.org (and follow links)

6.   Religion and Freedom of Expression
Amnesty International
http://www.ai.org

Oslo Coalition for Freedom of Religion or Belief
http://www.Ocfrb

Freedom House
http://www.freedomhouse.org

Human Rights Watch
http://www.hrw.org

OneWorld.net
(Portal link for in excess of 1000 NGOs worldwide)
http://www.oneworld.net

Statewatch (United Kingdom)
http://www.statewatch.org

United Nations Educational, Scientific and Cultural Organization (France)
http://www.unesco.org

United Nations Office of the High Commissioner for Human Rights (Switzerland)
http://www.unhchr.ch

7.   Writers and Freedom of Expression
Amnesty International
http://www.ai.org

Article 19
http://www.article19.org

Charter '88
http://www.www.charter88.org

International P.E.N. (Poets, Essayists, Novelists)
(and follow links to country-by-country networks worldwide)
http://www.www.intpen.org

Human Rights Watch (New York)
(and follow links to Hellman–Hammett Awards and freedom of expression)
http://www.hrw.org

Index on Censorship
http://www.index.org

OneWorld.net
(Portal link for in excess of 1000 NGOs worldwide)
http://www.oneworld.net

Statewatch (United Kingdom)
http://www.statewatch.org

Appendix IX

THE NOBEL PRIZE IN LITERATURE
AWARDS, 1901–2004

(Visit www.nobel.org for a history of the Prize, biographies of Award winners, Nobel acceptance speeches, and related materials)

2005	Harold Pinter
2004	Elfriede Jelinek
2003	J.M. Coetzee
2002	Imre Kertész
2001	V.S. Naipaul
2000	Gao Xingjian
1999	Günter Grass
1998	José Saramago
1997	Dario Fo
1996	Wislawa Szymborska
1995	Seamus Heaney
1994	Kenzaburo Oe
1993	Toni Morrison
1992	Derek Walcott
1991	Nadine Gordimer
1990	Octavio Paz
1989	Camilo José Cela
1988	Naguib Mahfouz
1987	Joseph Brodsky
1986	Wole Soyinka
1985	Claude Simon
1984	Jaroslav Seifert
1983	William Golding
1982	Gabriel García Márquez
1981	Elias Canetti
1980	Czeslaw Milosz
1979	Odysseus Elytis
1978	Isaac Bashevis Singer
1977	Vicente Aleixandre
1976	Saul Bellow
1975	Eugenio Montale
1974	Eyvind Johnson, Harry Martinson
1973	Patrick White

1972	Heinrich Böll
1971	Pablo Neruda
1970	Alexandr Solzhenitsyn
1969	Samuel Beckett
1968	Yasunari Kawabata
1967	Miguel Angel Asturias
1966	Samuel Agnon, Nelly Sachs
1965	Mikhail Sholokhov
1964	Jean-Paul Sartre
1963	Giorgos Seferis
1962	John Steinbeck
1961	Ivo Andric
1960	Saint-John Perse
1959	Salvatore Quasimodo
1958	Boris Pasternak
1957	Albert Camus
1956	Juan Ramón Jiménez
1955	Halldór Laxness
1954	Ernest Hemingway
1953	Winston Churchill
1952	François Mauriac
1951	Pär Lagerkvist
1950	Bertrand Russell
1949	William Faulkner
1948	T. S. Eliot
1947	André Gide
1946	Hermann Hesse
1945	Gabriela Mistral
1944	Johannes V. Jensen
1943	The prize money was with 1/3 allocated to the Main Fund and with 2/3 to the Special Fund of this prize section
1942	The prize money was with 1/3 allocated to the Main Fund and with 2/3 to the Special Fund of this prize section
1941	The prize money was with 1/3 allocated to the Main Fund and with 2/3 to the Special Fund of this prize section
1940	The prize money was with 1/3 allocated to the Main Fund and with 2/3 to the Special Fund of this prize section
1939	Frans Eemil Sillanpää
1938	Pearl Buck
1937	Roger Martin du Gard
1936	Eugene O'Neill
1935	The prize money was with 1/3 allocated to the Main Fund and with 2/3 to the Special Fund of this prize section
1934	Luigi Pirandello
1933	Ivan Bunin
1932	John Galsworthy
1931	Erik Axel Karlfeldt
1930	Sinclair Lewis
1929	Thomas Mann
1928	Sigrid Undset
1927	Henri Bergson

1926   Grazia Deledda
1925   George Bernard Shaw
1924   Władysław Reymont
1923   William Butler Yeats
1922   Jacinto Benavente
1921   Anatole France
1920   Knut Hamsun
1919   Carl Spitteler
1918   The prize money was allocated to the Special Fund of this prize section
1917   Karl Gjellerup, Henrik Pontoppidan
1916   Verner von Heidenstam
1915   Romain Rolland
1914   The prize money was allocated to the Special Fund of this prize section
1913   Rabindranath Tagore
1912   Gerhart Hauptmann
1911   Maurice Maeterlinck
1910   Paul Heyse
1909   Selma Lagerlöf
1908   Rudolf Eucken
1907   Rudyard Kipling
1906   Giosuè Carducci
1905   Henryk Sienkiewicz
1904   Frédéric Mistral, José Echegaray
1903   Bjørnstjerne Bjørnson
1902   Theodor Mommsen
1901   Sully Prudhomme

Appendix X

A TYPOLOGY OF DISSENT

The following are the conceptual contexts in which dissent of a prevailing worldview is likely to occur, and in which issues of freedom of expression, particularly its repression, are also to be expected.

1. The **Religious** (necessarily philosophical, political, concerned with a metaphysical, and sacred worldview, often but not necessarily theological, often but not exclusively idealistic — **in dialogue or conflict with the** — Ideological (necessarily philosophical, political, often but not necessarily secular, rationalistic, non-metaphysical and materialistic)
2. **Inter-religious (religion in dialogue or conflict with religion)**
3. **Intra-religious (religion in dialogue or conflict with its own tradition)**
4. **Inter-ideological (philosophical-political dialogue or conflict with other such)**
5. **Intra-ideological (philosophical–political dialogue or conflict with its own tradition)**

A Typology for the Interrogation of Dissent
1. What are the areas of greatest tension between freedom of religion or belief (political/ ideological/ theological) and freedom of expression (aesthetic — artistic, literary, musical — other) and in what media (electronic, film, print, reportage, other)?

2.   Is there a shift towards ideological repression? (Is this nation-State based or trans-national?)

Is there a shift towards increased religious repression? (Is *this* nation-State based or trans-national?)

Where does the pressure for *repression* of freedom of expression arise? (Is it governmental agency, inter-governmental or non-governmental organizations? Is it religiously led groups who institute pressure on governments — yet very often governments wish to separate religion from state — or governments who are instituting pressure on religiously led groups? Are there shifts in this trend motivated by particular events?)

Where does the pressure for *liberalization* of freedom of expression arise — from popular or religious sources or a combination of both? (Is it governmental agency, inter-governmental or non-governmental organizations? Is it religiously led groups who institute pressure on govern-ments — yet very often governments wishes to separate religion from state — or governments who are instituting pressure on religiously led groups? Are there shifts in this trend motivated by particular events?)

Index